The Daily Telegraph
GUIDE TO
BRITAIN'S
MARITIME PAST

The Daily Telegraph
Guide to
BRITAIN'S MARITIME PAST

Anthony Burton

Aurum Press

First published in 2003 by Aurum Press Limited,
25 Bedford Avenue, London WC1B 3AT

Copyright © 2003 Anthony Burton

Design by Robert Updegraff
Maps by Map Creation Ltd

A catalogue record of this book is available
from the British Library.

ISBN 1 85410 909 X (paperback)
ISBN 1 85410 920 0 (hardback)

1 3 5 7 9 10 8 6 4 2
2004 2006 2007 2005 2003

Printed and bound in Italy by Printer Trento srl

previous page **The National Maritime Museum, Cornwall.**
opposite **The light of the *Spurn* lightship.**

CONTENTS

FEATURES

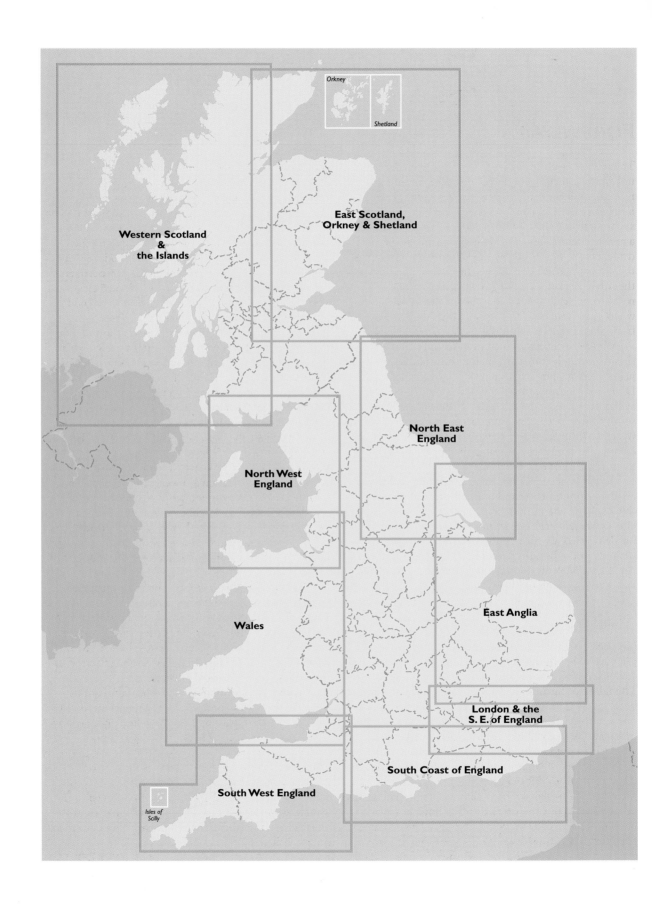

Orkney

Shetland

Western Scotland
&
the Islands

East Scotland,
Orkney & Shetland

North East
England

North West
England

Wales

East Anglia

London & the
S. E. of England

South Coast of England

Isles of
Scilly

South West England

FOREWORD

The word 'maritime' is a little vague – my dictionary, unhelpfully, gives five different definitions – and as readers are entitled to know what they are likely to find in a book, some explanation is called for. It is easiest to say what is not going to be included: this is not a book about the seaside and seaside holidays, nor will it be dealing with wildlife and natural history. At its simplest, the subject matter is ships and those who sailed them: the merchant ships carrying passengers and cargoes, the naval ships, ready for war. It is about the shipyards where they were built and the harbours they sailed from. It is, in short, about the working life of the sea.

We are fortunate in Britain in having a remarkably rich seafaring history, and there is far more to it than just the great names that appear in the history books, Drake and Nelson, Cook and Scott. Not so very long ago, great liners crossed the oceans from British ports, scruffy tramp steamers puffed their way around the world, carrying cargoes of every conceivable commodity and there were vast fishing fleets working throughout the year. There was a motley array of coasters, many of which were adapted to purely local conditions, from the famous Thames sailing barges to the sturdy Clyde Puffers of the Scottish west coast. Harbours were everywhere busy with trade and the bustle of working boats. The Royal Navy was the nation's pride, boasting the most powerful warships in the world. Now all that has changed. Small ports are still busy, but with pleasure craft, not trading vessels. The liners have gone, their role taken over by the new liners of the air. The Navy has shrunk to a fraction of its former strength. Happily, however, all has not been lost. Enthusiasts and institutions have worked to preserve much of the past. Coastal vessels still sail and steam, even if their cargo carrying days have gone. The fabric of historic docks, shipyards and ports has been restored. Important ships have been saved and opened up to the public, and the whole story of the maritime past is told in a number of fine museums. These form the raw material of this book.

The choice of what to include in this guide was, in general, not very difficult, but there was one area where difficulties arose: the boats and ships. There was no problem about the static exhibits, such as *Cutty Sark* in London or *Discovery* in Dundee. The difficulty appeared when considering the vessels that are still afloat and still in use. For a start, they do not, unlike museums, stay in one place. The paddle steamer *Waverley*, for example, moves round the coast throughout the summer months. In cases such as this, the vessel will be found listed under the appropriate home port. *Waverley* runs a regular passenger service, enabling thousands to travel on board every year; other vessels have more modest accommodation and can carry perhaps no more than a dozen passengers or only operate special chartered trips. Nevertheless, these vessels have been included for the very good reason that they represent some of the most interesting historic vessels to be found around Britain's coast. Such craft are fascinating even when tied up in harbour, though, of course, nothing quite compares with the excitement of going to sea. One of my happiest memories is of sailing in the two-masted Cornish lugger *Barnabas*, built in the nineteenth century, and overtaking a sleek, modern yacht!

Throughout the book you will find sections headed 'See Also'. This might suggest that these are also rans, the second bests. This is not the case. Sometimes, this is a response to a particular problem. There are, for example, a very large number of lighthouses spread around the coast. To describe each in detail would be tedious. I have included a short feature on lighthouses in general, made special entries for lighthouses that are open to the public and which have particular points of interest and put others, often very fascinating places to visit, in the 'See Also' sections. Similarly, there are certain types of site which are in some ways only marginal to the topic. Coastal forts and castles, for example, are an important part of the island story but they have been given a secondary role here. In the end, what appears on the following pages has been very much a matter of personal judgement.

Finally, the information is, I hope, accurate, or more precisely was accurate at the time when the work was completed. Opening times can alter, prices change; some museums close, others open. A particular problem in dealing with ships is that they can not only change ports but can change owners as well. While compiling the list I often found myself trying to trace a vessel which I thought was of special interest, but not always succeeding. I can only apologize for any omissions, and if there are errors, please write to me at the publishers.

ANTHONY BURTON

INTRODUCTION

No one can say when the first boat ventured out from some estuary or creek on the British coast and made its way to sea. One can hazard a guess at a sequence of events, which probably began with the simple discovery that, by holding on to a log, a man could float across a river. This could have led to a series of experiments with simple hollowed out trunks and rafts before the first recognizable boats appeared. Gradually, more sophisticated versions would have been built, until something that was capable of control and which could withstand the waves made what must have been that first great adventurous voyage into the deep. The story of the earliest craft, unearthed by archaeologists, is told in a separate feature (p.36). There are, however, two aspects of these craft which were to dominate British ocean-going and coastal vessels until quite

recent times: they had complex hulls, built up of planks of wood fixed to wooden frames, and could be driven by sails. This is not the whole story. Large ships were also built that were powered by oars, of which the most extraordinary were the quinquiremes, hymned by John Masefield in his famous poem 'Cargoes':

> *Quinquireme of Ninevah from distant Ophir*
> *Rowing home to haven in sunny Palestine,*
> *With a cargo of ivory,*
> *And apes and peacocks,*
> *Sandalwood, cedarwood, and sweet white wine.*

Whether quinquiremes ever existed is doubtful: certainly it is difficult to imagine a vessel rowed with five banks of oars. The uppermost set of oars would

A magnificent fleet of traditional craft, including Brixham trawlers, taking part in the annual Brixham Sailing Festival.

have been exceptionally long, and the effort to use them with any force would seem to be beyond human capability. We do, however, know something about the ships used by the greatest seafarers of the ancient world, the Phoenicians. A carving of a cargo ship shows a vessel with a main mast carrying a single square sail laced to a yard and what appears to be a bowsprit, with a second square sail beneath it. The vessel was steered by steering oars or boards slung at either side of the stern. In later developments, ships had the steerboard on one side of the ship, which became the steerboard or starboard. As this steering oar might have suffered damage if it came against a quay wall, ships were berthed on the opposite side, the port side.

The surviving Roman pharos at Dover Castle. This, Britain's oldest lighthouse, lies within the walls of Dover Castle. It was originally approximately 25m high; the present structure is original Roman work up to a height of 13m and medieval above that.

The Phoenicians were great traders, and to protect their merchant fleet they had warships. These were fitted with one, or more frequently two, banks of oars. The hulls were long and thin compared with the merchantmen, designed to move swiftly to the attack. The main weapon was the ram built into the bows. These ships were depicted as far back as 700BC, and it might seem as though they had little to do with the history of ship development in Britain. But there is very strong evidence that Phoenicians came to Cornwall to purchase tin, so that these magnificent vessels from the Mediterranean could have been seen at anchor in quiet coves in Britain more than 2000 years ago.

It is rather unfortunate that over the next centuries we know so little about vessels designed and built in Britain, though we know quite a lot about those of various invaders. The Romans followed the Phoenician tradition of building merchant ships and warships, but on a bigger scale. Grain ships were generally quite large, as much as 55m long by 14m beam, sometimes having three masts, as well as being rowed. They were kept busy supplying the Roman garrisons in Britain, protected by a fleet of warships stationed in the English Channel. The largest vessels had a hundred oars in two banks, powerful catapults and fighting towers for the soldiers, or as we would now call them, the marines. The Romans did more than just sail up to Britain: they built permanent harbours, often protected by imposing forts. One of the best examples is Richborough Castle in Kent, site of the first landings in AD43. The original wooden defences were demolished and replaced by more substantial works in stone, the whole dominated by an immense triumphal arch. It remained an important harbour, but over the centuries the sea has retreated, leaving it literally high and dry. The Romans were not only concerned with finding a safe harbour for their ships, but were equally concerned with getting their ships safely to it in the first place. The entrance to Dover Harbour was marked by two pharos or lighthouses, tall towers with fires on top, providing smoke in the day and flames at night. One has survived within the walls of Dover Castle. The lower part is of Roman construction, but the upper section was rebuilt in the Middle Ages. Many of the elements that were in place set the pattern for centuries to come. Ships were specifically designed for different roles, either as merchantmen or warships. Ports and harbours were constructed to give protection from the weather, and navigation aids were constructed on shore.

HMS *Britannia* and the fleet at Spithead in 1847, depicted in a painting by John Ward, and now on view at the Hull Maritime Museum. By this date steamships had conquered the Atlantic, but the ships of the Royal Navy had not changed since Nelson's day.

The Roman withdrawal led to the period generally known as the Dark Ages, largely because so little is known about it. The Angles, Saxons and Jutes, who moved in as the Romans left, were illiterate, and few documents describe their arrival in detail or their way of life. What little we do know does not have a great deal to say about seafaring. However, the one group about whom we do know is the Norsemen. A new Scandinavian tradition in boat building was imported into Britain with the arrival of the Viking long boats. One of the most famous of these was discovered in Norway at Gokstad, near Sandefjord, in 1880. This was quite a small vessel, 23m long by 5m beam, with fine lines and a great upsweep in the bows and stern. She had a mast for a square sail and the hull was pierced to take sixteen oars on each side. She was built around AD800, and a replica built in 1893 showed its seaworthiness by sailing across the Atlantic to be put on display at the Chicago World Fair. There is ample evidence that many Viking vessels were even grander than this, and by the eleventh century, although the basic design had changed very little, vessels as long as

50m were putting to sea. A feature of these ships was the square sail set amidships, which could be braced to allow the vessel to make headway against the wind, as explained in more detail in the feature on sailing ships (p.60).

Saxon ships were somewhat similar in design. Perhaps the best known feature of maritime life in these times came during the second half of the ninth century, in the reign of King Alfred of Wessex. This was the age of intensive attacks by the Danes, and it was Alfred who realized that there was a great deal to be said for attacking the Danish fleet before it had a chance to land men in Britain. He raised taxes to pay for his own fleet of warships, earning him the historic title of Father of the British Navy. This is not entirely accurate, since Britain was at the time divided between numerous kingdoms, but it was Alfred who established the principle that governed much of the country's history. A well-armed and well-organized fleet is the best protection an island kingdom can have against invaders. It was not, however, a policy that could guarantee success, as the events of 1066 were to prove.

The Age of the Sailing Ship

One of the first important innovations of the Middle Ages was the abandonment of the steering oar and its replacement by a rudder hung from the stern. No one is quite certain when it was introduced, but it would appear to be some time in the thirteenth century. At about this time ships were being built with no oars, true sailing ships. They were no longer the simple open boats in the style of Viking vessels, but had added superstructures. These were the Castles: one was in the bow, the forecastle (which was to develop into the familiar fo'c'sle); an aftercastle; and a third at the mast head. Clearly, these were intended for use in war, but were as likely to be found in merchant ships as in specialized warships. There was a steady movement towards bigger vessels, and different types of sail were used. The northern tradition had been based on the square sail, but in the Mediterranean the lateen sail was regularly in use. This is a triangular sail, still to be seen in Arab dhows. The sail was hung from a yard running at an angle to the mast and in a fore and aft arrangement, making it easier to sail close to the wind, though there was a price to be paid in the extra work needed to manoeuvre the sail round the mast on changing tack. With the growth of ships and the introduction of extra masts, it became common to have vessels using a combination of square and lateen sails. The most famous of these ships was the Portuguese caravel, the favoured vessel of the great explorers, including Columbus. Typically, it would have one or more square sails

A replica of Drake's famous ship, the *Golden Hinde*. She was built at the Hinks shipyard in Appledore, which itself has a long history, having been founded by Henry Hinks in 1844.

set on the foremast, and lateen sails on the main and mizzen masts. These ships were first built around 1400, but in time the lateen rig proved too unwieldy for long oceanic voyages and square sails replaced the former on the main mast. The end result of these changes was ocean-going vessels with three or even four masts, using a variety of different sail arrangements. One other great change that affected warships was the introduction of cannon or similar armament, mainly set alongside the sides of the ship to deliver broadsides. It was an arrangement that was to remain in use with variations for many years.

The sailing ship developed into a highly sophisticated vessel, adaptable to meet many different needs. In some the principal requirement was for speed. Perhaps the most famous were the China Clippers. China tea was a very expensive commodity, and huge premiums were paid for the first shipment to be brought back from the East as the new crop was picked. These vessels were noted for their fine lines, in particular their very sharp bows. Above a narrow hull, immense quantity of sail could be set, rising in billowing tiers, square sail above square sail, from the mainsail nearest the deck to the royal at the very top of the mast. Cargo space had to be sacrificed in order to achieve the high speeds, but this was not a major factor for high value merchandise. In contrast, another typical cargo vessel of the early nineteenth century, the East Indiaman, was bluff bowed with capacious holds, very similar in design to a naval man-o'-war. We are fortunate in having a superb surviving clipper in the *Cutty Sark*, but the sturdy everyday cargo ships of the great age of sail have all but vanished. One does survive as a hulk, with the hull intact, but the *Jhelum* ended her days in Stanley Harbour in the Falkland Islands. Built in Liverpool in 1849, she struggled round Cape Horn in 1870, almost sank and was abandoned. Liverpool's Maritime Museum has been actively engaged in conservation work on this last survivor. It is not surprising that so few great sailing ships survive, but we can still get a chance to see just how they would have looked from the builders' models, which form an important part of so many excellent maritime museums. Construction of replicas in recent years, such as the *Matthew* (based in Bristol) and *The Golden Hinde* (berthed in London), not only provides an opportunity to see how the ships of the past would have looked, but also to find out how well they sailed.

If ocean-going merchantmen and warships from the age of sail are few, the same cannot be said of coastal craft. All along the British coast one can find vessels specially adapted for the trade of a particular region. The best known are the spritsail barges, popularly known as Thames barges, but there are many more, from the basically simple Humber keel, a vessel in which any medieval sailor would feel quite at home, to grander ketches and schooners. All these will be featured in the main text. Sometimes, it might seem that if you have seen one sailing ship then that is it, but there is an almost infinite variety, and all kinds of special adaptations. A rig needed for deep-sea fishing, for example, might be quite unsuitable for a coastal trader, and years of experiment and refinement will have resulted in a hull and sail pattern that is just right for the particular job in hand. It is this fitness for the job that helped keep so many vessels in work for so very long. Just because the steamer had been invented did not mean that the sailing ship was finished. Fully rigged ships were still earning a living on the oceans of the world right up to World War II. Coastal barges survived even longer, and I have been privileged to sail with a number of skippers for whom a life trading under sail was a matter of personal memory and not something to read about in a book. Nevertheless, the arrival of steam inevitably led to the decline and eventual death of the working sailing ship.

The Steamship

The steam engine was one of the great inventions of the Industrial Revolution, which was adapted to moving vessels through the water before it was used to move vehicles on land. Given the central role of British engineers in developing the steam engine in the first place, it is perhaps surprising that the first successful experiments with steam on the water took place in France and America. Britain joined the fray in 1788 with an experimental boat, but the honour of starting the first commercial steamboat service went to an American, Robert Fulton, and his paddle steamer *Clermont* in 1807. Then in 1812 the first British steamer went into service on the Clyde. The engine of this historic craft, *Comet*, is in the Science Museum, and a replica can be seen at Port Glasgow. This was the first of a whole series of paddle steamers serving the Clyde, an unbroken line represented today by the last sea-going paddle steamer in the world, *Waverley*. It was not until 1836 that two engineers working independently came up with an alternative to the paddles: the screw propeller. There was a great debate over which type of propulsion was the more efficient. The argument was settled in dramatic fashion in 1845, when two naval frigates took part in a tug-of-war. They were fitted with identical engines; when the engines were started, the screw-propelled *Rattler* pulled the

The supremacy of the screw propeller over the paddle wheel was proved in a tug-of-war in 1845. *Rattler* on the left is shown steaming powerfully forwards, while *Alecto* is being dragged backwards.

The preservation of large steamships is an expensive business, but here is a fine survivor, the *Shieldhall*, berthed at Southampton. Built to carry sewage sludge, she now has rather more glamorous tasks, including taking passengers to view the Cowes regatta.

Alecto, paddle wheels thrashing, backwards through the water. The oldest screw propelled steamer still afloat is no grand ship, however, but the little launch *Dolly*, built around 1850 and now part of the superb collection of steam launches on Lake Windermere.

The other essential factor in the development of the steamer was the change from wooden hull to iron, a process that began modestly in 1787 when ironmaster John Wilkinson of Coalbrookdale built an iron barge for use on the Severn. All the elements – steam engine, screw propeller and iron hull – came together in Brunel's famous ship, the *Great Britain*, now being restored in Bristol. The great advantage of an iron hull was that it could be built far bigger than any wooden hull, and for the next century there was a steady advance in ship size and in the power of the engines. It was not only increased power that was necessary. If a steamship was to travel the oceans of the world, it needed to have enough coal to feed the boilers. So alongside the increased engine size came the search for ever-greater efficiency. The ultimate seemed to have been reached with the triple expansion engine, explained later in the book (p.146). Then, at the very end of the nineteenth century, Charles Parsons developed the marine turbine. The first

experimental craft to be fitted with the new engine, *Turbinia*, is preserved in Newcastle, and from a modest beginning the turbine was rapidly developed to power everything from the speediest naval craft to the mighty ocean liners of the early twentieth century.

The liners are among the most glamorous – and biggest – ships ever built, but they were not met with immediate and universal approval. During the nineteenth century, the old sailing packets competed for a while with the new-fangled steamers. Charles Dickens recorded his experience crossing the Atlantic by steamer and was clearly unimpressed by 'this utterly impracticable, thoroughly hopeless and profoundly preposterous box'. For much of the nineteenth century the sailing ships held their own, and their passengers held them in almost as much affection as their captains. One of the latter was delighted with the cheers of the passengers as they swept past a 'tea kettle'. The shouts were, he declared, 'good for the ears of sailormen to hear'. There was, however, another side to the passenger trade. While the wealthy could cross the seas in luxury, the emigrants often endured squalor and disease. Even worse were the conditions endured by the unhappy Africans abducted for the infamous slave trade. The recreation of the emigrant and slave experiences provides a sober but important part of the work of maritime museums, such as that in Liverpool. Sadly, we have little chance to see the great liners and to wonder at the opulence of their design. They were fitted out in a bewildering array of styles: anything, it seemed, as long as it was not associated with the sea. Arthur Davis, who did the interior design of the *Aquitania*, explained the philosophy: 'The people on these ships are not pirates, they do not dance the hornpipe; they are mostly seasick American ladies, and the one thing they want to forget when they are on the vessel is that they are on ship at all.' Today, the nearest most of us can get to appreciating just how luxurious sea travel can be is to take a trip up to Edinburgh for a visit to the former Royal Yacht *Britannia*.

The Steam Navy

Change in ship design came slowest in the Royal Navy. They quickly realized that paddle steamers were of little use as warships. Side paddles were vulnerable, though the Americans partly overcame the problem by setting the actual paddles between twin hulls. But there was little enthusiasm for steam: the paddles got in the way, the engines used too much coal – the men of the Admiralty were happy with their old wooden walls. Then technology moved on and everything changed. The old guns lobbing cannonballs gave way to a new range of guns firing shells. In a demonstration of the new ordnance in France in 1824 an old 80-gun wooden wall was simply blasted out of the water in minutes. The iron hull seemed an obvious answer but the iron available

The battleship *Blanco Encalada*, built for the Chilean navy at the Armstrong works at Elswick on the Tyne, is seen just before the launch in 1894.

was not just unable to stop a shell but actually made things worse. A direct hit sent metal splinters flying everywhere in a lethal shower. It was not until the latter part of the nineteenth century that a genuine, efficient armour-plated warship was built, the French *Gloire*. The British response was *Warrior*, launched in 1861 and now fully restored. In essence, however, she was still an old-style frigate, designed for firing broadsides. *Warrior* had not even entered service when everything changed again. Once more, the impetus came from overseas, America this time, with John Ericsson's iron warship *Monitor*, which had 11-inch guns mounted in a rotating turret. It saw action during the American Civil War, and though there were no victories to report, the idea of the rotating turret was soon accepted as standard in navies throughout the world.

One might think that the submarine would put in a much later appearance in naval history, but in fact experiments were being made as early as 1620 on the Thames. The first effort was not strictly a submarine, merely a boat loaded down so that it just showed above water and, unfortunately, the efforts to row it resulted in very little forward progress and an exhausted crew. But as early as 1776 the Americans actually used a submarine against the British fleet. It was an egg-shaped vessel, moved by hand operated propellers, submerged by flooding tanks with seawater. The idea was to move under a ship, attach a mine with a clockwork timing device to the hull and retreat as fast as possible. It worked up to a point, in that the charge went off as planned. Yet the Americans were

Boscastle is now known as a picturesque beauty spot, but in the nineteenth century it was a busy commercial port with as many as 200 ships a year calling in, some from across the Atlantic, bringing timber from Canada.

unaware that the new generation of warships had copper plating on the bottom of the hull to protect against the marine worm. The mine made no impression. The Americans, however, persisted and in 1864 there was the first 'successful' submarine attack. The warship was blown up and sunk using spar torpedoes. These devices were not unlike the lances of jousting knights, long poles with explosive charges at the end. Unfortunately, whatever the effect on the battleship, the submarine was also lost in the attack. The British Navy continued to show no interest in these developments, which they regarded as rather skulking and unfair. The answer of how to use a submarine efficiently was only solved with the invention of the self-propelling torpedo. At last in 1901 the British finally decided that they might look at these new-fangled devices after all, though not with great enthusiasm. It was the outbreak of war in 1914 that showed how devastating the new vessels could be. The Germans began the war with 29 submarines, and by the end had built 390, which between them sank 6000 merchantmen. The world of the warship had

come a long way from the rowed galleys used as battering rams to the unseen, underwater menace of the explosive torpedo. There was to be one further development in naval warfare in the twentieth century: when ships became mobile bases for aircraft. There is a chance to explore all aspects of the recent past of naval history from the submarine museum at Gosport to the Fleet Air Arm museum at Yeovilton, as well as more conventional warships such as HMS *Belfast*.

Home from the Sea

The ships are the most glamorous part of the maritime story, but they are only a part. They need somewhere to load and unload; they have to be steered across featureless oceans; they need protection from hazards of all kinds. The development of ports and harbours follows a natural progression, changing as the nature of the ships themselves changed. At first, vessels could simply be run up onto a beach or tied to a simple quay. As they got ever larger, they were often anchored in deep water and serviced by a fleet of smaller vessels, barges and lighters. On the coast, protection from storms was first found in sheltered coves, which could then be improved by the construction of breakwaters and piers. It was not until the nineteenth century that a new type of dock appeared, entered through lock gates so that water could be kept at a constant level, regardless of the state of the tides. An early example at Bristol is actually known as 'the floating harbour', and there are other splendid examples of closed docks in London and Liverpool.

As mentioned earlier, the first lighthouses in Britain were built by the Romans, and there were a few built around the coast in medieval times, of which one survives on the Isle of Wight. The main period of development began in the eighteenth century with the construction of splendid stone towers both on the mainland and on isolated rocks out to sea. Hazardous areas, such as sandbanks, do not necessarily have any convenient rocks nearby on which to build a lighthouse, so in 1732 the first specially built lightship was anchored at the Nore, soon followed by others on the Goodwin Sands. These, together with navigation buoys and other sea marks, helped to make coastal navigation considerably safer. The sea, however, is never completely safe and accidents still happen. For centuries there was no organized system for rescuing

sailors from wrecks. Locals would go out by boat, but often their interest was as much in salvaging cargo as in saving lives – and in the case of the notorious wreckers, the fewer sailors that survived the better. Again, it was only in the late eighteenth century that an award was made for the design of a specialist lifeboat, which, in the words of the advertisement in the Newcastle papers, was 'calculated to go through a very shoal, heavy, broken Sea'. The prize was won by Henry Greathead, and one of his lifeboats is preserved at Redcar. By the 1820s the Royal National Lifeboat Institution had been formed to co-ordinate rescues, a job it continues to do today, still relying on the volunteer efforts of local seamen.

There is one aspect of maritime life that is difficult to recreate and capture in a museum – navigation. The crew of a modern yacht has a whole range of navigational aids to give an accurate position, pinpointing the boat to within a few metres. They have excellent charts to direct them to their destination. It is hard to imagine life without them, or to grasp the huge daring of those who made their way into unknown waters with only the most primitive aids. Navigation lies at the heart of good seamanship, and it is a story that deserves to be better known. One good reason for looking at the early history of this

Britain's oldest surviving lifeboat, *Zetland*, seen here on her launching carriage. Built in 1800 she remained in service for eighty years and is now preserved in her own museum at Redcar.

A splendid sight: *Cuidad da Inca* on the left and *Marques* sailing off the quay at Stromness, Orkney. Sadly, the *Marques* was to be lost at sea not long after this picture was taken.

fascinating subject is that it gives one the opportunity to look at some of the superb workmanship of early instruments. They are as much works of art as practical tools.

This very brief look at some aspects of maritime history should give the reader at least some idea of what to look forward to. We are fortunate that so much has survived, particularly in relation to historic ships, which are incredibly difficult and expensive to maintain. This is particularly true of wooden ships, many of which were never expected to enjoy a long working life. It was said in the nineteenth century of sailing ships on the Atlantic run that they had a life expectancy of little more than five years. In that time they were driven hard, but many were constructed of cheap American timber which became waterlogged, slowing the ship down to the point where it could no longer compete, especially in the steam age. There were glorious sights to be seen and perhaps nothing man has made for practical use has ever had the beauty of a great barque with all sails set to make the most of a good wind. But if few ships survive for us to see from the great age of sail, and fewer still actually put to sea, it does not mean that the spectacle has been lost for ever. Ships can still be built to the old pattern. These are not replicas, in the

way that one might make a working replica of Stephenson's locomotive *Rocket*, for example. These are ships built to traditional designs, designs that have lasted down the ages and proved their worth. So I do not feel I need to limit the entries in this book to vessels built before a certain date, whether sailing ship or steamer. There are many vessels which if not especially old in themselves come as part of a very old tradition. I hope that readers will have a chance to see some of these craft, and perhaps even go to sea in them. But there are maritime museums, big and small, that are full of delights as well – and sometimes a tiny collection put together with love and knowledge can offer as much pleasure as a grander neighbour. And there is always a chance of seeing something that turns up quite unexpectedly. I remember opening the bedroom curtains of a hotel room overlooking the harbour at Stromness on Orkney and being confronted by the masts and spars of two square-rigged ships, which the next day sailed – not motored – off the quay. It was a magical moment. But one of the joys of going in search of our maritime past is that even without such happy coincidences, there is always the sea itself, ever changing in its aspects, always there to thrill the senses and to be enjoyed for its own sake.

To the lay eye this looks like an incomprehensible tangle of ropes, but for the professional riggers on board the *Thirlmere* in 1874, each line has its exact place and precise function.

About this book

Almost all the sites, museums and ships listed in this book are to be found on the coast, so that it seemed logical to arrange the entries in geographical order. Bristol was chosen as a starting point, partly because it has some of the finest ships and museums, but also because it made the arrangement of maps straightforward and logical. So from here, the sites follow in sequence down the Bristol Channel and on to Land's End before turning to the south Cornish coast and so on until an end is reached back at the Severn in South Wales. However, as readers will generally be looking for sites in a certain area, they have been broken down into regions. At the end of each regional description there is a 'See Also' section of sites which may not merit a long description, or are examples of a type already discussed in some detail. There are a number of sites included in this section that may not be open to the public, but which are interesting, important and well worth seeing.

The Ships

These present a special problem not found in most conventional guide books: they do not necessarily stay in one place. Here they are listed under their home ports. Some are readily accessible to the general public, others pay their way by taking passengers on day trips or longer cruises. The information provided for individual entries should be sufficient for readers to find out what will be where and when – and, if enthusiasm takes over, gives contacts to find out about charter and passenger fares. Wherever possible I have supplied a postal address, phone contact number and name of website for sites, museums and ships.

Ownership

Unlike ancient monuments, only a minority of sites is under the care of national bodies, and these are listed in the descriptions as EH (English Heritage) and NT (National Trust). As usual, members of these organizations will generally be admitted free of charge. There are a few sites which are simply there to be seen by anyone who cares to go and look, and these are indicated as 'Open Access'. Apart from the websites listed at individual entries, there are also a number which cover a much wider range, and these are listed below:

English Heritage: www.english-heritage.org.uk
National Historic Ship Collection: www.nhsc.org.uk
National Maritime Museum: www.nmm.ac.uk
National Trust: www.nationaltrust.org.uk
Northern Lighthouse Board (Scottish lighthouses): www.nlb.org.uk
RNLI: www.lifeboats.org.uk
Trinity House (English and Welsh lighthouses): www.trinityhouse.co.uk

Prices

Because prices change all the time, anything written now could well be out of date before publication. I have given a rough indication of the price band in which admission charges fall at the time of writing. They may tip over into a different band – a charge of £2.40 might rise to £2.60 for example – but the £ should serve as a good guide. Price bands are indicated by the following symbols:

£	£2.50 or under
££	£2.50 to £5
£££	£5 to £7.50
££££	Over £7.50

You should perhaps note that some in the top price brackets are big museums, where you can easily spend a whole day and where family admission rates often apply, so they can offer really very good value for money. Clearly, the price bands do not apply to charters and passenger fares.

Opening Hours

Again, these change all the time, so the best we can do is give the information available at the time of writing. All-day opening can be assumed unless indicated otherwise. The vast majority of sites add

A fine seventeenth-century stained glass window from the Elizabethan House, Great Yarmouth, showing a fishing buss.

Bank Holidays to their regular opening times. If in doubt, check with the local tourist board or contact directly using the information given at the head of each entry.

Directions

The directions should enable you to find the place you are looking for using an ordinary road atlas, and, in many cases, once you get within range, there are signposts to help find the exact location.

Please Note

Every effort has been made to make sure that the information is up to date and accurate, but one can never be absolutely certain. Even after work had started on preparing the material, I discovered that one historic ship was about to be moved from its 'permanent' berth to another several miles away. I trust, and hope, that no others slipped their moorings when I was not looking! If readers do find any errors in the information supplied, please do let me know by writing to me care of the publishers.

THE SOUTH WEST

This is an area of great contrasts, covering a whole range of coastal features, from the mud flats of the Bristol Channel, round the rocky coasts of Devon and Cornwall, to the wide estuaries and natural harbours of the South Coast. The Bristol Channel has the second highest tidal rise and fall in the world, surpassed only by the Bay of Fundy between Nova Scotia and New Brunswick. The upper reaches and the approach to the Severn have long been recognized as difficult waters to negotiate, which has ensured steady work for generations of Bristol pilot cutters guiding ships into the safety of the River Avon. Heading westward to Land's End, the coastline offers little shelter, and the fishing port is more characteristic of the area than havens for ocean-going vessels. Rounding the tip, however, brings a variety of larger harbours, from Penzance to the grandest of them all, the naval base of Plymouth. Alongside the splendidly rich variety of scenery is an equally impressive array of preserved historic craft of all kinds and a rich mixture of maritime museums.

BRISTOL

The city itself is full of reminders of a great maritime past, when it was the second most important port in Britain. The development of the port as anything other than a natural anchorage began as long ago as the thirteenth century. The River Frome entered the Avon after wandering through an area of marshland. The land was bought, the Frome diverted and a wide, deep artificial channel cut. Vessels could tie up alongside the new quays of St Augustine's Reach, and would settle down comfortably on soft mud at low tide. This was satisfactory for a long time and the port thrived, in later years profiting from the infamous slave trade. In the eighteenth century there were attempts to provide new docks, near the mouth of the Avon on the site of the old Roman port, at New Mills, and nearer to the city centre at Hotwells. All failed. It was obvious that something needed to be done, if only to counteract the threat from rapidly developing Liverpool, which was threatening to take over all the lucrative trade with America. The city fathers wrangled and argued until agreement was finally reached to build the floating harbour. Work began in 1804 under William Jessop. The Avon was diverted into the New Channel, and a new harbour constructed where water levels were protected behind lock gates. There were further improvements, but this is essentially the dockland that one sees today, though now the cargo vessels come no nearer than the new port complex at Avonmouth.

One can walk around the dock area, starting in the city centre with

Balmoral **making her way down the Avon under Clifton suspension bridge.**

the line of medieval docks preserved at St Augustine's Reach. On one side are the former Victorian transit sheds, now housing among other activities an arts centre, and on the opposite side by the harbour is a former tea warehouse, now the Arnolfini Gallery. There are more grand warehouses, built in an ornate style known as Bristol Byzantine, with a notably fine example on Welsh Back. Cranes still line the wharf of the Floating Harbour, which is also home to the Industrial Museum. There are more features than can be listed here, but one can easily spend a day walking round the entire complex, from the entrance locks at Cumberland Basin and round the other smaller basins and wharves. There is an easier way to see the docks, however, and a very appropriate one. Take a boat. There are a number of options.

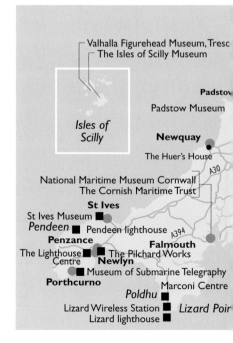

The *Bristol Packet*

££; Daily during school holidays, weekends rest of year; Tel: 01179 268157; Website: www.bristolpacket.co.uk

The trip round the docks is aboard an old working canal narrowboat, takes an hour and comes with a genuinely interesting commentary. Longer trips up river and down the Avon Gorge are available on the bigger trip boat, *Tower Belle*.

Bristol Ferries

These operate a regular service throughout the summer, and one very good trip that takes in much of the dock area starts from St Augustine's Reach, going past the SS *Great Britain* and further down to Cumberland Basin.

The *Balmoral*

Prices vary with trip; Tel: 0141 243 2224; Booking hotline: 0845 130 4647 Website: www.waverleyexcursions.co.uk

This is altogether grander: a motor cruise ship built in 1949, originally working for the Isle of Wight Steam Packet Company but bought by the famous operator of paddle steamers in the Bristol Channel, P & A Campbell, in 1980. She is now run as sister ship to the PS *Waverley*, offering a variety of excursions. Mostly starting in the heart of Bristol, the trips provide not only a good view of the docks but a chance to enjoy the River Avon gorge, passing under Brunel's famous suspension bridge.

Industrial Museum

Free; April to October Saturday to Wednesday; November to March weekends only; Princes Wharf; Tel: 0117 925 1470; Website: www.bristol-city.gov.uk/museums

This is an excellent museum covering all aspects of the city's industrial history right up to the modern aerospace industry and Concorde. There is, as one expects, a good deal about the history of the port, and exhibits are by no means confined to the inside of the building. Outside on the water are the museum's three craft. These are not just static exhibits, but regularly take visitors for trips around the docks, for which there is a charge. The oldest of these is the steam tug *Mayflower*, built

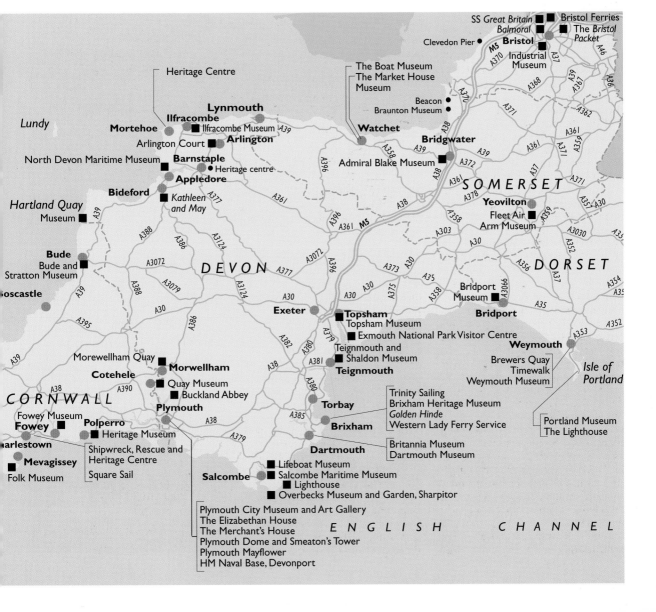

Bristol Industrial Museum's Fire Boat *Pyronaut* giving a demonstration of her abilities in Bristol docks.

ing replica engine. The plans include the recreation of the nineteenth-century dockyard surroundings.

Alongside the *Great Britain* is a full size replica of another famous ship, the *Matthew*. At a modest 50 tons she is dwarfed by her 1000-ton companion, but she too made a notable Atlantic crossing. In 1497 John Cabot set sail across the Atlantic where he discovered Newfoundland and made landfall on the North American coast. The replica repeated the voyage to mark the 500th anniversary, and is still sometimes absent at sea, so those who are only interested in this particular vessel should check in advance. The whole visit can be rounded off at the adjoining Maritime Heritage Centre, which tells the story of shipbuilding in Bristol.

in 1861, which has recently been joined by a former Bristol tug, *John King*. The third vessel is the 1934 diesel Fire Boat *Pyronaut*. Trips on this one give a very different experience: a demonstration of the water cannon. Water is pumped out of the dock and sent skywards as a high pressure jet.

The busy working life of the port is also well represented. Visitors can climb up to the cab of one of the big electric cranes, 30ft above the quayside, or see the splendid Fairbairn steam crane, installed in the 1870s, now restored and regularly demonstrated. The dock railway plays an important part in the story, and a section of the line has been restored, offering the opportunity to steam off for a visit to see Bristol's most famous preserved ship...

SS *Great Britain*

£££ includes Maritime Heritage Centre;
All year; Great Western Dock;
Tel: 0117 929 1843;
Website: www.ss-great-britain.com

Brunel's great ship has returned to the dock from which she was launched in 1843. She was the first iron hulled ship to be powered by steam and screw propeller, and can reasonably be called the forerunner of the ocean liner. After a successful career on the American service, she was also for many years involved in carrying emigrants to Australia. It seemed she was likely to end her days as a hulk in the

Falklands, but enthusiasts brought her home for the long process of restoration. The process still continues, but a great deal has already been done, and one can now see something of her former glory. This is a magnificent ship of worldwide importance, and everyone is looking forward to the full restoration, which will include a work-

BRIDGWATER
Admiral Blake Museum

Free; Tuesday to Saturday; Blake Street;
Tel: 01278 456127

This is the birthplace of Robert Blake (1599–1657), a General in the parliamentary army in the Civil War and who only joined the Navy at the age of

Brunel's famous steamer the SS *Great Britain*, seen here in the dock from which she was launched.

A reconstruction of a carrier flight deck provides an impressive setting for aircraft of the Fleet Air Arm Museum.

fifty. His most famous victory at sea was the attack on Santa Cruz, shown in the museum as a diorama. This also serves as a local history museum, with a number of items on Bridgwater's history as a port.

YEOVILTON
Fleet Air Arm Museum

££££; Daily; RNAS Yeovilton;
Tel: 01935 840565;
Website www.fleetairarm.com

The museum is based right next to an operational airfield, and a viewing gallery offers a chance to watch the Navy's modern aircraft at work, which certainly brings the story up to date. It is a story that begins with the Navy operating airships as early as 1909, and by 1912 the Naval Wing of the Royal Flying Corps had been established. A big step forward came in 1913, when two seaplanes operated in manoeuvres with the cruiser *Hermes*. It was not until 1917, however, that a plane was successfully landed on a warship – the seaplanes, of course, not needing to do so. As a result, the world's first true aircraft carrier, HMS *Argus*, was launched in 1918. From then on, it has been a story of bigger and more powerful carriers, and faster and more manoeuvrable aircraft. All are represented here. From one end of the time scale there is a Sopwith Pup, the plane used in the historic landing at sea in 1917, and the thought of landing this seemingly fragile plane of fabric and wooden struts on a moving ship is quite terrifying. At the other end

of the scale are the helicopters and the VTOL (vertical take-off and landing) Sea Harrier. Among the other famous planes on display is the Seafire, the naval version of the Spitfire. Although the site is far inland, there is a realistic exhibition of the carrier experience, with reconstructions of the operational areas and a flight deck, complete with genuine 1970s aircraft. This, being a very modern museum, makes full use of modern display technology, but in the end it is the aircraft everyone comes to see. And in amongst the military hardware is the remarkable Concorde.

WATCHET
The Boat Museum

Donation; Easter to end September
Tuesday, Wednesday, Thursday, Saturday,
Sunday afternoons; Harbour Road;
Tel: 01984 633117;
Website: www.wbm.org.uk

Housed in the former railway goods shed, this new museum deals with the many unusual small craft that plied the rivers and estuaries and penetrated the strange world of the Somerset Levels. These include the double-ended fishing boats known as flatners. The last to be used for fishing under sail, *The Ann*, was built in 1936, and was converted from spritsail to gaff rig in 1964. It is hoped that she will soon be back out on the water. Among the other specialist craft in the museum are withy boats, used to carry the cut willow sticks of the Levels and peat boats.

The Market House Museum

Free; Easter to end September; Market
Street; Tel: 01984 631345

The museum tells the story of the port, which in Saxon times was so important that it housed a royal mint, and it was still a working port engaged in foreign trade right up to the 1990s. Those days are gone, and the harbour has been rebuilt as a marina. It has one other claim to fame: it was in Watchet that Coleridge met 'an ancient mariner', whose story led to the famous poem. There are also a number of exhibits on the local lifeboat service, and an excellent collection of maritime paintings.

LYNMOUTH
Exmoor National Park Visitor Centre

Free; Daily; The Esplanade;
Tel: 01598 752509

An unlikely entry in the maritime lists, but the centre is home to a lifeboat very similar to the *Louisa II*, which was famously hauled overland to Porlock in 1899. Go outside and look up at Countisbury Hill and the full implication of what this trek meant in sheer hard work suddenly comes vividly alive.

The lifeboat *Louisa II* forms the centrepiece of a display at the Lynmouth Exmoor National Park Visitor Centre.

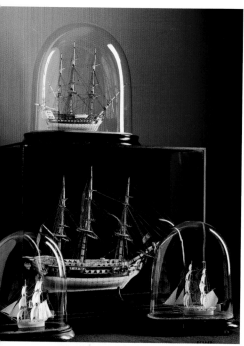

Part of Miss Chichester's splendid collection of ship models on display in the Ship Lobby at Arlington Court.

ARLINGTON

Arlington Court

NT; £££; Daily, except Tuesday end of March to November; Tel: 01271 850296

Readers might wonder what this grand country house with its typical overstuffed Victorian interiors is doing in this book at all. This, however, was the family home of the Chichesters, of whom Sir Francis Chichester, the solo circumnavigator, was an illustrious member. Other family members shared his love of the sea, and in amongst other fascinating collections in the house is a fine array of yachting pictures and ship models.

ILFRACOMBE

Ilfracombe Museum

£; April to October daily, November to March Monday mornings to Friday mornings; Runnymede Gardens; Tel: 01271 863541; Website: www.devonmuseums.net

The museum has a strong maritime interest, with models of a variety of craft from lifeboats to paddle steamers. One room is devoted to the history of Lundy.

MORTEHOE

Heritage Centre

£; Daily school summer holidays, otherwise Sunday to Thursday; Tel: 01271 870028; Website: www.devonmuseums.net

Housed in a splendid old village barn, the museum has numerous maritime displays, but the main focus is on shipwreck and rescue. The story of nearby Bull Point lighthouse is told and that of the local coastguard station. One of the exhibits – which is not always on display – is one of the very last of its kind, if not the last. It is a nineteenth-century Rocket Apparatus Wagon. Hauled by two horses, with a gang of twenty men in attendance, it was taken up to the cliff above the wrecked vessel so that life lines could be fired out to the crew. There is an attractive walk round the cliffs to Bull Point lighthouse.

BIDEFORD

Kathleen and May

Free; Afternoons Wednesday, Saturday, Sunday when in port; Tel: 01237 476375; Website: www.kathleen-and-may.co.uk

Here is a splendid survivor of what was once a famous class of vessels trading all round the British Isles: the topsail schooner. She has three masts, fore and aft rigged, with single topsails on the main and mizzen but able to carry two square-rigged topsails on the fore mast – hence the name topsail schooner. She was built in Wales and launched in 1900 as the *Lizzie May*, but was sold on in 1908 to an Irish owner, who renamed her after his two daughters. For many years she sailed back and forth across the Irish Sea, and finally ended her working days in Appledore. In recent years she has been restored, fallen into disrepair and is now restored once again and back under sail. She regularly returns to Youghal Bay where she spent so much of her working life. It is a great pleasure to be able to visit this handsome vessel – and an even greater pleasure to know that she is once again back under sail.

APPLEDORE

This is one of those little places that reward time spent on exploration. It seems just another small port with riverside quays but it has a long and honourable maritime history. Queen Elizabeth I was so impressed by the men of Appledore and their contribution to the defeat of the Armada that she declared it a free port, which it remains today. Real change came in the eighteenth century when the town began building ships as well as sailing them, and it was to become famous for its schooners. Ships are still built here but to see how it was in its prime means visiting the entirely delightful museum.

The 1836 coastguard wagon used for rockets firing life lines, seen outside the Mortehoe Heritage Centre.

LUNDY

NT/Landmark Trust; Tel: 01271 863636; Website: www.lundyisland.co.uk

The island is run by the Landmark Trust for the National Trust, and visitors can come for a day trip or a longer stay, renting a variety of historic buildings, from Government House to the Castle. You travel on the MS *Oldenburg*, either from Bideford or Ilfracombe, depending on the tide. Lundy, or Puffin Island, has had a decidedly colourful past, famous at one time as a base for smugglers and privateers. The island was also a hazard, sat right in the middle of the Bristol Channel. A lighthouse was built in the centre of the island, which remained in use from 1819 to 1897. It is a splendid structure, built of massive blocks of granite, with an equally grand home for the lighthouse keepers alongside. Fog signals came in the unlikely shape of two 18-pounder guns, which can still be seen at The Battery on the west cliffs. Visitors can climb to the top of the Old Light for spectacular views. Unfortunately, the light tended on occasions to be lost in low clouds, so two new lighthouses were constructed at the southern and northern ends of the island. For anyone contemplating a long visit who worries that a week on such a small island could be boring, I can only say that I thought the same way once – but after the first visit, came back for a second.

The old lighthouse of 1819 on Lundy, which though it no longer has a light, is open to visitors, who can also rent the lighthouse keepers' quarters as a holiday home.

North Devon Maritime Museum

£; May to September daily, Easter to end of April and October afternoons only; Odun House, Odun Road; Tel: 01232 422064; Website: www.devonmuseums.net

It is not difficult to spot the museum from the figurehead poking out from the wall above the porch. Inside there are some splendid models of schooners, which were still being built here in the early twentieth century, even though wooden hulls had by then largely given way to steel. Fishing was also important locally, and a former Taw estuary salmon boat has recently been restored. The museum covers other aspects of the town's history – and there is a special mention of the man who had a print works out in the old coach house, Jerome C. Jerome, whose famous son wrote the classic *Three Men in a Boat*.

THE CHANGING COAST

There are two scales of change: the almost incomprehensible hundreds of millions of years of geological time, and the far shorter period during which the British Isles existed. The first humans were living in Britain at a time when it was still joined to Europe, some 500,000 years ago, a mere blink of the eye in geological times. So, even within the times of human settlement, the landscape changes have been immense. And change never stops. The sea eats away at the land, and what is eroded in one place will be washed up in another.

We can still see the way in which the huge forces of moving water have sculpted our coast. One of the most spectacular areas is the Dorset coast, where the sea has attacked joints in the rock, then broken through, creating arches such as Durdle Door, and flooded through to create coves such as Lulworth. In other places the arches have fallen to create sea stacks – and both arch and stacks can be seen close together as the Elegug stacks and the Green Bridge of Wales off the Pembrokeshire coast. Of a very different nature are the shifting sands and shingles of the east coast of England. The Holderness region north of the Humber is

changing at a remarkable rate, faster than anywhere else in Europe. The sea is advancing at an average rate of two metres a year, and it has been estimated that since Roman times, more than thirty villages have been lost beneath the waves. One of the more spectacular recent events in the north east occurred when the cliff collapsed in Scarborough, taking an entire hotel with it.

The shifting of sand and shingle could have a disastrous effect on ports along the east coast. Dunwich was a prosperous Norman port until 1286 when storms threw a barrier of sand across the harbour entrance, and the River Blyth was moved out of its old channel. Worse was to follow as the sea steadily advanced, reaching the market place in 1677; in 1920 the church also collapsed into the waves. The story of Dunwich's losing battle with the sea is told in the local museum. A similar story can be found further south at Orford. Once again, there was a prosperous port in Norman times: this time the sea has not eroded the coast, but built up an immense spit of sand, Orford Ness, effectively cutting off the old port. One can still see the former importance of Orford, with its castle and imposing church, and there are still

Orford Ness and the lighthouse. The shingle beach has moved dramatically through the years.

traces of the old harbour, now dry and abandoned.

The ever-changing coastline can throw up its surprises. Some 5000 years ago, in the New Stone Age, there was a small community settled on the coast of Mainland, Orkney. Then a storm blew up and the villagers fled as sand whipped over the land, covering their tiny houses. We would never have known of their disaster if another storm in 1850 had not reversed the havoc caused by the earlier gale, blowing away the sand and revealing the hidden village of Skara Brae. And what an extraordinary place it is, with its stone huts connected by covered stone alleyways. The most remarkable features are the interiors, complete with stone furniture: stone box beds, cooking hearths and what look for all the world like stone Welsh dressers. The remains show that this was a community that looked to the sea for its living. These were fishermen, and stone tanks were built which, it seems, were filled with water and used to soak limpets for use as bait. This could well be one of Britain's first fishing villages.

For centuries man has attempted to hold back the ravages of the sea. Groynes and breakwaters have been built to break the force of the waves and dissipate their energy. High sea walls have been constructed to save towns from flooding. In recent years more elaborate precautions have been taken in estuaries and tidal rivers to guard cities against a combination of high tides and strong winds. Moveable barriers, which in normal weather allow shipping to pass, can be closed in an emergency. Notable examples can be seen, for example, in Hull and most dramatically in the River Thames. What history tells us is that in the long term the coast cannot be preserved as it is. Change must come. Overall, Britain has actually gained rather more land than it has lost in recent centuries. The new trend is to accept the inevitable. A natural feature such as the huge Chesil Beach in Dorset is recognized as an important sea defence, and where once the stones were carted away for building material or ornament, there is now a strict ban on their removal. In other areas the sea is being allowed to encroach on the land, creating areas of marsh which themselves act as flood barriers, harmlessly absorbing the power of the waves, as well as providing valuable wildlife habitats. An attempt is being made to balance the loss of low lying land and the crumbling of cliffs with the need to protect coastal towns. With the threat of global warning likely to produce a steady rise in sea levels, the one certainty is that change will continue, and nothing man can do will ever stop it.

The remains of the *Johanna* at Hartland Point, one of the wrecks featured in the Hartland Quay Museum.

HARTLAND QUAY
Hartland Quay Museum

£; Easter to end September daily afternoons; Tel: 01237 441218

This is a most inhospitable stretch of coast, with no safe refuge for ships until three famous Elizabethan sailors, Drake, Hawkins and Raleigh, promoted an Act of Parliament for the construction of the tiny harbour. The perils, however, remained. Sailors had a landmark in the 130ft high tower of St Nectan's Church a mile inland, and a lighthouse was built at Hartland Point. Tragically, none of this prevented wrecks from occurring. The two stories of the harbour and shipwrecks are told in the little museum through artefacts and photographs. The nearby hotel was converted from coastguards' cottages.

BUDE
Bude and Stratton Museum

£; Easter to October daily; The Lower Wharf; Tel: 01288 353576; Website: www.budemuseum.com

This is a local history museum covering all aspects of Bude life, which include the lifeboat service and shipwrecks, illustrated with dramatic videos. It also tells the story of the very unusual Bude Canal. The museum itself stands on the old canal wharf. Work began in 1819 in constructing a new harbour and canal. The present embankment was built out into the bay and a sea lock constructed to give coasters access to the basin. The canal itself was primarily used for carrying sand from the beach, which was a valuable fertilizer for inland farms. The sand was carried in tub boats, hauled up a series of inclined planes to reach a height of 450ft above sea level. The first of the inclines can be reached by following the towpath.

BOSCASTLE

NT; Open access

One of Cornwall's oldest and most remarkable harbours, Boscastle came into existence as the only natural haven in some forty miles of rugged coastline. The Normans built a castle here, and the quay itself is of uncertain date but was rebuilt in 1584 by Sir Richard Grenville. A breakwater was added later. The natural inlet follows a serpentine course and ships had to be towed into harbour by hobbler boats, manned by eight oarsmen. In spite of the difficulties, some 200 ships a year, mainly ketches and schooners, were using the harbour in the nineteenth century. It is now preserved by the National Trust.

PADSTOW
Padstow Museum

£; Easter to October Monday to Friday and Saturday morning; Market Place

The museum is housed in the former Men's Institute, which it now shares with the public library. This is a small museum with a lot to say. There are items on lifeboats, shipwrecks and the local fishing harbour. Padstow is itself something of a curiosity, in that the sands of the estuary are constantly changing: a flat sandy beach is likely to disappear from one side of the estuary while another appears across the water. One of the best features of the museum is its collection of marine paintings.

ST IVES
St Ives Museum

£; Easter to October Monday to Saturday; Wheal Dream; Tel: 01736 796005

The site has a long history: first quarry, then lime kiln, pilchard curing cellar, British Sailors Society Mission and eventually, after many other uses, a museum. The exhibits cover a similarly wide range but inevitably there is a strong emphasis on the history of the port, shown through both artefacts and in the work of the many artists who have come to this famously picturesque area. There are stories of the steamship company founded here by Edward Hain in 1878, of the local fishing industry and the life of the harbour. Down in the old fish cellar is an example of the famous breeches buoy, which has saved many lives at sea.

PENDEEN
Pendeen lighthouse

TH/TT; £; Easter, May Bank Holidays, July and August weekends; Tel: 01736 788418; Website: www.trevithicktrust.com

The lighthouse occupies a splendid position on a headland overlooking sandy Portheras Cove. Built in 1900, it stands 195ft above the sea, a rugged structure built of rough-hewn stone. Visitors can see the main lighthouse, the engine room and the mighty 12-inch siren, the last survivor in England of these deafening sound machines.

The deafening but shapely siren at Pendeen lighthouse.

PORTHCURNO
Museum of Submarine Telegraphy

TT; ££; End March to September Sunday to Friday, April to November Sunday and Monday, July and August daily; Tel: 01736 810996; Website: www.porthcurno.org.uk

This tiny, sandy cove earned its place in history in 1870 when a cable was laid that ran to Bombay, establishing the first long-distance telegraph service in the British Empire. It gained new importance in World War II when it became a major communications centre, hidden away in tunnels. Now the secret site houses a museum that includes a great deal of the early equipment, much of which is still in working order.

NEWLYN
The Pilchard Works

££; Easter to end of October weekdays; Tolcarne; Tel: 01736 332112; Website: www.pilchardworks.co.uk

There was a time when fleets of boats went out regularly to chase the shoals of pilchards and bring them back to port for processing. This is a solitary survivor, a factory which has been preparing salted pilchards for the Italian market since 1905. Traditional drift net fishing using special nets at Newlyn, Mousehole and Mevagissey keeps the works supplied. The museum

The engagingly mixed displays that greet visitors to the local history museum at St Ives.

contains seventy-year-old presses and the oldest surviving pilchard net-making machine. The process involves packing the fresh fish with salt, then gradually pressing them to extract water and oil, before packing them into wooden boxes. A bare description cannot do justice to a place like this, which provides a most satisfying example of a tradition that has continued, producing the same excellent results ever since the beginning of the twentieth century.

PENZANCE
The Lighthouse Centre

££; May to October Monday to Saturday; Wharf Road; Tel: 01736 360077

The museum is housed in the old buoy store and it is easy to find, as there is a selection of large, colourful buoys outside. Just as one would expect, there is a good display of lighthouse equipment, but there are also things that some of us may never have thought of at all. For example, the specially curved furniture that had to be built to fit the round towers. Audio-video displays help to recreate the lonely, and often dangerous, life of that now vanished group of men, the lighthouse keepers.

Much of the Isles of Scilly Museum is taken up with telling the stories of ships that foundered in the surrounding waters.

ISLES OF SCILLY

The islands can be reached from the mainland by sea or air.

The Isles of Scilly Museum

£; Early April to late October Monday to Saturday, winter Wednesday afternoons; Church Street, Hugh Town, St Mary's; Tel: 01720 422337;
Website: www.aboutbritain.com/islesofscilly museum.htm

The museum tells the whole history of the islands, much of which deals with the sea. One of the most imposing exhibits is the 1873 pilot gig *Klondyke*. Vessels such as this were rowed out to ships in the area, and gig racing is still a popular and highly competitive pastime. That pilots were necessary here was vividly demonstrated in 1707 when Admiral Sir Cloudsley Shovell's flagship *Association* was lost with all hands after hitting the Bishop and Clerk rocks. A bronze gun salvaged from the wreck is on show.

Valhalla Figurehead Museum, Tresco

£££ Entrance price includes visit to the gardens; Daily; Tel: 01720 424105; Website: www.tresco.co.uk

The museum is set in the sub-tropical gardens: handy for a day trip, as the Penzance helicopter lands more or less outside the front door. The theme is shipwrecks, in particular figureheads collected over the years from wrecks around the islands. The oldest date back to the seventeenth century.

POLDHU
Marconi Centre

NT; Free; May, June and September Tuesday, Wednesday and Sunday, September, July and August Tuesday, Wednesday, Friday, Saturday and Sunday afternoons; Walk up the hill to the point from the Cove; Tel: 01326 561407; Website: www.mulliononline.com

Part of the clockwork drive for the St Mary lighthouse optic by the famous glassmakers Chance Brothers, on show at Penzance.

This is a historic site in the story of radio communications. In the spring of 1901 a transmitter was set up at Poldhu and contact made with Ireland. A far more ambitious project succeeded in December that year, when three dots, the Morse letter 'S', were sent out and received in Newfoundland, and the first radio link to America had been made. The new centre tells the story, and local amateur radio enthusiasts explain and demonstrate equipment. The story is continued at The Lizard.

THE LIZARD
Lizard Wireless Station

TT/NT; Donations; January to May and October to March Wednesday afternoons, June Sunday and Wednesday afternoons; July to September Sunday and Tuesday to Friday afternoons; Bass Point, reached by footpath from Lizard village, or along the cliffs from the lighthouse;
Tel: 01326 290384

Marconi came here in 1900 and acquired land for a coastal radio station, building what became known as the Marconi Bungalow. A transmitter and receiver were installed, and signals were received from the Isle of Wight. In 1910 the station recorded receiving the SOS from *Titanic*. The buildings have been carefully restored to their 1901 condition with replicas of the original equipment. Communications still play an important part in the life of The Lizard, represented today by the Goonhilly Earth Station, which began tracking its first communications satellite in 1965. Technology has come a long way since a century ago, when the transmission of just one letter in Morse was considered almost miraculous.

Lizard lighthouse

TH/TT; £; April, May, September and October Sunday to Thursday, June Sunday to Friday, July and August all week; Tel: 01326 290065;
Website: www.trevithicktrust.com

The lighthouse was built in 1751, replacing an earlier light. Apart from enjoying a splendid situation on the southernmost point of mainland Britain, it also has exhibits that tell the story of lighthouse development. There is an early 'caloric engine' for generating electricity, and the original 'magneto machine', installed here in 1878, has also been preserved.

The National Maritime Museum, Cornwall, under construction in readiness for an opening in 2002. Boats will be seen both inside and out on the water.

FALMOUTH
National Maritime Museum Cornwall

£££; Daily, closed January; Discovery Quay; Tel: 01326 313388;
Website: www.nmmc.co.uk

This is a brand new museum of national importance, opened to the public in 2002. The building has been designed to show off the exhibits to the greatest advantage, while at the same time paying due respect to a long tradition of maritime architecture. It will be home to the National Maritime Museum's collection of small boats, 120 craft, which had formerly put in only occasional appearances at the main museum at Greenwich. They cover the full range from old wooden working boats to the modern sail boards. These will not just be static, indoor exhibits. A good number will be out on the water at the museum's jetties and will regularly put out to sea. This being a wholly modern museum, it offers more than just a chance to stand and admire a lot of boats: there are water tanks where visitors can try sailing model boats; demonstrations of boat construction; displays on navigation; and memories of Falmouth's own importance as a deep-water harbour, home to the Falmouth Packet Service.

The Cornish Maritime Trust

Offices: 35 Mongleath Avenue, Falmouth;
Tel: 01326 317890

This is not a museum, but an organization dedicated to preserving some of Cornwall's historic craft. There are three vessels based at Falmouth, all of which are regularly sailed and shown to the public, and there are opportunities for individuals and groups to experience the thrill of sailing on one of these magnificent craft. Having been fortunate enough to enjoy the experience myself, I can vouch for the fact that sailing a vessel that is already over a hundred years old is like no other sailing experience. The oldest vessel is *Barnabas*, a 40ft two-masted mackerel driver built in 1881. There were once hundreds of such craft that crowded the fishing harbours of Cornwall, but now she is a rare survivor. She has a dipping lugsail, which means hard work for the crew, but that gives her a truly surprising speed through the water. *Ellen* is a 17ft Gorran Haven crabber, just a year younger, built in 1882. She is again two-masted, with spritsails on the main and mizzen and a foresail. *Softwing*, built in 1900, is an oyster dredger with a conventional gaff rig, and is currently undergoing restoration. The Trust works closely with the new museum.

MEVAGISSEY
Folk Museum

£; Easter to October; East Quay;
Tel: 01726 843568

The most interesting exhibit as far as maritime history is concerned is the building itself. This was established as a boat builder's workshop in 1754 and has changed very little structurally. The roof is supported on three old masts, the beams carved using that traditional boatbuilder's tool, the adze. Old ship's timbers were used throughout the building, and an old hand-operated lathe is still in place. The exhibits are varied and include several related to the town's history as a fishing port.

CHARLESTOWN

Even if there were no museum and no old ships, Charlestown would still be worth a visit. The harbour was specially created to serve one local industry: china clay. It was built in the 1790s to designs by John Smeaton. Chutes can still be seen, down which the clay was slid into the waiting holds. In 1908 an underground railway connected with a tunnel at the port, linked to clay pits at Carclaze.

Diving equipment, ancient and modern, make spectacular exhibits at the Shipwreck, Rescue and Heritage Centre.

Shipwreck, Rescue and Heritage Centre

££; March to end October daily;
Tel: 01726 69897;
Website: www.shipwreckcharlestown.com

Housed in an old china clay works at the end of the harbour, the museum does rather more than its name suggests. It does indeed deal with rescue, and the lifeboat *Amelia* greets visitors when they arrive. It also has good exhibitions on the history of Charlestown and the local mining industry. The main emphasis, however, is not just on shipwrecks, but rather more interestingly on how they are located, explored and salvaged. There is a superb collection of diving equipment, from the oldest dating back to 1715, to a modern armoured suit that seems to have wandered across from a science-fiction movie. Material found in local wrecks is displayed, including a selection of porcelain recovered from a Dutch East Indiaman, which appears to have survived the plunge to the seabed without collecting a single crack or chip. Visitors can walk down one of the old clay tunnels, along which wagons rolled, for a view out over the harbour.

Square riggers line the quay at Charlestown, the harbour built for the china clay trade and now home to Square Sail.

Square Sail

Square Sail Shipyard;
Tel: 01726 70241;
Website: www.square-sail.com

The company uses Charlestown as the home port for their magnificent square-riggers. The vessels are the three-masted barque *Kaskelot*, a ship square-rigged on main and foremast, fore- and aft-rigged on the mizzen; the two-masted, square-rigged brig *Phoenix*; and a second three-masted barque, *Earl of Pembroke*. All these ships are in regular use, out on charter or, very often, on film location. So there is no guarantee as to which, if any, will be in harbour at any one time. There is also no guarantee that a ship you have seen on one visit will look the same on the next: when I called in, one vessel was being made over for a new *Hornblower* film. However, several varieties of passenger trips are available, from modest weekend trips to longer voyages.

Barnabas may now be well into her second century, but she can still show a fine turn of speed as she sails away from the camera boat.

The hundred-year-old former Looe lifeboat, which could be rowed or sailed, at Polperro.

FOWEY
Fowey Museum

£; April to November daily; Trafalgar Square; Tel: 01726 833513

A small museum but interesting, particularly for a set of photographs of life under sail in the late nineteenth century. Fowey harbour is reached down a narrow channel, and sailors have been guided to its entrance for almost two centuries by a striking red and white beacon on Gribbin Head.

POLPERRO
Heritage Museum of Smuggling and Fishing

£; Easter to end of October daily;
Tel: 01503 272423;
Website: www.polperro.org

A splendid situation right on the harbour and an appropriate building, once used as a pilchard factory, all add to the appeal of the museum. Polperro had its very own smuggling mogul at the end of the eighteenth century, the splendidly named Zapheniah Job. He organized everything, right down to paying for lawyers to defend anyone caught in the act. But even he could do nothing for Tom Potter, executed for murdering a customs official in 1798. This gory tale is matched by the workaday world of the fishermen and of the gaff-rigged drifters that once worked out of Polperro. There is one other particularly interesting exhibit out on the water: the former Looe lifeboat *Ryder*, built in 1902. It is a classic self-righting lifeboat, which could be sailed or rowed by ten oarsmen.

COTEHELE
Quay Museum

Donations; April to October;
Tel: 01579 50830;
Website: www.nmm.ac.uk

A simple quay, with stone wharf building and dock cut into the bank of the Tamar, this is typical of many small quays along tidal rivers and estuaries. That large vessels were not expected can be guessed from the simple hand crane. Today it is an outpost of the National Maritime Museum, who restored the old ketch-rigged Tamar barge *Shamrock*, now berthed here. She looks very handsome, but was built in 1899 for the very unglamorous trade of carrying animal manure. She was later converted for coastal trading and worked in a variety of different capacities right up to 1973. The full story of the little port is told in the museum, housed in the warehouse.

BEGINNINGS

Excavations have revealed substantial remains of a number of ancient boats, covering three periods. The earliest are from the Bronze Age, which lasted from approximately 2000 to 500BC; the next is from the succeeding Iron Age; and the last from the Dark Ages, between the end of Roman rule and the Norman Conquest. With so few craft representing a period of some 3000 years, it is impossible to draw even general conclusions. One of the surprises is that the Iron Age boat seems considerably cruder than the Bronze Age vessels built 1000 years earlier. That may not be significant. It might simply mean that we have not found crude Bronze Age boats nor sophisticated examples from the Iron Age. What we can say, however, with complete confidence is that right back in 1500BC men were building vessels that could go to sea.

Four Bronze Age vessels were discovered in Britain in the twentieth century, one at Dover and the other three at North Ferriby on the Humber. A boat found at Brigg in Lincolnshire in 1886 was only partly excavated. Two of the Ferriby boats were found in 1938, and they set a real problem for their discoverers, E.V. and C.W. Wright. They were close to the low water mark and were submerged for much of the day. Work began on the painstaking task of recording and recovery but was interrupted by the outbreak of war. When excavations restarted there was an attempt to lift one boat from its muddy grave, but in the lifting it collapsed into fragments. Boat number two fared rather better, and was cut into manageable pieces for removal and study. Then in 1963 a third boat was discovered on the same site, and once again it was found to be all but impossible to remove the ship undamaged. The remains of the Ferriby boats can be seen in the Hull and East Riding Museum. Then in 1992 another Bronze Age boat was discovered at Dover, and its timbers have been accurately dated to 1550BC. Excavation techniques and preservation technology had improved by this time, and it has been reassembled at the Dover Museum.

The first thing that strikes one about all these vessels is that these are very far from being the crude affairs one might expect from the dawn of shipbuilding. There are similarities between them all. The base of the vessel, the keel, would have been made by splitting a log from which two bottom planks could be made. As well as being carved to shape, cleats were cut out of the solid wood. These were wooden loops through which transverse timbers could be slotted to hold the bottom planks together. Rails were added to strengthen the hull, and wedges were driven through slots in the rails to help keep the planks together. Side planks or strakes were fixed, sewn together by strips of yew. The vessel was made wateright by packing the spaces with moss, which was then covered by laths. None of the boats was found complete, and some doubts remain about the shape of the bow and stern. One possibility is that the bow bent upward, rather like that of a modern punt, or it may have been formed by the side strakes converging to a point. For good seaworthiness they probably had a transom stern, a straight back piece. It also seems probable that the crew used paddles rather than oars.

The original excavation at Sutton Hoo in 1939 revealed the outline of a great Saxon ship preserved in the sandy soil of what was once the grave of a king.

Moving forward 1000 years to approximately 450BC we get to the Hasholme Iron Age boat, also found by the Humber. Here construction could scarcely be simpler. The main hull is simply a hollowed-out oak log, over 12m long. This time the

The burial mounds at Sutton Hoo as they are today. A new museum shows some of the spectacular finds revealed by excavation.

stern was intact, a simple transom slotted into a groove in the hull. Frustratingly, the bow had once again been damaged, but what remained was indeed rather like that of a punt. Conservation work is still continuing in Hull.

One of the most remarkable discoveries of modern archaeology was the burial ship of a Saxon King found at Sutton Hoo in Suffolk. Within the burial mound was the shadowy outline of the great ship itself, and a rich treasure trove of coins and jewels, rich artefacts and everyday objects. At first it was the goods that attracted attention, but work began on the boat in 1939. Careful records were made and photographs taken, but once more war intervened. When the archaeologists returned, they discovered that the army had dug a trench through the site and roared all over it in their armoured vehicles. Nevertheless, we have a very good picture of what the ship looked like and how it was constructed, and the technology has moved on a long way since the Iron Age. This was an open rowing boat, roughly 27m long by 4m beam, powered by twenty pairs of oars and steered by a single steering-oar at the stern. Here the keel ends in separate stem posts and stern posts. The hull is clinker built, the overlapping planks held together by metal rivets. Strength is provided by twenty-six heavy wooden frames inside the hull. The hull is extended upwards by a gunwale, with claw holes to hold the oars. Superficially, this looks like a Viking long ship, but the lines are nowhere near as fine. There is one last boat to consider: the vessel discovered at Graveney in Kent, dating from around AD900. It is like Sutton Hoo in some ways but there are important differences. The stern post is set at an acute angle to the keel, so that there is considerable curvature of the lower strakes. The frames are lighter and held in place by wooden pegs or trenails. Joints are made watertight by caulking, being packed with twisted hair. In looking at the Graveney boat we are viewing all the elements that were to be developed through many generations of wooden ships.

MORWELLHAM QUAY

££££; Open daily but limitations in winter; Tel: 01822 832766;
Website www.morwellham-quay.co.uk

Morwellham was, in its day, the greatest copper ore port in the world. The whole area was rich in mines, and the opening of the Tavistock Canal in 1817 not only connected the mining area to the port, but excavations during construction of the canal tunnel located still more rich veins. Then in 1844 the biggest mine of them all, eventually known as Devon Great Consols, was opened up. This created Morwellham's boom period, when as many as six schooners could be lying alongside quays heaped with ore. Morwellham flourished while the mines flourished, and declined when the mines declined. Now the whole Victorian port has been restored as a major open-air museum, recreating the scene as it would have been in the 1860s. This does not just apply to the quay itself, but includes, for example, one of the copper mines, where visitors get the chance to see underground workings. The port itself is unique, with an overhead railway bringing trucks to the quayside. The *Garlandstone*, a Tamar ketch built at nearby Calstock in 1909, has a permanent berth here. This is an immense site, full of interest, which really needs a whole day set aside to do it justice.

The *Garlandstone*, a handsome Tamar ketch, at the quay built to serve the old copper mine, Devon Great Consols, at Morwellham.

Sir Francis Drake looks out over Plymouth Hoe, where he famously played bowls while waiting for the Armada.

PLYMOUTH

Plymouth Sound is a fine natural anchorage, made even safer in the early nineteenth century by the construction of the immense breakwater. From a fishing village, Plymouth developed into an important port, with a long and varied history. Drake famously played bowls on the Hoe – or not, as seems rather more likely – and refused to sail to face the Spanish Armada until his game was over. Whatever the truth of the story, his statue still stands on The Hoe and bowls is still played nearby. The Pilgrim Fathers set sail from here in the *Mayflower* and their embarkation point on the harbour is still known as The Mayflower Steps. The other important event in the maritime history of the area is the development of the naval base at Devonport, once separate from Plymouth but now very much part of the whole urban area. All these different aspects are touched on in museums and buildings in the area. Quite the best way to get an overall view of the port and the dockyards is to take a boat trip. There are two regular services, one starting at Mayflower Steps and the other at Phoenix Wharf.

Plymouth City Museum and Art Gallery

Free; All year Tuesday to Saturday; Drake Circus; Tel: 01752 304774; Website: www.plymouth.museum@plymouth.gov.uk

This is a good, all-purpose city museum, which has recently opened a new gallery entirely devoted to marine paintings.

The Elizabethan House

£; April to October Wednesday to Sunday; 32 New Street; Tel: 01752 304380; Website: www.plymouth.museum@plymouth.gov.uk

New Street was actually new in the sixteenth century when houses were built for merchants and sea captains. The Elizabethan House has memories of the sea built into the fabric: the spiral staircase, for example, winds its way round a ship's mast. It has been furnished as a captain's house, complete with sea chest. It is full of atmosphere and is even said to have its very own benevolent ghost, which rocks the cradle in the main bedroom.

The Merchant's House

£; April to October Wednesday to Sunday; 33 St Andrews Street; Tel: 01752 304774; Website: www.plymouth.museum@plymouth.gov.uk

This is a grander version of the Elizabethan House, jettied out over the street, its carved oak-framed windows contrasting with the rough stone of the walls. Rather than being furnished in a single style, this is a museum depicting different aspects of the life of the city, and reflecting the fortunes that could be made in trade – or in the case of one previous owner, piracy.

Plymouth Dome and Smeaton's Tower

££ Dome only, £££ Dome and Tower, £ Tower only; Dome open end March to end October daily, Smeaton's tower open end March to end October daily, winter, end October to end March Tuesday to Saturday; Follow signs to Hoe and seafront; Tel: 01752 603300

The Dome is now an unmistakable Plymouth landmark, a high-tech addition to the city's range of exhibitions. It uses modern display techniques to recre-ate the sensations of the past, whether strolling around the Elizabethan harbour or experiencing the devastating air attacks of World War II. It is even possible to visit a virtual Eddystone lighthouse – particularly useful for those who do not want to climb the staircase of the next attraction, Smeaton's Tower. This is the upper section of the Eddystone light built by John Smeaton, taken apart and reconstructed on The Hoe. Even if it does not have the dramatic setting of a lonely rock far out to sea, it is still a mightily impressive structure and offers magnificent views from the top.

Plymouth Mayflower

Daily; Tel: 01752 306330; Website: www.plymouth-mayflower.co.uk

A new 'museum' in a new building, opened in 2002; it tells the story of the harbour, from the first record of cargoes leaving Plymouth in 1211 to the present day, using videos and graphic displays, but virtually nothing in the way of historic artefacts. There are models of the two most famous ships ever to sail from Plymouth, the *Golden Hinde* and *Mayflower*, and hands-on exhibits. The best way to complete the visit is to join one of the guided tours through the old Barbican quarter. The centre is run in conjunction with the National Maritime Aquarium, and joint tickets are available.

John Smeaton's Eddystone lighthouse, re-erected on The Hoe at Plymouth.

HM Naval Base, Devonport

Parties by arrangement;
Tel: 01752 552593; Open Days,
Information at Tourist Information or
Website: www.navydays.com

This is an unusual site in that there is an immense amount of interest here but access is currently limited. However, plans are well advanced for a major visitor centre, which will open up a great deal of the historic dockyard. What you can see at the moment is a rich and varied mixture: a small museum exists, just outside of which is the dock police station and the very early fire station of the 1850s. Among the eighteenth- and early nineteenth-century buildings are the immense ropery and the very beautiful Number 1 covered slip, which now provides cover for a display of figureheads. Sadly, much of the magnificent officers' terrace, built in the 1690s, was destroyed in the bombing raids of the 1940s. The aim of the visitor centre will be to tell the entire story of the docks and to bring it right up to date, with HMS *Courageous* on display, a nuclear submarine, launched in 1970. This really is a story of continuity, and the visitor is highly conscious of the fact that buildings designed for the needs of the sailing Navy are still part of a complex serving the fleet of today. The open days provide the opportunity to see the whole, covering three centuries of naval history.

A famous relic, Drake's Drum, in the Great Banqueting Hall, Buckland Abbey.

The brig *Mary Dare*, painted by J.M. Huggins, Jnr in 1842, is just one of many fine marine paintings at Overbecks.

BUCKLAND ABBEY

NT; ££; April to October daily except
Thursday, November to March weekends;
Between Plymouth and Tavistock;
Tel: 01822 853706

Few houses could have more illustrious maritime connections: converted by Sir Richard Grenville, it was bought by Sir Francis Drake after he returned to Britain in the *Golden Hind* in 1580. It is packed with Drake memorabilia, from his commission to command the fleet signed by Queen Elizabeth, to the carefully itemized accounts incurred in beating the Armada, with payments covering such unlikely combinations as 'to drummers, carpenters, cooks, mariners, surgeons'. The best known exhibit is Drake's drum, which, it is said, will bring the old sea dog back whenever Britain is threatened by invasion.

SALCOMBE

Lifeboat Museum

Easter to Christmas daily; Lifeboat
Station, Unity Street;
Tel: 01458 842975/842158

This is very much a local museum, and why not? Inside are models of every Salcombe lifeboat since the service was founded in 1869, together with a photographic record of their work.

Salcombe Maritime Museum

£; Easter to the end of October daily;
The Old Council Hall, Market Street;
Tel: 01548 842522;
Website: www.devonmuseums.net

In the nineteenth century these were sailors' rooms, where they could come to use the library, play games or simply exchange seafarers' gossip. Now it holds a particularly diverse collection. There are excellent paintings of sailing vessels, tools, models and photographs, all good serious stuff, but there is also a lot laid on especially for children. There are salvaged goods, including a bar of soap rescued from a vessel that went aground in 1939. It may not seem much today, but in the days of wartime rationing, bars of soap were as welcome as bars of gold. One surprising fact I learned: the town once had a busy trade in acorn cups! They were not used for mini-drinking cups, but in the less romantic tanning industry.

Overbecks Museum and Garden, Sharpitor

NT ££; April to end of July, September
daily except Saturday, August daily,
October daily except Friday and Saturday;
Tel: 01548 842893

An Edwardian house, with subtropical gardens overlooking the sea, it was the home of Otto Overbeck. Here is a collection relating once again to Salcombe's own maritime past. A strongly featured vessel is the *Phoenix*, built here in 1836 and lost with all hands on a voyage to Spain. An interesting exhibit is the collection of sailors' snuffboxes, a sort of marine picture gallery in miniature. Overbeck himself may have been interested in the sea, but his money came from his bizarre invention, the Electric Rejuvenator, guaranteed to cure most known diseases!

START POINT
Lighthouse

£; April and October weekend afternoons, May Thursday to Sunday afternoon, June Wednesday to Sunday afternoons, July and August daily, September Tuesday to Sunday afternoon, November Sunday afternoon; Tel: 01803 770606

This is a classic lighthouse, built in 1836, with a circular granite tower rising 92ft above the cliffs. There is no direct road access, and the best approach is along the coastal path from Bickerton for the scenery; there is also a shorter walk on the road from Kellaton.

DARTMOUTH
Britannia Museum

April to end of October Wednesday, Saturday, Sunday afternoons; Britannia Royal Naval College; Tel: 01803 677233; Website: www.devonmuseums.net

This is part of the very grandiose Royal Naval College, built in 1903, which quite dominates the Dartmouth skyline. The museum itself is housed in the no less imposing vaulted Cadet Gun Room. It is worth visiting if only for a chance to see inside the college, but once there the exhibits are full of interest. The main concern is to tell the story of the college. However, what really grabs the attention is the collection of Napoleonic ship models, carved out of bone by French prisoners of war.

Dartmouth Museum

£; April to October all day except Sunday, November to March afternoons except Sunday; The Butterwalk; Tel: 01803 832923; Website: www.devonmuseums.net

The former Brixham trawler, Trinity Sailing's *Leader*, a magnificent sight with all sails set. Seeing such a beautiful craft, it is difficult to remember that she was built for work, not pleasure.

Another museum with a most attractive home, only this one is housed in a merchant's house of 1640. Like the museum described above, it has Napoleonic bone models, along with a number of excellent, more conventional ship models.

BRIXHAM
Trinity Sailing

Sailing Details from Trinity Sailing, The Sail Loft, Pump Street, Brixham, TQ5 8ED; Tel: 01803 883345; Website: www.brixhamheritage.org.uk

The first sailing trawlers were built at Brixham towards the end of the eighteenth century. They developed into supremely efficient vessels, characterized by great driving power supplied by a gaff rig and jibs attached to a long bowsprit. Even when steam power came to the fishing industry, the Brixham trawlers kept on working. When working days ended, many were bought up and converted for pleasure boating. Two of these splendid craft, *Provident* and *Leader*, are run by Trinity Sailing, taking passengers on holiday cruises in the English Channel, calling in on the

The Royal Naval College, Dartmouth, gives no hint in its wedding cake façade that it was actually built in the twentieth century.

Ship models, half models and shipwrights' tools form part of the maritime display at the Brixham Heritage Museum.

French coast, the Channel Islands and the Scillies. The third of their craft, *Golden Vanity*, is built on traditional lines, but as a yacht. It was owned by Arthur Briscoe, a marine artist who often painted Brixham trawlers, following them out to sea to catch the true atmosphere of boats at work. All three were built at a shipyard on the River Dart, between 1892 and 1924.

Brixham Heritage Museum

£; Monday to Friday and Saturday morning but reduced hours in winter; The Old Police Station, Bolton Cross; Tel: 01803 856267; Website: www.brixhamheritage.org.uk

Although covering many aspects of Brixham life – and the museum itself is housed in the 1902 police station – the main emphasis is on fishing and shipbuilding. There is a good display of navigational instruments, going right back to the backstaff and the quadrant, and an excellent collection of ship models, with a strong local bias. Among the typical, often rather naive, paintings of boats and ships at sea, there are some much more unusual pictures. These were made from wool by sailors whiling away the time between watches. For a quite small museum this has a surprisingly wide range of interesting exhibits.

Golden Hinde

£; March to October; Tel: 01803 856223

A full-sized replica of Drake's ship can be visited at the quay.

Western Lady Ferry Service

May to October; Tel: 01803 297292/852041; Website: www.torbayenglishriviera.com

The ferry service runs between Princess Pier, Torquay, and New Pier, Brixham. Normally such services are not included in this book, but this one is a bit different – and the difference is the boats. They are Fairmile 'B' Motor Launches, BMLs, built not for tranquil trips to Torquay but for coastal defence, mainly patrolling the English Channel during World War II. Even with seats and canopies replacing guns and depth charges, the vessels still have an air of sleek efficiency.

TORBAY

Free; Open access

This area is so famous as a holiday resort that it is difficult to imagine it as ever having had any sort of role in maritime history. But in the past the wide bay provided a good, safe anchorage, well sheltered from the prevailing westerlies. William of Orange landed here with his troops in 1688. In the mid-eighteenth century, during the Seven Years War against France, the bay was the base for the Channel Squadron under Admiral Edward Hawke. It was from here that he controlled the blockade of the Port of Brest and led the fleet to the decisive victory of Quiberon Bay in 1759. Torbay once again provided a safe haven during the Napoleonic Wars, a place to which the fleet could retire if

adverse weather forced them out of the Channnel. And it was here that Napoleon was brought on the *Bellerophon* after his surrender in 1815; he is said to have remarked on how attractive the bay looked. So those who today loll on the sands or take their ease in the deckchairs may like to contemplate the days over two centuries ago when men of war, not yachts and dinghies, crowded the waters of Tor Bay.

TEIGNMOUTH

Teignmouth and Shaldon Museum

£; Easter, May to November Monday to Saturday; 29 French Street; Tel: 01626 777041; Website www.lineone.net/~teignmuseum

The old house is easily spotted from the large anchor outside the front door, indicating that maritime history is the main ingredient. It certainly has a varied story to tell, from that of the local fishermen who spent half the year catching cod off Newfoundland to the discovery of a sixteenth-century Venetian trader, armed with a bronze swivel gun, now on display. One room is devoted to local hero Edward Pellew, who ran away to sea at the age of thirteen. He rose to the rank of Admiral, and his most famous exploit was the bombardment of Algiers in 1816, which resulted in the freeing of thousands of Christian slaves. He rose from midshipman to end his career as Sir Edward Pellew, Viscount Exmouth. Other exhibits include figureheads and a collection of paintings by marine artist Thomas Luny (1759–1837).

TOPSHAM

Topsham Museum

£; April to November Monday, Wednesday, Saturday all day and Sunday afternoon; 25 The Strand; Tel: 01392 873244; Website: www.devonmuseums.net

The museum has a handsome setting in a group of seventeenth-century houses overlooking the Exe estuary. The representation, however, is very up-to-date, including touch-screen displays. The main maritime collection is in the old sail loft, with models, paintings and exhibits relating to the history of shipbuilding in the area.

THE SOUTH WEST **43**

BRIDPORT

Bridport Museum

£; April to October Monday to Saturday; South Street; Tel: 01308 422116; Website-www.westdorset-dc.gov.uk

This is a local history museum covering a wide range of subjects, including the town's most important industries: making ropes and nets for the fishing trade. Some of the old machines are still to be seen and demonstrations are often given.

WEYMOUTH

Brewers Quay

The development is based on a former Victorian brewery complex beside the harbour, with a variety of attractions, from ten-pin bowling to a craft market – and there are two very different interpretations of the town's history

Timewalk

££; Daily, closed last two weeks in January; Tel: 01305 777622

There are recreations of scenes from different times in the town's history and a major section which, though not strictly maritime, is certainly of interest to most sailors: brewing beer.

Weymouth Museum

Free; Daily

Because Weymouth is now thought of primarily as a seaside town, it is often forgotten that it has a long history as a port – but there are reminders here. There are artefacts from the East Indiaman *Abergavenny*, material on the busy paddle steamers that plied the coast and on the local lifeboat. Each year also brings a new exhibition, which may or may not deal with the sea.

PORTLAND

Portland was an island until 1839, when it was joined to the mainland by causeway and bridge; but long before that time it was important for its stone quarries and as a naval base. The latter two aspects come together at the harbour. Henry VIII built a castle to protect the natural anchorage at Weymouth Bay, a sturdy structure, now open to the public (EH). It has overseen many notable events, and in recent times has served as a focal point for the military, a seaplane base in World War I and a rallying point for the D-Day forces in World War II. The harbour also has an interesting history of the civil life of the island. Look up the hillside and you can still see the long straight line of a railway incline that used to bring Portland stone down for shipment.

Portland Museum

£; April to July, August to October Friday to Tuesday, August daily; Wakeham; Tel: 01305 821804

This is a delightful local history museum with an interesting story of its own. It consists of two cottages, one of which, dated 1640, featured in Thomas Hardy's novel *The Well-Beloved*. They were bought by the birth control pioneer Dr Marie Stopes in 1932. She was a frequent visitor to the old Higher lighthouse, which was used as a holiday home, and it was she who began the collection.

The Lighthouse

£ Lighthouse tower, Visitor Centre Free; April to September Sunday to Friday; Tel: 01305 820495

In fact, there is not one lighthouse here but three. The two oldest survivors, replacing one that was even older, were built in 1869. The Lower Lighthouse is now a bird observatory, the Higher privately owned. Both became redundant in the early twentieth century with the construction of the new, taller light on Portland Bill. The Visitor Centre is at the latter.

See Also
Clevedon Pier

£; October to March daily except Wednesdays; Tel: 01275 878846

A graceful pier, opened in 1867 and restored in 1998, complete with the exotic Chinese Pavilion at the end. It is still used by trip boats.

BURNHAM-ON-SEA
Beacon

Open access; Exterior only

A very strange beacon perched up on nine legs with weather-boarded sides, built in 1832 to warn sailors about the mud flats that literally stretch for miles from high water mark.

Braunton Museum

Free; Monday to Saturday all year, plus Sundays in school holidays; The Bakehouse Centre, Caen Street; Tel: 01271 816688; Website: www.devonmuseums.net/braunton

A local history museum with a maritime section, including exhibitions on sail making and a model ship collection.

BARNSTAPLE
Heritage centre

£; April to November Monday to Saturday, November to March Tuesday to Saturday; Queen Anne's Walk, The Strand, Barnstaple; Tel: 01271 373003; Website: www.devonmuseums.net/barnstapleheritage

Set in an elaborate colonnade, presided over by the statue of Queen Anne herself, the museum covers all aspects of the long history of town and port.

NEWQUAY
The Huer's House

Open Access; Exterior only

A little whitewashed house stands at the southern end of the Towan Head peninsula, overlooking Newquay Bay. Here the huer waited, on the look-out for shoals of pilchards; once sighted, he shouted out 'Heva' to the fishermen down below, a word that lends itself to a wide-open mouth to make a lot of noise – try shouting pilchards.

THE ELIZABETHANS

No period of Britain's maritime history has ever seemed as romantic as that of the Elizabethans, and the names of the great men resound still with ideas of high adventure, daring and skill – Drake, Hawkins, Raleigh, Frobisher and Grenville. It is unfortunate that the great story begins with perhaps the most infamous trade of all, the slave trade. Sir John Hawkins was born in Plymouth in 1532. He went into business with his brother William, trading mostly with the Canary Islands. It proved highly profitable, but there was more money to be made in slaves. Ships went on triangular voyages, carrying trade goods to Africa which were exchanged for slaves, taking the slaves to the New World, where they were sold at an immense profit, before returning to England. There was only one problem: the Spanish regarded the New World as their own domain and resented interlopers. Everyone today is, quite rightly, disgusted by the slave trade, but attitudes were very different in the sixteenth century. After the first successful expedition, there were to be two more in which the Queen herself was not only a shareholder, but lent Hawkins one of her own vessels,

Jesus of Lubeck, on which the royal standard flew above the miserable human cargo. The second expedition passed without incident, but the third proved to be a disaster that set in train events that would end in war.

Hawkins set out in 1567, taking with him his young cousin, Francis Drake. Drake, another Devonian, was born *c.*1540 and was apprenticed on a small coaster. At its master's death he inherited the vessel and began a successful career, which included sailing to the coast of Guinea and the Spanish Main with Captain John Lovell. He was already an experienced sailor by the time he joined Hawkins as commander of the comparatively small 50-ton barque *Judith*. Hit by storms, Hawkins was given permission by the Spanish to anchor at the Mexican port of San Juan de Ulloa for reprovisioning. But the Spanish had other ideas and attacked the unprepared ships. *Jesus of Lubeck* was an old-fashioned ship, slow to respond and was easily overcome. Drake was able to escape in the nimbler *Judith*, and the third vessel in the enterprise, *Minion*, managed to rescue Hawkins and some of his crew. The rest were slaughtered. This episode had a

Richard Grenville converted the thirteenth-century Buckland Abbey into a fine house, with this magnificent great hall. It was bought by Sir Francis Drake, and it was from here that he planned the attack on the Spanish Armada.

profound effect on Hawkins and Drake, whose lives were now to be dominated by a deep hatred of the Spanish. They began to plan their revenge.

Hawkins' role was in many ways the more decisive. He was appointed Treasurer and later Comptroller of the Navy. He had seen the fate of the sluggardly *Jesus of Lubeck* and began designing a new type of vessel. The high forecastle went, the sides were made lower and the underwater hull more streamlined. The result was a vessel that was fast and could sail closer to the wind than earlier, grander warships. More accurate guns with longer range replaced the older cannon.

Drake took a different approach: he attacked the Spanish directly wherever he could, determined to break up their American monopoly. To the Spanish he was a common pirate, to the English a national hero, who had the covert, though not very covert, support of the Queen. His most famous exploits included the attack on a Spanish treasure train between Nombre de Dios and Panama, after which he returned to England in 1573, his expedition ships fully loaded with gold and silver. It was during his time in the area that he climbed a tree and saw in the distance another ocean, the Pacific. He was determined to visit this ocean, and set off in 1577 in the *Pelican*, which in the course of the voyage was renamed the *Golden Hinde*. This was one of the great voyages of the age, and a profitable one, as Drake captured a Spanish treasure ship and held many towns on the west coast of South America to ransom. They had no preparations for English ships appearing in the Pacific. He completed his great circumnavigation in 1580.

By 1585 Spain and England were at war. It was obvious that England was not going to send an army to fight Spain, and the only way that a Spanish army could fight on British soil was to send an invasion fleet. The English Navy was far the smaller of the two fleets and needed time to prepare. Drake gave the English time. In what was the most astounding episode in an incredible career, he sailed right into the harbour of Cadiz. Defence in southern Europe was still entrusted to fast, rowed galleys. Drake simply blew them out of the water and set about destroying the Spanish ships. There was to be no invasion that year.

It was in 1588 that the famous Armada set sail, an imposing fleet of 132 vessels, described by the Spanish as 'invincible'. The ships looked grand but were built to the old pattern, high sided, with tall fore and aft castles. The English, however, had Hawkins' new craft, which were at least a knot faster than the Spanish, could sail closer to the wind and had longer barrelled guns firing with greater range and accuracy. The big Spanish ships made ideal targets. The destruction wreaked in the battle was compounded by gales that battered and wrecked much of the Armada, so that out of the great fleet only fifty-three vessels limped home. Drake and Hawkins were commanders, under the Lord High Admiral: they had their revenge. The two men set off on one last raid to the West Indies in 1795 but both were struck down by disease and were buried at sea.

Sir Walter Raleigh, the third of the great Devonians, was born *c.*1552 but had a very different early career. He was a courtier, accomplished poet and historian. He famously sent out expeditions to attempt to establish colonies in North America in the 1580s. Where the Spaniards had returned with gold and silver, Raleigh's men brought back the potato and tobacco. He himself was convinced that there really was a famous city of gold, El Dorado, and set out to find it when he led an expedition to South America in 1594. The death of Elizabeth in 1603 brought a drastic reverse to his fortunes. James I made peace with Spain, and Raleigh found himself in The Tower charged with high treason. He was released and went on one last South American expedition. The king was more interested in appeasing the Spanish than in the fate of Raleigh who, on his return, was condemned to death. He faced his execution as fearlessly as he had the dangers of the sea. Feeling the executioner's axe, he calmly noted, 'Tis a sharp remedy, but a sure one for all ills.'

The other famous seamen of the age, Frobisher and Grenville, were again quite different characters. Frobisher is the odd one out of the West Country set, born in Yorkshire in 1539. His early years at sea were spent as what was officially known as a privateer, though pirate might have been a more accurate description. He sailed with Drake to the West Indies and plundered Spanish shipping around the Azores. He played a heroic role in the Armada battle, fighting off four Spanish vessels near Portland Bill, but is best known for his attempts to find the North West passage. He made his way to the Arctic and traded with the Inuit. A robust character, Martin Frobisher died in battle in 1594.

Sir Richard Grenville was born in Cornwall *c.*1541. He came from a seafaring family but not a lucky one. His father commanded the *Mary Rose* and died when she sank. Richard Grenville led Raleigh's first expedition to America, but is famous not so much for how he lived as for how he died. He was a commander in Lord Howard's Azores fleet in 1591, when they had an unexpected encounter with a far larger Spanish fleet. Grenville's ship, the *Revenge*, became separated from the rest and stood alone to fight against fifty-three Spanish warships with the inevitable result. History is divided over whether he was exceptionally heroic or foolhardy and incompetent. Tennyson described the action in verse, and left no one in any doubt that to Victorian England he was a hero, fit to stand among the ranks of the other great Elizabethans.

THE SOUTH COAST

The images that come to mind with the words 'South Coast' are many and varied. For most of us the first association will be with seaside resorts, from the pebbly beaches of Georgian Brighton to the sands of sub-tropical Torbay. Then there is the scenery, again offering contrasts from the white chalk cliffs of Dorset and those that bring the South Downs to abrupt closures, to the marshes of Romney. There is another factor, however, that does not appear on the map of Britain itself, but which has had immense influence on the history of the region: the South Coast looks out across the Channel to France. So ports have developed to carry trade to and from the continent – Dover because it is the nearest good harbour to France,

Southampton because it enjoys the natural protection of the Solent. Relations between Britain and her nearest neighbours have not always been friendly, so the South Coast is also peppered with fortifications, from the forts of the Romans, through the Martello towers erected when Napoleon seemed the greatest threat, to more modern installations. For centuries, however, Britain's greatest protection was her Navy, and there are few places where the glories of the past are more impressively celebrated than at Portsmouth. Add to the list the old fishing villages, the yachts of Cowes and so much more, it is not difficult to see why this section is crowded with maritime sites covering a period from the Bronze Age to the present day.

Lulworth Cove is a beautiful natural harbour, all but surrounded by high chalk cliffs.

LULWORTH COVE
Heritage Centre

Free; Open daily; Tel: 01929 400587

No one really needs an excuse to visit Lulworth Cove. It is an extraordinary natural phenomenon, a bay that is almost a round pond, created when the sea broke through the cliffs. There are wonderful, though decidedly strenuous, walks along the cliffs, one of which comes out above the natural arch of Durdle Door. The Centre tells the history of the area, with a good deal about the more nefarious goings on when this was the haunt of smugglers.

POOLE
Waterfront Museum

£; Monday to Saturday, Sunday afternoons; High Street; Tel: 01202 262600

Every year thousands pass through Poole on their way to the ferry terminus and quite fail to notice the much older port that survives alongside the new. Here, amid a wealth of old dockside buildings, is the museum, housed in a former mill rising on the site of the medieval Town Cellars. It tells the story of the town from Roman times, with a very strong emphasis on the history of the port and local shipwrecks – perhaps not one to visit just before boarding the ferry. A joint ticket can also be purchased to include the nearby fifteenth-century merchant's house Scaplen's Court.

BUCKLER'S HARD

££; Daily; Tel: 01590 616203; Website: www.bucklershard.co.uk

This is an extraordinary survivor, an eighteenth-century shipbuilding centre that has remained virtually unchanged. It was originally intended to be a port. In 1709 the Duke of Montagu, of nearby Beaulieu, had the idea of creating the port on the Beaulieu River to take produce from a colony he intended to establish in the West Indies. Unfortunately, he never acquired the colony, so Montagu Town was useless. It had been laid out as a model town with

a broad main street leading down to the water, making it ideal for shipbuilding. Timber from the New Forest could be hauled down the street, and boats could be built and launched into deep water. Montagu Town became Buckler's Hard.

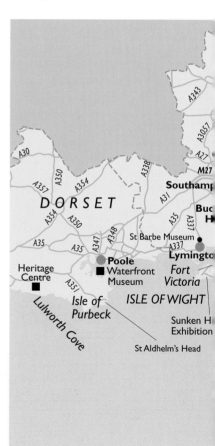

Apart from the slipways, there are none of the familiar signs of shipbuilding as we know them today. But it was here that the great ships of Nelson's Navy were built, including his own favourite command, *Agamemnon*. The museum in the village has a display showing the shipyard as it was at the beginning of the nineteenth century.

In a sense, the whole village is now a museum, with reconstructions of how a labourer's cottage would have been, contrasting with the far grander accommodation of a master shipwright. The man who oversaw the great years of Buckler's Hard was shipbuilder Henry Adams, and his house still stands. There was an eyrie at the top, where he sat with his telescope in his latter years. Each workman had a number, and if Adams saw any slacking or mistakes, he rang a bell and hoisted the number on the flagpole.

Cruises are available on the river between Easter and October, and the boat trip takes visitors past another, more recent, scene of marine engineering: the docks where sections for Mulberry Harbour were built before being floated across to France on D-Day, 1944.

SOUTHAMPTON
Maritime Museum

Free; Tuesday to Saturday, Sunday afternoon; Town Quay;
Tel: 023 8063 5904;
Website: www.southampton.gov.uk/leisure/heritage/maritime.htm

This is as good a place as any to begin an exploration of Southampton's maritime history. For a start you get a reminder that it does go back a very long way, as the building itself is a former wool warehouse, built *c*.1400. Inside, one of the most striking exhibits is a model showing the docks in the 1930s when the greatest liners of the world were regular visitors.

For many, the grandest of them all was the *Queen Mary*, and there is a magnificent model of the ship. Seeing the museum exhibits might well encourage visitors to visit what is still to be seen in the docks area, and happily the age of steam still survives.

SS *Shieldhall*

Prices vary; Dock Gate 4, Berth 48, Information on sailings from Blue Funnel Cruises, Tel: 02380 223278

The *Shieldhall* was built in 1954 for the unglamorous task of taking sewage sludge down the Clyde for dumping at sea. Now she has the more pleasant job of taking passengers for cruises around the coast and to special events such as the Cowes Regatta. She is a steam enthusiast's delight, with power supplied by a pair of triple expansion engines and no fewer than nineteen auxiliary engines. Visitors are welcomed on board when she is in dock. Lying nearby is the 1930 tug *Calshot*, built by the local firm Thornycroft, still at work as Vosper Thornycroft. It is hoped that she, too, will be restored to full working order.

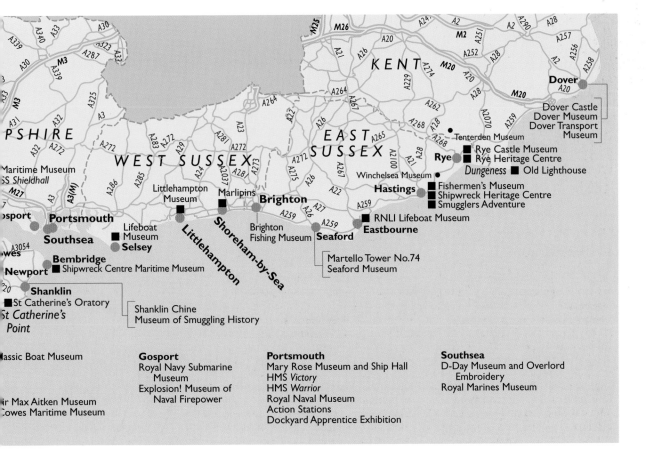

Gosport
Royal Navy Submarine Museum
Explosion! Museum of Naval Firepower

Portsmouth
Mary Rose Museum and Ship Hall
HMS *Victory*
HMS *Warrior*
Royal Naval Museum
Action Stations
Dockyard Apprentice Exhibition

Southsea
D-Day Museum and Overlord Embroidery
Royal Marines Museum

The submarine *Alliance*, sleek and deadly.

BEMBRIDGE, ISLE OF WIGHT
Shipwreck Centre Maritime Museum

££; April to November; Sherbourne Street; Tel: 01983 872223

A good mixture of exhibits is spread over six galleries. Shipwreck is matched with salvage, and there are some interesting examples of early diving equipment. Not all of the latter inspire a great deal of confidence. Other sections deal with the days of sail and the paddle steamers that served the island.

COWES, IOW
Sir Max Aitken Museum

£; May to September Tuesday to Saturday; 83 High Street; Tel: 01983 292191

Sir Max Aitken's personal collection of marine paintings, nautical instruments and yachting memorabilia.

Cowes Maritime Museum

Free; Monday to Wednesday, Friday to Saturday; Tel: 01983 293341

A small museum where the main emphasis is on photographs and plans from local boat builders. There is a modest collection of boats on loan, including one of the well-known dinghies designed by Uffa Fox.

FORT VICTORIA, IOW
Sunken History Exhibition

£; Easter to November; At Fort Victoria Marine Aquarium near Yarmouth, off the A3054; Tel: 01983 760283; Website: www.globalnet.co.uk/~pblake/aquarium.html

The museum is part of a complex that includes a marine aquarium, a planetarium and a model railway. Sunken History is far more than just a story of shipwrecks. It sets out to show the work of marine archaeologists, ships being only a part of that story. The oldest discovery dates back to the end of the last Ice Age when the Solent was a river valley submerged by the rising waters. This is a world that has been submerged for thousands of years, and only now is this underwater landscape being revealed. More familiar exhibits show the exploration of a sixteenth-century wreck. One grim story is that of the 'first fleet', the convict ships sent out to Australia.

NEWPORT, IOW
Classic Boat Museum

££; April to October daily; Seaclose Wharf, Newport Harbour; Tel: 01983 533493

This is the sort of museum where you see people standing around with dreamy looks in their eyes, for it has a wonderful collection of around forty small boats, just the sort of thing that

many of us would love to get our hands on. Some people will even have handled similar boats, such as the famous Mirror-class dinghies that brought cheap boating to a whole generation of enthusiasts. Those who look for classics might go for a local boat, a Bembridge Redwing such as *Circus Girl*, built in 1898. Another Redwing, *Kestrel*, was once owned by Lord Brabazon, who gave it a unique Autogyro rig with a propeller on top of a steel mast. Or you might care to imagine yourself travelling in suitably jaunty style in the motor boat *Jazz*, built in 1912, with an engine adapted from a sports car. Not everything relates to leisure, at least not directly. Many an amateur sailor has had reason to be grateful for the presence of the lifeboat service, and the museum is home to an exceptional early example. This is the self-righting, rowing lifeboat *Queen Victoria* of 1887. All the boats are properly maintained and regularly seen out on the water.

ST CATHERINE'S POINT, IOW
St Catherine's Oratory

EH/NT; Free; Open Access; North of the A3055; Map ref: 196/493772

This extraordinary building is popularly known as 'The Pepperpot', but what it actually looks like is a stone rocket. It has a pointed roof and buttresses that look like the fins. In fact, it is a rare survivor, a medieval lighthouse built in the fourteenth century on the highest point of the island. It was endowed by Walter de Godyton, who paid for a priest to say masses for the family and to light the beacon each night. Its work has long since been done by a conventional lighthouse at the Point. Built in 1838, the octagonal tower was once much higher, but the light was often lost in mist and so it was shortened in 1875.

SHANKLIN, IOW
Shanklin Chine

£; April to November daily;
Tel: 01983 866432

It has to be said that the main reason people come here is to enjoy the splendours of the natural gorge with its spectacular waterfall. But it does also have a Heritage Centre, with changing displays, generally on a maritime theme; there are also remains of PLUTO, the pipeline under the ocean, built to supply fuel following the invasion of Normandy in 1944.

VENTNOR, IOW
Museum of Smuggling History

£; April to September daily; Botanic Gardens; Tel: 01983 853677

This might seem an odd place to find a smuggling museum, but it is not so much *in* the gardens as *under* them. Here in extensive vaults is a tale of smuggling, a popular trade for islanders for some 700 years.

GOSPORT
Royal Navy Submarine Museum

££; Daily; Haslar Jetty Road;
Tel: 023 9252 9217;
Website: www.rnsubmus.co.uk

There is no question about the main attraction here: the A-class submarine *Alliance*, built in 1945 and in its day one of the biggest submarines in the Royal Navy. Seen from the outside, the vessel looks suitably menacing but quite roomy; once inside reality becomes clear. Two-thirds of the hull is taken up with ballast and fuel tanks, and only the top third is available for all the machinery, armaments and the crew of seventy-four. Everyone has to be crammed together: the stokers' mess, for example, is just 12ft by 8ft and was home to a dozen men sleeping in three tiers of bunks. As one watch went on duty, the other took over the bunks. It is not a good place for claustrophobics. And if you want to know just how complex life could be in a submarine, just try understanding the instructions for flushing the loo – or, in naval parlance, the heads. The museum is no less interesting, with models of the horribly unlikely and dangerous looking prototypes. The latest addition to the collection is the Navy's very first submarine, *Holland I*, salvaged in 1982 after seventy years on the seabed and now restored.

Explosion! Museum of Naval Firepower

££; Daily; Priddy's Hard; Tel: 023 9250 5600;
Website: www.explosion.org.uk

The buildings are eighteenth century and most appropriate for this new museum, as they once held the Grand Magazine, an immense gunpowder vault. Everything else, however, is very twenty-first century, using all the latest multimedia techniques. In spite of the sensational name, this is more than just about a lot of guns going bang. It also tells the equally interesting story of munitions, how they were made and what life was like for the men and women who made them.

The multi-media film show takes place in the appropriate setting of the old gunpowder vault at Explosion!

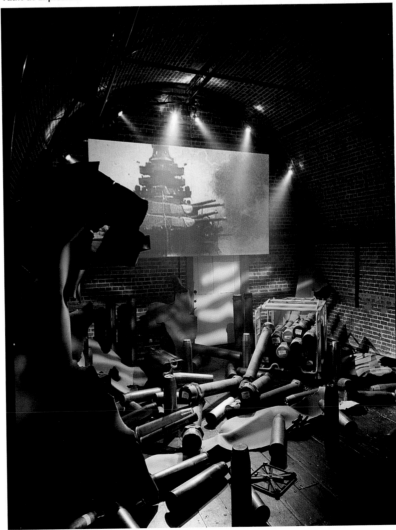

PORTSMOUTH The Historic Dockyard

There really is nowhere quite like this in Britain for its combination of historic site and famous ships. Here is a dockyard that has grown through the centuries, where you can wander freely, admiring buildings, some of which date back to the eighteenth century. Within the complex are three historic warships, from the sixteenth, eighteenth and nineteenth centuries, and three separate museums, each dealing with a different aspect of naval life. There are also harbour tours by boat to see whatever modern warships are in port, and a separate trip can take you to land on Spitbank Fort, a mile out to sea. Visitors can buy tickets covering all the exhibits, opt for a three-for-the-price-of-two tickets, or buy individual tickets. The prices quoted below are for individual entries:

The following information covers the whole site, all museums and ships:

Daily; Tel: 023 9286 1533; Website: www.historicdockyard.co.uk

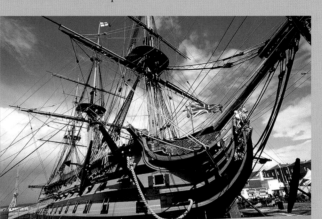

Probably the most famous ship of the Royal Navy, Nelson's flagship *Victory*, on which he died at Trafalgar.

Mary Rose Museum and Ship Hall

£££

The *Mary Rose* was built at Portsmouth for Henry VIII in 1509–10, and named after the king's sister. The ship was soon in action against the French, and a report was sent back to Henry that this was 'the flower I trow of all ships that ever sailed'. She was a four-masted carrack and after a refit had a formidable armament of forty-three heavy guns and thirty-seven lighter weapons. When she set out for battle she carried a crew of over a hundred sailors and nearly 300 soldiers and gunners. In 1545 she sailed out again to meet the French fleet and, watched from the shore by the king, the great ship foundered and sank. In 1982 a substantial part of the hull was recovered from the Solent and is now on display in this special ship hall. She remains awesome and provides a unique opportunity to admire the work of Tudor shipwrights. The museum displays the artefacts found with the wreck. There are the essentials of a warship of the period, including a bronze gun and large numbers of long bows. Perhaps the most affecting finds are the personal possessions, such as a roughly carved flute or a still immaculate backgammon board.

HMS *Victory*

£££ includes entry to Royal Naval Museum

This is probably the most famous British naval ship of all time, forever associated with Admiral Lord Nelson. She is the last surviving First Rate ship, a name used in the eighteenth century, when she was built, to describe a vessel carrying more than 100 guns. Work began on her in 1759, and by 1797 she was demoted to the lowly rank of hospital ship. Thanks to the Napoleonic Wars she was given a complete refit, and in 1805 she sailed off to Trafalgar and a place in history. Today's visitors get guided tours of what is now largely replica. The old wooden masts, for example, have been replaced by lighter metal ones, but it is still a great ship.

HMS *Warrior*

£££

When I first saw the ship in 1981 she was little more than a hull, having finished an unglamorous career as a pontoon at Pembroke, her decks encased in concrete. The restoration to her present condition seems all but miraculous. Launched in 1861 she was the navy's first true armour-plated battleship (see p.124), powered by sail or steam, and when both were used together on a trial run she exceeded 17 knots. She is a fascinating mixture of the old and the new. Technically, she was classed as a frigate, and was still firing broadsides just as *Victory* had done. The restoration has been so thorough that it seems as if one were visiting a ship just fitted out and ready for a maiden voyage. Every detail is correct, right down to the fixtures in the cabins.

Royal Naval Museum

££

This is more or less what the name suggests, a museum devoted to telling the history of the navy up to the present day. It has recently been updated with modern interactive displays, and the new 'Victory at Trafalgar' gallery recreates the atmosphere of the battle.

Dockyard Apprentice Exhibition

£

The one area devoted to the work of the dockyard itself, this gives an idea of the skills and technology employed in building a battleship at the beginning of the twentieth century.

Action Stations

£££

This is the latest addition to the complex, opened in 2000, with all the very latest whizz-bang displays to recreate life on a modern warship.

SOUTHSEA

D-Day Museum & Overlord Embroidery

££; Daily; Clarence Esplanade;
Tel: 023 9282 7261;
Website: www.portsmouthmuseums.co.uk

The embroidery is the twentieth-century equivalent of the Bayeux Tapestry, though considerably larger, with a total of thirty-four panels stretching out to a length of 272ft. Much of the museum is devoted to Britain at war, but there is also a series of displays recreating the greatest seaborne invasion force ever to leave Britain.

Royal Marines Museum

££; Daily; Eastney Esplanade;
Tel: 023 9281 9385;
Website: www.royalmarinesmuseum.co.uk

The main room setting, the former Artillery Officers' Mess, is sumptuous, grander than most Grand Hotels. The marines were founded in 1664 as 'sea soldiers' and officially established in 1775; this is their story. It is part conventional museum, with a collection of over 7000 medals, trophies and paintings, and part up-to-the minute audio-visual and interactive displays.

SELSEY

Lifeboat Museum

Free, but contributions welcomed;
Easter to October daily; East Beach;
Tel: 01243 602833;
Website: www.selseylifeboat.fslife.co.uk

Although there is still a lifeboat here, this is more than just a museum of local interest. It shows the work of the RNLI all around the British coast, and has lifeboat models and videos of lifeboats at sea.

LITTLEHAMPTON

Littlehampton Museum

Free; Tuesday to Saturday; Church Street;
Tel: 01903 738100

One section of this local history museum is 'The Sea Room', which is very much what the name suggests, a collection devoted to the port and its seafarers. There are artefacts, photos and paintings, but what sets this museum apart is the collection of over 200 miniature ships. There is also a separate area for temporary exhibitions.

SHOREHAM-BY-SEA

Marlipins

£; May to September Tuesday to Saturday;
Tel: 01273 462994

The museum, housed in an early twelfth-century building, has always had an extensive collection dealing with maritime subjects, covering everything from a lighthouse lamp to figureheads. But at the time of writing it has been closed for a major refurbishment and reorganization. It is scheduled for reopening in the summer of 2003, so anyone planning a visit should telephone for an update.

The Artillery Officers' Mess of 1868 now houses the Royal Marines Museum and looks out across the Memorial Gardens.

THE CINQUE PORTS

The early history of the Cinque Ports is a little vague. The name certainly dates back to the early years of Norman rule, when these were the five important ports for the protection of south east England from invasion – though the name is not pronounced as the modern French 'cinque' but as 'sink'. It was probably in the eleventh century that the old system employed in Saxon times of hiring mercenaries and their ships to defend the country was replaced by one in which ports provided ships for what was, in effect, the Royal Navy. The first five were Hastings, Romney, Hythe, Dover and Sandwich. The situation was later formalized and the official Cinque Ports established. Each of the ports had to meet quotas of ships and men when called on by the crown, and in return they enjoyed special rights and privileges. The overall standard quota was for fifty-seven

ships, each fully manned, to be available for a maximum of fifteen days a year. That was considered quite sufficient when the main threat came from raiders rather than invaders. In return, the ports were excused taxes and customs duties, were awarded special trading rights and allowed to hold their own judicial courts. To ensure that the ports met their obligations they were set under the control of the Lord Warden, who also held the offices of Admiral of the Cinque Ports and Constable of Dover Castle. In its time this was an important position which carried a great deal of prestige and responsibility, but with the decline of the ports it became a purely honorary post, which in recent years has been held by Sir Winston Churchill and the Queen Mother.

In their prime the Cinque Ports represented the front line of defence against invasion from continental Europe.

The name 'Cinque Ports' survived, even after Rye was added to the original five. The old town climbs up the hill above the harbour.

To meet the growing demand for men and vessels two more ports were added – Rye and Winchelsea. These were the head ports, and assisting them were a number of 'limbs', such as Lydd and Faversham. They all prospered mightily as a result of their privileged status, but it was not to last. It was not enemy attacks that brought them down, rather the great storms of 1287. In that year south east England was lashed by immense gales, which moved shingle, changed the course of the River Rother, and left the port of Romney quite literally high and dry. Southampton, protected to the south by the Isle of Wight, began to grow in importance, and soon only Dover of all the original Cinque Ports could still be said to have a major role in either defence or trade. It was not all a dead loss for the other ancient ports. As the coastline changed, so the marshes and creeks became an ideal home for smugglers. As the permanent Navy developed, the influence of the Cinque Ports diminished. They were soon unable to meet anything like their quota of ships, and when the fleet was assembled to sail out against the Spanish Armada in 1588, they could only muster five ships.

An old warehouse on the quay at Faversham, a Cinque Ports 'limb'.

New Romney achieved its official status as a Cinque Port in the twelfth century, but it is difficult to imagine how it must have been before the Rother moved and the sea retreated. Visit the church of St Nicholas, however, and you can still see the tide marks on the pillars of the nave. Nearby Hythe has at least kept a tenuous connection with the sea, even though the old town centre is now half a mile inland. It retained something of its role in defence with the construction of the circular Martello towers, built to fend off the Napoleonic invasion that never was. Hastings lost its harbour in the Great Storm, and the centre of the town shifted eastwards to gain some protection from the overshadowing hills, though it never regained its former pre-eminence among the Cinque Ports. Sandwich is now almost two miles inland, but boats still tie up at its ancient quays, having followed a tortuous route up the winding channel of the Stour from Pegwell Bay. With its town walls, guarded by the twin towers of the Barbican Gate

and the even older Fisher Gate of 1384, Sandwich is the epitome of the medieval town. Streets and alleys make the most of every inch of space within the confines of the walls, there are three medieval churches and the Guildhall has exhibitions and regalia on the Cinque Ports.

Dover has, of course, thrived where the others have dwindled in importance: here the harbour is the work of twentieth-century engineers, not medieval builders. The story of Dover's long history is told in the Dover Museum, where there is a reminder of just how far back the maritime history does stretch in the form of a Bronze Age boat. Here, too, there is a great deal of information about the history of the Cinque Ports.

The 'Two Antient Towns', which were added to the original five head ports, Rye and Winchelsea, are both delightful spots – and both have been deserted by the sea. The narrow streets of Rye climb the hill to the Norman church, while Ypres Tower remains as a fragment of the once mighty castle. Strand Quay survives, but Rye's actual quay is over a mile away. Winchelsea is, in some ways, the most interesting of all the towns. The old town was all but obliterated in the thirteenth-century storm and a new town built miles away on a hilltop site. It fared no better, as shingle built up over the years and cut off all access to the sea. Merchants abandoned the town for nearby Rye, and Winchelsea remained almost fossilized in its design: this is how New Towns were planned in the thirteenth century. Here a regular grid of streets is laid out within the town walls, where three of the ancient gateways have survived. Its early history can be seen in the fine public buildings, such as the Court Hall; once again, you can see just why the Cinque Ports were created. The town was attacked by the French in the fourteenth century and much of the church of St Thomas the Martyr was destroyed. Inside the surviving fragment is a resplendent effigy to the first Admiral of the Cinque Ports. It could also serve as a monument to the men and ships under his command and his successors' who defended the English coast for so many years.

The entrance to the Royal National Lifeboat Institution at Eastbourne celebrates almost two hundred years of life saving in the town.

HASTINGS

Fishermen's Museum

Free, donations welcomed; Daily; Rock-a-Nore Rd; Tel: 01424 461446

The museum should really be seen together with the real thing, for they go together to make a unique experience. Starting with the present-day scene, Hastings is unusual in that fishing boats are to be seen lined up along the shore, a privilege that goes with the town's status as a Cinque Port. Even stranger are the old net shops, which have been described as 'skyscraper huts'. There are rows of these black weather-boarded huts, tarred all over, multi-storeyed and jostling for space. The story of these and other facets of the fishing industry are told in the museum, housed in the nearby former fishermen's church. One of the larger exhibits is the lugger *Enterprise*, built locally in 1909.

The figurehead, a survivor from the *Peruvian*, wrecked on the beach at Seaford in 1889.

BRIGHTON

Inevitably one thinks first of Regency Brighton, with its finely controlled, elegant architecture rather overshadowed by the oriental flamboyance of the Royal Pavilion. Then there is the Victorian contribution: the Palace Pier of 1896, with its elaborate ironwork, and the even grander West Pier, designed in 1865 by the greatest of pier engineers, Eugenius Birch, but now in sad disrepair. Yet long before the idea of seaside holidays had been formulated, Brighton had a workaday life as a small fishing port.

Brighton Fishing Museum

Free; Daily; The Arches, King's Rd; Tel: 01273 723064

The Arches were once used by local fishermen to store their gear, but are now mostly occupied by artists, craft shops and gift shops. One survives to tell the story of working Brighton, with boats, collections of fishing gear and illustrations. It also holds the archive for Sussex lifeboats and has a number of models. For kids, there are half a dozen boats outside they can clamber all over.

SEAFORD

Martello Tower No.74 – Seaford Museum

£; Easter to end of Summer Time Sundays and afternoons, Wednesday to Saturday, Winter Sundays; Tel: 01323 898222; Website: www.seafordmuseum.org

Here is a rare chance to see inside one of the Martello Towers. Built to defend Britain against Napoleon, they were never used, but this one at least provides a home for a museum telling the story of the town, once an important member of the Cinque Ports. The maritime section includes a fine pair of glamorous figureheads.

EASTBOURNE

RNLI Lifeboat Museum

Free; Easter to Christmas daily; King Edward's Parade; Tel: 01323 730717

There has been a lifeboat station at Eastbourne since 1822, so it is appropriate that it should also be home to England's first lifeboat museum. The collection of models of lifeboats through the years and photographs was given an update in 2002 with video and interactive displays.

The outline of a lugger on the wall identifies the Fishermen's Museum at Hastings.

Shipwreck Heritage Centre

Free; Daily; Tel: 01424 437452

This is both a serious and an absolutely fascinating museum, showing the work achieved by marine archaeologists. The oldest remains are from a ship of the Roman period, which appears to have sunk on her way to London with a cargo of stone. Only the ribs and some nails survive, but that is enough to recreate how the ship was held together. It is quite unlike other early ship construction techniques, involving bending the nails round to act as both conventional nails and as a form of small clamp. There are finds from the Dutch East India Company cargo ship *Amsterdam*, which came to grief on the Hastings beach in 1749 and has been stuck there ever since. The remains can still be seen off St Leonards at low tide. The other major find is a Victorian river barge.

Smugglers Adventure

£££; Daily; Cobourg Place;
Tel: 01424 444412; Website:
www.smugglers@discoverhastings.co.uk

It is the location that makes this visit so exciting, a warren of caves and passages burrowing under West Hill. Here visitors get something like the old, fairground ghost-train experience, with eerie noises and evocative lighting as they move between a series of tableaux and exhibitions. This is one for the children, largely because it plays down the brutality associated with The Gentlemen of the eighteenth century.

RYE

Rye Castle Museum

£ per site (reduced price for joint ticket);
April to October Thursday to Monday,
November to March weekends
Ypres Tower only; Tel: 01797 226728;
Website: www.ryetourism.co.uk

The museum is divided between two sites. The older of the two is housed in the Ypres Tower, built in 1249 as part of the town defences but used for many centuries as a gaol. So the emphasis here is on law and order, and on this stretch of coast the principal illegal activity was smuggling. Smuggling, by its nature, leaves few artefacts behind, but this museum has a few. One is a curious device called a spout lantern. It is a bit like a watering can, with the light shining out to sea down the spout, undetectable by watchers on the land.

The other collection is housed in East Street, and is concerned with the overall history of Rye. There is also a special section devoted to the history of the Cinque Ports, including the magnificent regalia worn by officials.

The thirteenth-century Ypres Tower at Rye has a suitably gaunt appearance for a museum devoted to law and law-breakers.

SMUGGLERS AND WRECKERS

The first smuggler probably began his nefarious trade on the day the first duty was imposed on goods. There had been sporadic attempts to impose duties in Saxon times, but the system only became formalized when Edward I imposed a permanent customs system. From taxes imposed on just a few goods, the system grew, until by the eighteenth century there were over 2000 items subjected to duty. This was the heyday of the smuggler. No one has ever calculated just how many people were involved directly or indirectly in evading duty, but it was a huge number, and communities around the coast saw it as a perfectly acceptable way of supplementing an income. It was so widely accepted that local papers could openly run adverts, such as this one from a Sussex paper of 1785, offering 'A very useful CART, fit for a malster, ash-man, or a smuggler ... and many articles that are very useful to a Smuggler.' Local magistrates did not just turn a blind eye but were happy to fill their cellars with contraband goods. Smuggling in the eighteenth and early nineteenth century was a two-way traffic, with goods carrying a high tax, such as wool, being taken out of England to pay for the goods for the return journey. The popular image is of barrels of brandy being rolled into a cave, with connections to some cliff-top house or inn, and there were many such places. By far the most profitable commodity for the eighteenth-century smuggler was tea.

Many smugglers were honoured members of their community and regarded as very honest men. Harry Paulet, a notorious Hampshire smuggler, was sailing back from France in 1759 when he spotted the French Admiral and his fleet leaving Brest and heading for England. Although he risked his life if caught smuggling, he sailed up to Admiral Hawke's squadron with the news. The British set off with Paulet on board and the result was a decisive victory for the English fleet at the Battle of Quiberon Bay. Paulet's cash reward enabled him to give up smuggling and enjoy a comfortable retirement. There are many stories of 'honest' smugglers. John Carter of Cornwall was known as the King of Prussia Cove, and the cove itself was indeed famous for its complex cave system and secret tunnels. He suffered the indignity on one occasion of having goods seized by the revenue men, which he had promised to one of his regular customers. This was a severe blow to his honour and prestige. He broke into the Customs House and reclaimed 'his' property but left everything else untouched. The Customs men had no doubt who was responsible but took the matter no further: just another episode in the long-running contest between the smuggler and the excise men. The smugglers also provided work for many local craftsmen. They needed to have fast boats to outrun the revenue cutters, and ports such as Polperro became famous for their speedy luggers. This is the side of smuggling that has led to it being romanticized, as in Kipling's famous poem:

> Brandy for the Parson,
> 'Baccy for the Clerk;
> Laces for a lady, letters for a spy,
> Watch the wall, my darling, while the Gentlemen go by!

However, not everything was as cosy as that verse suggests. There were bands of smugglers who effectively terrorized whole areas and were more than ready to murder to protect their trade. None was more ferocious than the infamous Hawkhurst gang of Kent. They were so powerful that the Customs officers were quite unable to challenge them. An official report of the 1740s described how they could raise 500 armed men in less than an hour to defend their goods and 'that not one person in ten in the country but would give them assistance'. But when faced with opposition, as at Goudhurst in Kent in 1747, they declared they would burn the town and murder the inhabitants. There was a pitched battle with a militia raised by the local gentry, and in the end the town was saved. The arrogance of the big gangs was terrifying. They would ride into a small town, shooting off their muskets, demanding free drinks at the inns and defying the law to approach them. It was not a good idea to enquire too closely into the gangs. There was the case of an inquisitive young man taken off by the smugglers and never seen again. One of the most audacious acts was the raid on the Customs House at Poole. A load of tea had been captured and the smugglers marched on Poole where the contraband had been taken. Even though there was an armed sloop in the harbour, the Hawkhurst gang broke in and recovered the goods. Later on, a local shoemaker who had accepted a gift of tea from the smugglers was held by Customs and agreed to turn informer. He and an officer, William Galley, were captured by the gang, tortured and murdered. A mythology has grown up around smuggling – every cave is a smuggler's cave, every old inn has its secret passages. This all helps make parts of the coast seem very exciting. The brutality and viciousness of the big, organized gangs tend to be largely overlooked.

If smuggling was often far more savage than its popular image suggests, wrecking was not quite the evil pastime it is supposed to be. Wreckers are generally perceived as unscrupulous men luring ships

Prussia Cove in Cornwall was the base of operations for the famous smuggler John Carter.

onto the rocks by false lights. There are stories of a light fastened to a hobbling horse, so that it bobbed up and down in imitation of a masthead light, leading the unwary captain to assume that it was safe to come further inshore. The Wirral was an area said to be particularly bad for luring sailors to their doom. Yet there is very little evidence to support such stories, and the truth is that there was not much need to lure ships to their doom: there were quite enough shipwrecks around the coast as it was. Areas such as the Scillies were notorious for their treacherous waters, as the splendid collection of old figureheads on Tresco elegantly testifies. A rather more telling testimony came from a visitor who noted just how much timber was used in houses and buildings on treeless islands. The truth is that the vast majority of wreckers descended on ships wrecked by natural causes. There was no legal right to take anything from such vessels but they were generally accepted as being gifts from nature. Even the clergy were disinclined to argue the opposite, and some went further. An old story tells of a vicar calling to the congregation to stop rushing from the church before he'd had time to leave the pulpit.

Stop! Stop! Cried he, at least one prayer,
Let me get down, and all start fair.

The wreckers were locals who would break a whole ship up for its timber and rigging, and carry off the cargo. In many cases the wreckers who had gone out to a ship had saved the lives of the crew – but not always. There were many recorded instances of a ship going aground that could have been floated off at the next tide if the wreckers had not got there first. There were also cases of survivors losing their clothes and valuables – and in a very few instances, their lives at the hands of wreckers. Acts of real barbarity seem to have been very rare. Far more common were the stories of ships carrying a cargo of wine and brandy being emptied and the entire local populace getting roaring drunk on the proceeds. In modern times there was the famous case of the SS *Politician* running aground on the Scottish island of Eriskay in 1941 with a cargo of whisky. It formed the basis for the comic novel and film *Whisky Galore*. In the eyes of the law, the islanders were wreckers, just as much as any eighteenth-century wrecker on a wild Cornish shore.

The extraordinarily well-preserved remains of the 3500-year-old Dover Boat.

DOVER

Dover has the distinction of having the largest artificial harbour in the world. A modest start was made in 1495 with the building of a pier, though the first real attempt to make a protected harbour came in the reign of Elizabeth I. There were further improvements over the years, but the greatest changes came in the nineteenth century, culminating in the decision taken in 1895 to enclose the harbour with breakwaters. When work was completed it was said to be capable of containing the entire British fleet.

Dover Castle

EH; £££; Daily; Tel: 01304 205108

Dover stands at one end of the shortest sea crossing between England and France, so that few places have a greater strategic significance. As 'Dubris', it was the headquarters of the Romans' British Fleet, which needed to be protected against enemies and required the building of a fort. The fleet also needed to be guided safely into harbour. So, some time in the first century a pair of lighthouses was built, one of which still stands within the walls of the later Norman castle. The castle itself developed and grew through the centuries, and was connected to the outer defences on the cliffs via a network of tunnels. The tunnels were to play a major part in one of the most remarkable events in Britain's naval history. It was here in 1940 that

Vice-Admiral Ramsay set up his headquarters to mastermind the evacuation of troops from Dunkirk. This is one of those rare places where one can see evidence of great historic events covering a span of more than 2000 years.

Dover Museum

£; Daily; Market Square; Tel: 01304 201066; Website: www.dovermuseum.co.uk

Now we are travelling even further back in time, to the Bronze Age. Here is an outstanding discovery that leads us right back to the very beginning of Britain's maritime story, the remains of a 3500-year-old boat (see p.36). It has, and deserves, a gallery all of its own, and it is worth coming here even if you march past everything else in the museum with averted eyes. But that would be a mistake, for the rest of the museum is crammed with interesting information on this, one of the country's most important ports.

Dover Transport Museum

£; Easter to October Wednesday to Saturday afternoons and Sunday all day; Tel: 01304 204612

The main emphasis is on road vehicles, but there is a maritime room with ship models and a good deal of information about the harbour.

Rye Heritage Centre

£; Daily; Strand Quay; Tel: 01797 226696; Website: www.rye.org.uk

This is a very different way of getting to see and understand the history of a town. It is based on a model, and an audio-visual show takes you on what is literally a miniature tour. It does not end there. It can be followed up by an audio tour of the modern town, for which a separate charge is made, so that everything seen in the town model can be related to what one can see today walking round Rye.

DUNGENESS

Old Lighthouse

£; Summer, closed Mondays; Tel: 01794 321300

There has been a lighthouse on this site since 1615, and few places had more need of one: in the worst year of disasters over 1000 sailors lost their lives on the ness. The longest lasting light was built in 1792 and remained in use right up to 1904. It still exists, converted into flats. So what is now called the 'Old Lighthouse' is really a comparative newcomer. It is unusual in being a circular tower built of brick rather than stone. It originally stood close by the sea, but the shifting shingle now gives it an incongruous position, well inland. Enthusiasts may climb the 167 steps to the top for a magnificent view impeded only by the nuclear power stations. The present lighthouse was opened in 1961. The local lifeboat station is also open to visitors at weekends.

See Also

St Aldhelm's Head, Isle of Purbeck

Free; Open Access

The simple square Norman chapel on the headland was said to have been built by a father whose daughter and her husband drowned at the foot of the cliffs. A beacon was kept alight on the roof to warn other sailors of the danger. A modern coastguard station now stands next to it.

LYMINGTON

St Barbe Museum

££; Monday to Saturday; New Street; Tel: 01590 676969; Website: www.stbarbe-museum.org.uk

A general museum that lays on lots of activities for children; displays include boat building and smuggling.

Winchelsea Museum

£; Tuesday to Saturday, Sunday afternoon May to September

Housed in one of Winchelsea's oldest surviving buildings, the Court Hall, the museum tells the story of this medieval planned town and important member of the Cinque Ports Confederation.

Tenterden Museum

£; April to June and October afternoons only, July to September all day; Station Rd; Tel: 01580 764310; Website: www.ukpages.net/kent/museum.htm

It is strange to think of the town as a port, but it was one of the Cinque Ports. The museum is based on an attractive weather-boarded coach house and stables, and covers many aspects of local history, including shipbuilding at Small Hythe.

The interior of Winchelsea Court Hall, with its rough-hewn timbers, provides a suitable setting in which to tell the story of the ancient port.

SETTING SAIL

The notion of using a sail to move a boat through the water must have occurred fairly early on in the history of boat building. It is easy to imagine a man standing up in a vessel and holding out his cloak in the wind, feeling the pressure of the air at his back and sensing that the boat was responding. It would have been obvious that the same effect could be obtained more efficiently by replacing the man with a mast and the cloak with a specially manufactured sail. In northern waters, at least, all the earliest sailing vessels were square-rigged. They were equipped with a single mast, on which a square sail fastened to a horizontal yard, suspended at its mid-point, could be hoisted. The yard was set at right angles to the fore and aft line of the boat. Now it is easy to see how this works at its simplest. The wind gets behind the sail and blows the ship along. But what was the sailor to do if the wind was not blowing in the direction he wished to travel? If a sail was entirely rigid then all would be lost – but it is not. It is pliable, curving as it takes the wind: in modern terms it acts rather like a flexible aerofoil. Power can be produced by the action of air blowing across the face of the sail. So a square-rigged vessel can be sailed close to the wind by pulling the sail round so that it runs more in a fore and aft

direction instead of being set athwart the line. This was how the Vikings sailed and how a great square-rigger sails, and it can be seen at its simplest in a vessel such as the Humber keel. A vessel such as this is equipped with standing rigging, which is used to steady the masts and spars, and the running rigging, which is used to alter the direction of the sail in relation to the hull. The lower corner of the square sail is pulled towards the bows by the tack, and the opposite corner towards the stern by the sheet.

Even with this arrangement, it is not always possible to make headway in exactly the right direction, so the vessel has to zigzag or 'tack'. This involves reversing the direction of the sail: the tack is slackened on one side and pulled taut on the other, and similarly with the sheets. While tacking is under way, the sail has a period where it simply hangs slack before taking the wind again. One problem with a square rig is that there is a limit to which the sail can be moved without fouling the standing rigging. And, because the yard is suspended from its centre point, the sail is always symmetrically placed on either side of the mast. There are advantages in having a sail that is set asymmetrically, so that there is more sail astern the mast than there is ahead of it. A simple variation

St Nicholas rebuking the Tempest **by Bicci di Lorenzo. The painting shows a typical medieval ship with square rig and high fore and aft castles. The hull may be different, but the sail arrangement is very similar to that of** *Comrade* **on the opposite page.**

on the square sail is to be found in a number of fishing boats, such as the lugger *Barnabas* in Cornwall and the Scottish fifies of Anstruther and Shetland. Here the sails are not entirely square. The yards carrying the sails – and these are two-masted vessels – are suspended close to the narrower side of the sail. This is all very well, but in tacking, if the sail was simply allowed to swing across as with the square rig, everything would then be the wrong way round, with most of the sail now in front of the mast instead of behind it where it is needed. The answer is to dip the sail, carrying both it and the yard right round the mast and hoisting it again on the opposite side. It all sounds very cumbersome, but the advantages of better sailing close to the wind outweigh the effort involved.

An alternative is the fore and aft or gaff rig. Here, all the sail is permanently behind the mast, suspended from a spar, known as the gaff. This rig can be seen at its simplest in the wherry *Albion*, with its tall mast and single sail. The position of the sail is controlled through the sheets and sheet block. Unlike the lugger, the wind can be taken on either side of the sail. If the tiller is pushed across, the sail shakes loose for a moment before the breeze catches the other side. The block controlling the sail shoots across an iron rail, known as the horse. The sheets control the movement into and away from the centre line. Another obvious feature of *Albion* is that the area of sail can be reduced in a strengthening wind by rolling up the foot of the sail and securing it with reef points – tied, of course, with the famous reef knot. There are numerous variations on the fore and aft rig – the spritsail barge is a familiar example. The grandest fore and aft rigged vessels are the schooners, with two, three or more masts. Some also carry small topsails, and *Kathleen and May* is an example of a

The Humber keel *Comrade*, a square rigged vessel that, although built in 1923, is essentially very little changed from its medieval predecessors.

topsail schooner. There are many other variations. A fully rigged ship would have square sails on the masts, triangular staysails in between, and triangular jib sails on the bowsprit. Many also had a gaff sail on the mast nearest the stern, the mizzen. As sailing ships developed, they employed a bewildering mixture of square sails and fore and aft sails, each having its own name. It all sounds very confusing, but the variety of sails was developed to meet the different needs of different types of vessel. A pilot cutter dashing out to be the first to greet a ship making for harbour and to win the contract for guiding it safely to port has very different needs from the cargo vessel making long ocean voyages. In larger vessels there are sails that provide the main thrust through the water, and others that ensure stability or are used for fine trimming. A ship could be manoeuvred out of harbour simply by using the staysails, which could be quickly trimmed for carefully controlled movement. It is this infinite variety that ensures that the study of sailing ships is a subject to which there is no end.

There is one aspect of the sail that should never be overlooked – the skill of the sailmaker. On land, the sailmaker generally works in a sail loft, with a large floor area allowing the whole sail to be spread out. Dimensions and shapes are carefully established, then strips of canvas are cut to size and sewn together. The sailmaker uses a palm, a piece of leather with a thumb hole and a hardened area in the centre, which performs the same function as the familiar, if rather more delicate, thimble of the domestic sewing basket. Rope is then stitched round all the edges to prevent fraying and to supply fixing points for the sails. Ships carried their own sailmakers to repair or replace sails during the longer voyages.

LONDON AND THE SOUTH EAST

The whole area is dominated by London and the Thames estuary. The city is both the country's capital and, until very recently, its greatest port. Such a vital centre of political power, commerce and trade demanded protection, so the area was provided with a series of naval bases at Chatham, Sheerness and Greenwich. Consequently this is an area of the very first importance in maritime history, an importance reflected in major museums. Great cargo ships and warships only represent a part of the story. Scurrying in amongst them were a variety of smaller craft, notably fishing boats, including specialist craft such as the oyster yawls of Whitstable. But one class of small sailing vessel was of paramount significance. Popularly known as the Thames barge – though they also plied the Medway and the east coast – these were among the most successful and most efficient coastal traders in the age of sail. Fortunately, many have survived, and there is even a specialist museum devoted to them at Sittingbourne.

ST MARGARET'S BAY

St Margaret's Museum

£; Easter and end of May to early September afternoons Wednesday to Sunday; Beach Road; Tel: 01304 852764; Website: www.pinesgardenandmuseum.co.uk

The museum is opposite the Pines Garden created in 1970 by Fred Cleary, and most of the artefacts in the collection come from him. Many are of maritime interest, including ship models and a figurehead. There is a strong emphasis on the area as the gateway to Europe, from the Roman invasion to the Channel Tunnel. There are also a few surprises, including a Bronze Age skeleton called 'Marguerite'.

South Foreland Lighthouse

NT; £; 1 March to 31 October daily; Tel: 01304 852463

The lighthouse on the cliffs above the bay is famous for being the scene of the first experiments in lighting with electricity (in 1858) and for the installation of a new type of arc light (in 1862). The light itself was constructed to warn ships about the dangers of the Goodwin Sands, and in 1897 Marconi established the first ship-to-shore telegraph communication with the East Goodwin lightship. The guided tour includes a visit to the generating room and a chance to inspect the rotating optic with its ingenious clockwork mechanism.

The granite obelisk to the north is a memorial to the Dover Patrol and the sailors of two world wars who died in protecting the South Coast.

Walmer Castle

EH; ££; April to November daily, December and March Wednesday to Sunday; Tel: 01304 364288

Situated on the coast, immediately to the south of Deal, the castle was built by Henry VIII to defend against possible attacks from France or Spain after the break with Rome. It became the official residence of the Lords Warden of the Cinque Ports. As the role of Warden diminished in terms of naval requirements and the post became largely ceremonial, so the fortress became ever more domesticated. The interior is more that of a stately home than a fortress, and the grounds have been laid out in formal gardens. It does, however, still have a strong message to deliver on the former importance of the Cinque Ports.

DEAL

Maritime and Local History Museum

£; April to October Monday to Saturday afternoon; St George's Road; Tel: 01304 381344

One of Deal's best known residents was Captain John Willis Jr, owner of the *Cutty Sark*. There are elaborately carved panels from two of his other ships, and the somewhat grotesque figurehead of *Zenobia*, a ship built for him in Bombay in 1851. The lady was Queen of Palmyra, and one can only hope for her sake that it is not an accurate portrait. Among the boats, both inside the museum and outside in the courtyard, is a rare example of a rowed galley, *Saxon King*. In the Armoury there is a display relating to the Royal Marines, who have a long association with the town. Upstairs is more concerned with the history of the town as it gradually changed its role from important port to seaside resort.

The South Foreland lighthouse is unusually ornate and makes a striking appearance above the famous White Cliffs at Dover.

Walmer Castle was built for defence but now provides the official residence for the Warden of the Cinque Ports.

naval escorts during the Napoleonic Wars. Inside the museum are exhibits on time, navigation and communications at sea. In later years nearby Richborough became immensely important as the main depot for supplying men and material to the Western Front in World War I.

SANDWICH

Guildhall Museum

£; April to September Tuesday to Saturday, Sunday afternoon, October to mid-December, March Thursday and Saturday, afternoons only Tuesday, Wednesday, Friday and Sunday; Tel: 01304 617197

Sandwich now lies almost two miles from the sea, but the town fortifications still tell of the time when this was one of the Cinque Ports. This is the main story told in the museum displays.

RAMSGATE

Royal Harbour and Maritime Museum

£; March to September daily, October to February Tuesday to Friday; Tel: 01843 587765; Website: www.ekmt.ssnet.co.uk

The Royal Harbour was given its grand name in 1821 when George IV embarked from here, and the buildings

Time-Ball Tower

£; July and August closed Monday; Victoria Parade; Tel: 01304 360897

An essential aid to navigation in the nineteenth century was the chronometer, and sailors needed to be able to check it against the standard of Greenwich Mean Time. So in 1854 the tower was built with a massive ball able to slide up and down a pole on the roof.

It was hoisted to the top and then, at exactly 1 p.m. GMT, it dropped. It still does, now controlled by an electrical connection with Greenwich. This was particularly useful for the ships anchored in The Downs, the stretch of water between Deal and the Goodwin Sands. It was here that vessels waited for a favourable wind to take them into the Thames, and was a gathering point for merchantmen waiting for

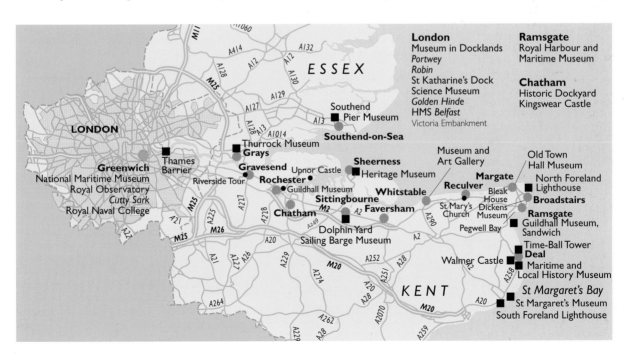

London
Museum in Docklands
Portwey
Robin
St Katharine's Dock
Science Museum
Golden Hinde
HMS *Belfast*
Victoria Embankment

Ramsgate
Royal Harbour and
Maritime Museum

Chatham
Historic Dockyard
Kingswear Castle

Thames barges are still repaired and restored at the Dolphin Yard Sailing Barge Museum, Sittingbourne.

of the early nineteenth century still dominate the area. One of these, the Clock House, is home to the museum. The name is appropriate, for not only is there a prominent clock tower, but it was also a place where ships' chronometers could be corrected. The four galleries deal with all aspects of the area's maritime heritage, including displays on two great engineers: John Smeaton, closely involved with the construction of the harbour, and John Rennie. The story is continued outside in the harbour. Smeaton's dry dock of 1791 has recently been restored. Three vessels are also on display: the steam tug *Cervia* of 1945, which visitors can board; the motor yacht *Sundowner*, a former Admiralty steam launch of 1912; and the 1930 pleasure boat *New Britannic*. Both of the latter were among the many privately owned boats that took part in the evacuation of Dunkirk in 1940.

NORTH FORELAND
Lighthouse

£; Weekends, Easter to end of September plus Tuesday to Friday, school summer holidays; Tel: 01843 60049

There has been a lighthouse on this site for 500 years. A new tower was built in 1634, with a coal fire light, and the tower was increased in height in 1790 with improved oil lamps. Improvements followed over the years, and in 1998 it was the last manned lighthouse in Britain to be converted to automatic operation.

MARGATE
Old Town Hall Museum

£; April to September daily, October to March weekends; Tel: 01843 231213

The town hall consists of an original seventeenth-century building, extended in the nineteenth century, reflecting the growth of Margate itself from a fishing village to a seaside resort. This is the story the museum tells, with a maritime display of model ships, including the paddle steamers that were once regular visitors to the popular resort with its bathing machines and pierrots.

WHITSTABLE
Museum and Art Gallery

Free; July and August Monday to Saturday plus Sunday afternoon; Oxford Street; Tel: 01227 276998; Website: www.whitstable-museum.co.uk

Think of Whitstable and you think of oysters, either with an anticipatory sigh of delight or a grimace of repugnance. There seems to be no half-way point: you love them or detest them. Either way, oyster fishing is still important, and a good part of this museum is concerned with this specialist form of fishing and its boats. There are also exhibits on diving and shipping, and changing exhibitions at the art gallery. The story is continued outside, where the old oystermen's huts and sail lofts line the harbour and where oysters can be bought and consumed. Conventional fishing boats still use the harbour.

SITTINGBOURNE
Dolphin Yard Sailing Barge Museum

£; Sundays and Bank Holidays, Easter to end of October; Off Crown Quay Lane; Tel: 01795 424132; Website: www.Thamesbarge.org.uk

The museum is based on the former Burley's Barge forge and sail loft. The main building may not be glamorous but it has history built into its fabric, with colourful, intricately carved barge tillers used as pillars. Inside, the museum is devoted to the history of the Thames barge. The old machinery is still in use, for this is literally a working museum, a place where barges are brought for repair and restoration. You will certainly see barges here, but which barges at any particular time depends on work in hand. One barge, however, is assured of a home here for some time to come. *Cambria* was built in 1906 and in her working days regularly travelled right up the coast as far as the Trent. She was the very last sailing vessel to trade under the British flag. When restoration is complete she will have a permanent berth here but will also be regularly sailed. This is a delightful place, and one of the pleasures in coming back over the years lies in seeing what looked like an abandoned hulk emerge as a splendid sailing barge, with traditional red sails spread in the wind.

SHEERNESS
Heritage Museum

£; Daily; Off High Street; Tel: 01795 663317

The dockyard was begun in the seventeenth century but greatly enlarged in 1812 under the direction of the engineer John Rennie. As part of the enlargement, new houses were built for the dockyard workers. They were modest cottages of clapboard on a wooden frame, and the museum is housed in one of the few survivors. It has been refurnished as it would have been in the nineteenth century, and there are dockyard plans and mementoes of the dockyard's role in the last world war.

CHATHAM
Historic Dockyard

££££; February, March and November Wednesday, Saturday and Sunday, April to October daily; Tel: 01634 823807; Website www.chdt.org.uk

This is a magnificent site, a great dockyard with a long history, which would be well worth visiting just for the astonishing buildings even if there were no museum here at all. It was founded in the sixteenth century, and if little survives from that early period, there is a great deal from the eighteenth and nineteenth centuries. These vary from the classical elegance of the Commissioner's House of 1704 to the seemingly knock-together roughness of the mast house and mould loft of the 1750s. Best of all are the covered slips. Number 3 of 1838 is like an immense upturned ship, while Number 7, built just seventeen years later, is Victorian hi-tech, glass and iron, a sort of maritime Crystal Palace.

HMS *Ocelot*, the last submarine built at Chatham for the Royal Navy.

The museum itself covers the whole period of Chatham history, right up to the closure of the working yard in 1984. It is interesting to come here after Portsmouth, to continue the story of warships on to the modern age. HMS *Gannet,* built in 1878, catches the Navy in a time of transition. She is a sloop, built with an iron frame but with teak planking, and she could travel under sail or use her steam engine. When the Victorians wanted to send a gunboat, this was the sort of ship they had in mind. HMS *Cavalier* also shows a new technology being introduced, though not quite so obviously. This World War II destroyer, built in 1944, had a partially welded hull in place of the usual riveted version, producing a smoother surface; the extra speed earned her the title of fastest in the fleet. Taken out of service in 1972, the ship has been fully restored, and visitors can enjoy a tour of the whole ship. HM Submarine *Ocelot* is altogether more mysterious: built at the height of the Cold War, her service career still remains secret. Indeed, secrecy is what this submarine was all about. Designed for silent running, one can guess at the kind of surveillance voyages carried out in foreign waters.

Since much of what one can see was built in the days of wooden warships, it is appropriate that one major part of the exhibition is simply called 'Wooden Walls'. It follows a young apprentice on a walk through the streets of eighteenth-century Chatham, where he is met by his master and set to work on the 74-gun ship of the line, *Valiant.* He is introduced to many of the different trades involved in building the ship and ends up with a chance to visit the gun deck. The story is based on real characters who worked in Chatham, and housed in old buildings, including the mould loft, where, tradition has it, the lines for *Victory* were laid down.

There is a section on lifeboats, with fifteen boats from the early pulling and sailing version to modern inshore craft. The one other really major feature is the ropery. This was fully dealt with in the companion volume *Britain's Working Past*, so it is sufficient to say here that this is not to be missed. Seeing the practical demonstrations is one of the highlights of the whole tour. To do Chatham justice a day is scarcely enough time, but if all this leads to an irresistible urge to get out on the water, then the *Kingswear Castle,* described below, provides the perfect answer. An inclusive ticket can be bought or a ticket just for the excursion.

Kingswear Castle

Early May to late October; Prices and timetable vary, with a variety of trips from 45 minutes to a full day, for details Tel: 01634 827648; Website: www.pskc.freeserve.co.uk

Paddle steamers are rare enough, but this one is unique, the last still to raise steam in a coal-fired boiler. This is a slim, elegant craft, quite modest by paddle steamer standards. She was built in 1924 in Dartmouth for use on the River Dart, but was fitted with an even older compound engine of 1904. She did splendid work on the Dart right up to 1965 and two years later she was bought by the Paddle Steamer Preservation Society. Then came the long work of restoration, ending with successful trials in 1983. Now her regular runs from Chatham Dockyard are deservedly popular.

HISTORIC NAVAL DOCKYARDS

Throughout the Middle Ages the country's fighting fleet consisted of armed merchantmen requisitioned for occasional service through organizations such as the Cinque Ports (p.52). It was not yet an official navy, but even so, a fleet still needed to be provisioned and protected against attack. In 1212 King John ordered the Sheriff of Southampton to 'construct a good and strong wall round our dock at Portsmouth without delay'. It scarcely qualified as a true dockyard, since there were no facilities for working on ships and there was still no navy. It was Henry V who first ordered fighting ships for what was to become a Royal Navy, and the process expanded greatly under the Tudors. Now the first true naval dockyards were commissioned. The first dry dock was built at Portsmouth in 1495. It was a simple excavated pit, lined with wood and closed by gates. After a vessel had entered, the gates were closed with clay and the water pumped out. Ships were repaired and built here as well, including the famous *Mary Rose*, begun in 1509. Henry VIII went on to establish other dockyards at Deptford and Woolwich, and in 1547 a storehouse on Jyllingham Water was acquired, and the anchorage was shortly dignified by a new name – Chatham. There was then something of a lull before the next generation of naval dockyards was established, Sheerness in 1665 and Devonport in 1689.

The dockyards were big and, in the days of the sailing ship, complex places. Their main function was the construction, repair, fitting out and victualling of ships. There were often grand quarters for the officers in charge, but no need for extra housing, as the civilian workforce lived outside the dock area. There were wet docks where ships could float and dry docks where the hull was exposed for repairs. There were extensive storehouses and all kinds of specialist workshop areas: forges, ropewalks, sail lofts, rigging houses, yarn houses and more. Timber for masts was kept in special mast ponds. It was, in effect, a large industrial complex. Daniel Defoe visited Chatham in 1722 and was overwhelmed by the variety of materials kept ready for use. Here is his list:

Pitch, tarr, hemp, flax, tow, rosin, oyl, tallow; also of sail cloth, canvas, anchors, cables, standing and running rigging, ready fitted, and cordage not fitted; with all kinds of ship-chandlery necessaries and gunners' stores, and also anchors of all sizes, grapnells, chains, bolts, and spikes, wrought and unwrought iron, cast-iron work, such as potts, caldrons, furnaces, &c. also boats, spare-masts and yards; with a great quantity of lead and nails, and other necessaries (too many to be enumerated) whose store looks as if it were inexhaustible.

A view of Plymouth Dockyard in 1735. It shows wet and dry docks and the imposing officers' terrace, part of which still survives.

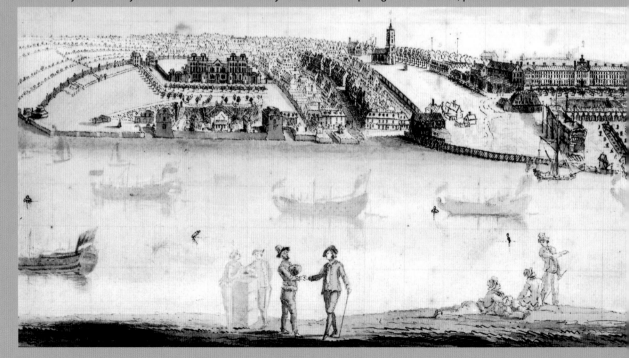

Many old buildings have survived at the great dockyards of Chatham, Devonport and Portsmouth. Among the most imposing are the roperies. Ropes were made by spinning the yarns into strands and then laying the strands up into ropes. Twisting was achieved by rotating hooks, and the rope maker moved backwards down the ropewalk to ensure that there was an even lay. The walks themselves needed to be long: the biggest naval ropewalk built at Devonport in 1775 stretched to 400m. Ropemaking in the old way is still demonstrated at Chatham. Most dockyard architecture is functional but can have an almost accidental beauty. One of the most attractive surviving buildings is the Slip No.1 at Devonport, with its original timber roof, reminiscent of a particularly majestic tithe barn. Among the more surprising buildings generally found within the dock complex is the alehouse. As early as 1689 there were complaints at Portsmouth that it was becoming common for workmen 'to keep Ill companies in the Tapp house drinking and Tippling to the loss of their time and great disservice to their majesty'. The practice was continued because the work was hard, men needed refreshment and the beer was considerably safer to drink than the water.

Mechanization was slow to appear, largely due, many said, to the innate conservatism of the Admiralty. Isambard Kingdom Brunel wrote in exasperation that they 'have an unlimited supply of *some negative* principle which seems to absorb and eliminate everything that approaches them'. Yet it was his father, Marc Brunel, who first introduced the notion of mass production to the dockyards. A sailing ship needed a vast array of blocks, which could be of many sizes and used singly or in combination. But the fundamental shape and method of construction scarcely varied. Between 1802 and 1806 he designed forty-five different machines, installed at Portsmouth and which turned out 140,000 blocks a year. Where 100 men had once been employed, there were now only ten. Although the building that housed the machinery has survived, the machines have almost all gone. There was one new dockyard begun in 1814 when a site on the fine natural harbour of Milford Haven was chosen as a location. Pembroke Dock was to be the scene for the launching of some memorable vessels, including the pioneering steam man of war *Tartarus* in 1834. It soon gained a reputation as one of the most modern shipyards in the world, and was used for the building of five royal yachts. But its location, far from other naval yards, told against it and it was closed in 1926. Of the historic dockyards, only Devonport and Portsmouth remain active. It is possible to see the former by boat trips from Plymouth, and the excellent Naval Base Museum can be visited by special arrangement. Portsmouth has a fine museum housed in three Georgian storehouses, but the great attraction here are two of the most famous ships ever built in naval dockyards: *Victory* and the *Mary Rose*. Chatham was closed in 1984 but has been redeveloped as The Historic Dockyard, offering a unique opportunity to see four centuries of development in the history of naval dockyards.

WOOLWICH
Thames Barrier

£; Daily; Tel: 020 8305 4188;
Website: www.environment-agency.gov.uk

The information centre and exhibition area is at the southern end of the barrier. Whether this is strictly a maritime centre is arguable, but it is mightily impressive and certainly has a real effect on shipping movements. The barrier is normally open, but if exceptional tides and floods threaten the river, the barrier is raised and shipping movements stop. The centre has a working model and video, and it is possible to get a close-up of the barrier itself on a Thames cruise. The shining metallic hooded piers house the hydraulic machinery. A few statistics help to give an idea of the scale of engineering involved. The main gates each has a span of 61m, rises to a height of 20m and weighs around 3700 tonnes.

GREENWICH
National Maritime Museum

Free; Daily; Tel: 020 8312 6565;
Website: www.nmm.ac.uk

It really does seem that there is no aspect of maritime history that this museum does not cover, all the way from the excavations of prehistoric boats to the present day. The first thing that strikes everyone who comes here is the magnificence of the setting and the architecture. Some of the greatest of all British architects worked here – Wren, Inigo Jones, Vanburgh. At the heart is Queen Anne's House, built by Jones in the early seventeenth century. It has a spectacular hall, designed as a 40ft cube, and is an integral part of the museum, housing much of the art collection. From this core, colonnades lead away to the exhibition halls. There is an almost bewildering array of things to see and do, with the world of sail nudging up against the world of steam. Children have not been forgotten. New galleries make use of interactive displays. It is the obvious starting place for anyone who wants to look at the broad spectrum of the maritime past. One gallery deals with London and the river, and a splendid day out can be rounded out with a return to the city by one of the many river passenger boats. Like a lot of national museums, there is really too much to take in at one go. But with constantly changing exhibitions and new galleries being opened – the latest, still in preparation at the time of writing, deals with the nature of oceans – there is every excuse to make more than one trip. In any case, there are other important sites and exhibits to visit in Greenwich.

The famous clipper *Cutty Sark*, still the epitome of maritime elegance even when high and dry at Greenwich.

Royal Observatory

Free; Daily; Tel: 020 8858 4422;
Website: www.nmm.ac.uk

What has this got to do with maritime Britain? The answer is: everything. The Observatory was founded in 1675 specifically to help in finding a means of determining longitude, essential for navigators making long voyages out of sight of land. The architect was Sir Christopher Wren, himself an astronomer. As a result of the work done here, longitude was established from a basic meridian passing through Greenwich and chronometers were calibrated to Greenwich Mean Time. The time signal is given daily by the dropping of the time ball, similar to that at Deal (p.63). Now the observatory contains a fine collection of navigational instruments, chronometers (including the famous pioneering instruments designed by Harrison) and astronomical instruments. These are not only practical devices, but often works of great beauty.

The Thames barrier, showing just a few of the ten movable gates built to protect London from floods. The whole structure is 520m long and the biggest gates are the height of a five-storey building.

Cutty Sark

££; Daily; Tel: 020 8858 3445;
Website: www.cuttysark.org.uk

The clipper ships are among the most beautiful vessels ever built, with shapely hulls and steeply raked bows. Where most cargo vessels are built to carry as much cargo as possible, the clippers were designed for speed to bring high value goods quickly back to the home port. *Cutty Sark* was commissioned in 1869 for the race to bring back the new crop of China tea. Then the Suez Canal was opened and the trade passed to the steamers. The ship began a new career in 1883, bringing back wool from Australia, making fast runs culminating in a voyage back from Sydney in sixty-seven days. Now she has a permanent berth in dry dock at Greenwich. If she is no longer in her natural element, at least one has the opportunity to see the details and admire the fine lines of the hull, including the copper-zinc-sheathed bottom that kept the teredo worm at bay. This is a sailing machine that could carry as many as thirty-four sails, which between them would cover an area of three-quarters of an acre. In her latter days all this was managed with a crew of just nineteen. Sir Francis Chichester's yacht *Gipsy Moth IV,* in which he completed his solo circumnavigation, lies alongside.

Royal Naval College

Free; Daily; Tel: 020 8269 4747;
Website: www.greenwichfoundation.org.uk

In 1692 the Queen decided to make the King's House, Greenwich, into a hospital for retired seamen, the naval equivalent of Chelsea Pensioners. Then in 1694 the decision was taken to create a new hospital and the commission went to Wren. It was stipulated that nothing should obscure the view of the river from the Queen's House, so two identical wings were designed, with a gap in the middle to create the magnificent view enjoyed from the river today. In 1873 the hospital closed and the buildings became the Royal Naval College. There are two stupendous rooms open to the public: the painted hall with its immense ceiling painting by Sir James Thornhill and the chapel.

The National Maritime Museum at Greenwich is the world's oldest maritime museum and has recently been imaginatively extended to create even more display space.

LONDON

Museum in Docklands

The museum will open in 2003. No further information is available at present. Tel: 020 7001 9800

This is a brand new museum housed in a former warehouse on West India Quay, built to hold the produce of the Caribbean – sugar, rum and molasses. It is part of the whole major dock building scheme that began at the end of the eighteenth century, with the cutting of the City Canal across the Isle of Dogs and the creation of the import and export sections of the West India Docks. So the museum lies at the very heart of the most important developments for shipping on the River Thames since Roman times. The tag line is self-explanatory – the river, the port and the people. The story is told in thirteen galleries, covering the history from Roman times to the present day using all the latest display technology. There are even 'aromatic effects', though whether these will include a realistic representation of what the great Elizabethan writer Ben Jonson described as the 'merd-urinous' river remains to be seen. There will be models, including a 6m-long representation of medieval London Bridge, with its shops and houses, panoramas and paintings. There will be the

recorded memories of those who knew the old working river, and a display of the extraordinary paintings of William Ware, who painted the docks right through the years of the Blitz. This is a museum which truly covers all aspects of London's river, from the frivolity of the famous frost fairs when the Thames froze over to the degradation and filth of the nineteenth century when scavengers literally scraped a living out of the mud.

Portwey

Free; Wednesday afternoon and early evening; For visits at other times phone 01268 769583; Port East, West India Dock; Website: www.stportwey.co.uk

The steam tug is a small vessel packed with power. Built in 1927 by Harland and Wolff, she has the traditional tug lines, high in the bow and low in the stern. The twin screws for manoeuvrability are powered by a pair of compound engines, and there is more steam available on board. A 1918 Robey engine could generate electricity, and there are fire pumps capable of sending out water at a ton a minute. In her working days at Dartmouth she put out a fire on a waterfront hotel before the fire brigade arrived. In

Very much the traditional tug, with high bows and low stern, *Portwey* is one of the few survivors of thousands of steam tugs that were once the workhorses of British ports.

London's docklands may no longer see any ships unloading cargo, but it is good to find this robust reminder of the working port, the old cargo steamer *Robin*.

2000 the tug was bought by a Trust, who have already carried out extensive restorations and she now steams again. She can be visited at the dock.

Robin

Free; Exterior only; Canary Wharf;
Website: www.ssrobin.com

Here is the classic 'dirty British Coaster', built in 1890. The profile is very much of the period, particularly the funnel, nicknamed the 'Woodbine' because it looked like a thin cigarette poking up to the sky. Forward of the funnel is the bridge, a rather handsome affair, faced with timber. Her power comes from a triple expansion engine by Gourlay of Dundee, so in her day she was at the forefront of technology. Now privately owned, *Robin* is undergoing essential restoration, but she is well worth visiting as the last of a whole fleet of ships carrying the trade of a nation.

St Katharine's Dock

Open access

Britain has just two great examples of early enclosed docks, and this is the earliest – the other is Albert Dock, Liverpool. The dock itself was designed by Thomas Telford and the surrounding warehouses by Philip Hardwick. In its day it was absolutely the latest thing and it is still mightily impressive. Everything is beautifully planned, with warehouses overhanging the wharf and supported on pillars to make maximum use of space, recesses for cranes and a very efficient lock system to allow ships in and out. It must have been immensely impressive when it opened in 1828, and it still is. Trading vessels have long since outgrown the dock, and the warehouses are now home to everything from bars to tourist shops, but nothing can destroy the air of grandeur.

Science Museum

Free; Daily; Exhibition Rd; Tel: 020 7942 4000;
Website: www.nmsi.ac.uk

Britain's premier museum of science and technology is a delight, and many of us can date an interest in the subject to a visit, pressing buttons to make things work. The museum has moved on a bit since then but it still fascinates. Although it covers a wide range of subjects, maritime matters are not neglected and it is particularly strong on marine engineering, with exhibits ranging from the original engine of the paddle steamer *Comet* of 1812 to Parsons' experimental turbine for *Turbinia*.

Golden Hinde

£; Daily; St Mary Overie Dock, Cathedral Street, SE1;
Tel: 020 7403 0123; Website: www.goldenhinde.co.uk

Not the real thing, of course, but the next best thing, a full-size replica of Drake's ship, built using traditional methods and materials. The details are impressive, right down to the sails, woven out of flax and sewn by hand. And, like the original, she, too, has sailed round the world before finishing up here as a museum. As well as the self-guided tours, a slightly more expensive guided tour is available, and for those who really want to immerse themselves in the past, it is possible to stay overnight and join in costumed re-enactments of life on Drake's ship.

HMS *Belfast*

£££; Daily; Tel: 020 7940 6300; Website: www.iwm.org.uk

Moored in the Thames by Tower Bridge, *Belfast* is in a way as much a survivor of a bygone age as *Victory*. She was built in 1936 at a time when cruisers had a clearly defined role: to protect cargo ships and, when the opportunity arose, sink the enemy's cargo ships and engage enemy cruisers. The main armaments are the mighty guns, mounted in rotating turrets. The 6-inch guns have a maximum range of 14 miles, which means that pointed north they could shell the M25 ring road. So here we have a formidable fighting machine, as she proved in wartime, on escort duty with the Russian convoys and in the Battle of North Cape, which saw the sinking of the German battle cruiser *Scharnhorst*. Active service did not end with World War II, however. *Belfast* was among the first British warships to be sent to Korea in 1950, and spent 404 days on active patrol. Visitors can now explore the entire ship,

The replica of Drake's *Golden Hinde*.

from the mighty turbines of the engine room to the Operations Room, from which the firepower of the *Belfast* was controlled.

The cruiser HMS *Belfast* occupies one of the best sites in London, under the shadow of Tower Bridge, a quiet resting place for a ship that saw service in two wars.

GRAYS

Thurrock Museum

Free; Monday to Saturday; Thameside Complex, Orsett Road; Tel: 01375 382555; Website: www.thurrock.gov.uk/museum

This is a local history museum, but with a history closely tied to the working Thames. The scale of interest is certainly broad. The Thames barges come in for a good deal of attention, with exhibits on building and repair, but so, too, do Tilbury Docks, having a special emphasis on the golden years when P & O steamers carried passengers around the world.

SOUTHEND-ON-SEA

Southend Pier Museum

£; May to November Tuesday, Wednesday, Saturday and Sunday; Tel: 01702 611214

Housed in the old pier workshops below the pier station, this tells the story of the world's longest pleasure pier, over a mile and a third of it. The pier has had a chequered history. Promoted locally as the mile-long pier, work began in 1830 but only reached its full length in 1846. It was intended as a steamer pier to bring excursionists to the resort. Unfortunately it failed: the company went bankrupt and the local authority took over. The entire pier was rebuilt in 1888–90 and finally showed a profit. The museum has pictures and antique slot machines. The main exhibit is the pier itself, which visitors can use to walk far out to sea – or travel the easy way by train.

See Also
Pegwell Bay

Open Access

A picnic site is the slightly incongruous setting for a full-sized replica of a Viking long boat, the *Hugin*, which sailed here from Denmark in 1949 to commemorate the 1500th anniversary of the landing by Horsa and Hengist.

BROADSTAIRS
Bleak House Dickens Museum

£; Mid-February to mid-December daily, January to mid-February weekends; Fort Rd; Tel: 01843 862224

Dickens stayed here while writing *David Copperfield*, but as well as memorabilia of the author, there are displays on the maritime past, smuggling and wrecks.

RECULVER
St Mary's Church

EH/TH; Open Access

There was a Roman fort here, a Saxon church and a Norman church. When the latter began to crumble away, Trinity House stepped in to repair the two towers, preserving them as the only landmark on the coast from Herne Bay to Margate.

FAVERSHAM

Open Access

An ancient port, with old timber-framed warehouses by the quay, and well worth exploring. Thames barges are regular visitors, and the local gunpowder mills began supplying the Navy as early as the seventeenth century.

Upnor Castle

EH; ££; April to October daily; Tel: 01634 827980

Built on the orders of Queen Elizabeth I to protect the Medway from foreign fleets, it notably failed to do so in 1667 when the Dutch fleet sailed past to attack Chatham. The story of the Battle of the Medway is told in the fortress.

ROCHESTER
Guildhall Museum

Free; Daily; High Street; Tel: 01634 848717

Housed in two very different buildings, one of 1687 and the other 1909, the museum covers all aspects of local history. One gallery, however, is devoted to the infamous prison hulks of the Medway.

GRAVESEND
Riverside Tour

Open Access: Guided Tours ££; First Wednesday of the month; Tel: 01474 337600; Website: www.towncentric.co.uk

A walk along the river front takes in the town pier, built for steamers in 1834 and the oldest surviving cast iron pier, and the Thames and Medway Canal, built in 1824 to take ships between the naval dockyards on the two rivers. The guided tour includes a visit to the Customs House Museum, which is otherwise closed to the public.

LONDON
Victoria Embankment

Open Access

A number of vessels are permanently moored along the embankment, some of which are open to the public as restaurants, bars and so forth. Among the most interesting are the World War I sloop HMS *Chrysanthemum* and the paddle steamer *Tattershall Castle*.

LONDON'S DOCKLAND

As London's dockland disappears under new developments and old warehouses become fashionable apartments, it is difficult to appreciate that this was once one of the greatest trading ports in the world. It may also be surprising to discover that the history of the docks extends back no more than two centuries.

Until the end of the eighteenth century there was not a single wet dock in London, nowhere where ships could lie alongside wharves and quays at all states of the tide. Instead, vessels moored up below London Bridge in the Pool of London, where they were loaded and unloaded by a fleet of barges and lighters. When the situation was assessed in 1794, a count revealed that there were 800 vessels crammed together in the Pool, tied together in places in ranks of up to sixteen vessels. The situation had become intolerable, and to add to the problems there was large-scale theft from the open quays where the lighters dropped off their cargoes. At first, development was centred on the Isle of Dogs, created by a great loop in the Thames. A ship canal was cut across the narrow neck of land, and three new sets of docks created – West India, East India and London. Work began in 1800, and they were immense undertakings. The West India dock designed by William Jessop, for example, was a complex system. There were two docks, both the same length, approximately 800m, but the import dock was almost twice as wide (55m) as the export dock. There were holding basins at either end. The larger of the two,

The Pool of London in 1810, a crowded scene with ships lying at anchor, waiting to be loaded or unloaded by fleets of barges and lighters. The new generation of closed docks was already being opened further downstream.

Blackwall Basin, was approached through an entrance lock, which was then the biggest built in Britain, 50m by 12m. At the far end of the docks was the smaller Limehouse basin, used by the lighters that carried cargo on up river. There were six grand warehouses built along the north quay, so that when it opened as London's first new dock, it was a vastly impressive undertaking.

Not everyone was happy with docks so far from the city centre, so in 1827 work began on a new dock close by the Pool of London, named St Katharine's Dock after a hospital which was demolished to make way for it. In 1823 Parliament had passed the Warehouse Act, which allowed goods to be held duty free in bonded warehouses. So the decision was taken to create a closed dock surrounded by secure warehouses, and this time the engineer was to be Jessop's old associate, Thomas Telford. The locks covered ten acres (4 hectares) and the approach was through a lock similar in size to that of the earlier London docks. In order to speed movement Telford installed a Boulton and Watt steam engine to pump water from the river to fill the entrance lock, supplementing that with conventional sluices from the basin. The result was that the huge lock could be filled in just five minutes. The surrounding warehouses, designed by Philip Hardwick, used the available space to great advantage. The upper storeys were carried out above the quay on iron pillars and cranes were set into recesses in the warehouse walls. Its function may have changed but the fundamentals remain as a splendid reminder of the engineering skill of the men who began the transformation of the Port of London.

The new system was marvellous, but it was designed to meet the needs of the great age of sail. By the middle of the nineteenth century the steamer was beginning to take over world trade and steamers were getting steadily bigger. There was also a new form of transport to think about – the steam railway. The first of the new generation of docks was built as a speculation by three of the most famous of railway contractors: Samuel Morton Peto, Thomas Brassey and Edward Ladd Betts. They acquired land in east London on the old Plaistow Marshes, and with foresight they bought enough of it to allow for future expansion. Everything about the new dock was to be modern: there was hydraulic machinery supplied by Sir William Armstrong, a 25m (80ft) wide entrance to accommodate steamers and, of course, a railway connection. It was opened in 1855 and named Victoria Dock, to be followed over the years by the Royal Albert (1880) and the King George V (1921) to complete the Royal group of docks. South of the river, docks had been developed from 1807 onwards, eventually merging to form the Surrey Commercial Docks. They thrived by specialization on timber and

grain, adding the big Canada Dock specifically for grain cargoes in 1876. They were rather more successful than another late comer, the Millwall Docks of 1868. There was one other comparatively small dock built for trans-shipment between ships and the boats of the Regent's Canal (1820).

In 1882 the focal point for development shifted right down river, when work began on a new complex at Tilbury. It was not immediately obvious at the time, but Tilbury was to thrive and the upriver docks would close one after the other. It was not simply a matter of ships getting bigger: the twentieth century also introduced whole new concepts for cargo handling, centred on containerization. The working days of the old port finally came to an end. There is still a great deal to see. St Katharine's is easily accessible and now fully open to the public. One can walk round many of the other docks as well, but undoubtedly the finest way to see the whole complex is on the Docklands Light Railway. One branch goes down across the Isle of Dogs, while the other heads east across the Royal Dock complex. The story is fully told in the new Docklands Museum, housed in a former West India Dock warehouse. What you will not see is the whole system filled with shipping and scurrying barges and lighters; for that you will need to use your imagination.

The grand opening of St Katharine's Docks on 25 October 1828, with the *Elizabeth*, dressed overall, entering the basin from the Thames.

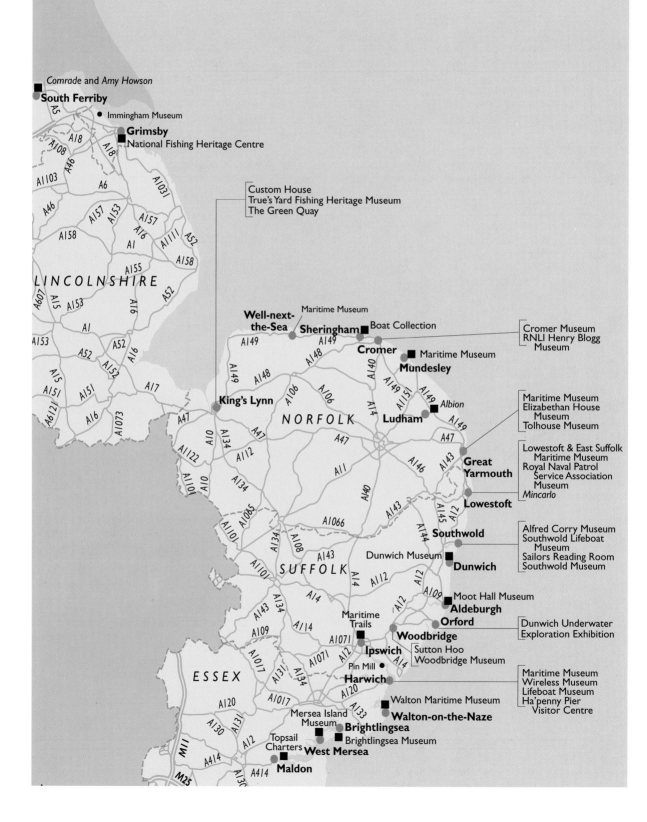

Comrade and *Amy Howson*

South Ferriby

• Immingham Museum

Grimsby
National Fishing Heritage Centre

Custom House
True's Yard Fishing Heritage Museum
The Green Quay

L I N C O L N S H I R E

Maritime Museum

Well-next-the-Sea

Sheringham

Boat Collection

Cromer

Cromer Museum
RNLI Henry Blogg Museum

Maritime Museum

Mundesley

King's Lynn

N O R F O L K

Maritime Museum
Elizabethan House Museum
Tolhouse Museum

Albion

Ludham

Lowestoft & East Suffolk Maritime Museum
Royal Naval Patrol Service Association Museum
Mincarlo

Great Yarmouth

Lowestoft

Alfred Corry Museum
Southwold Lifeboat Museum
Sailors Reading Room
Southwold Museum

Southwold

Dunwich Museum

Dunwich

S U F F O L K

Moot Hall Museum

Aldeburgh

Orford

Dunwich Underwater Exploration Exhibition

Maritime Trails

Woodbridge

Ipswich

Sutton Hoo
Woodbridge Museum

Pin Mill •

Harwich

Maritime Museum
Wireless Museum
Lifeboat Museum
Ha'penny Pier Visitor Centre

E S S E X

Walton Maritime Museum

Walton-on-the-Naze

Mersea Island Museum

Topsail Charters

Brightlingsea

Brightlingsea Museum

West Mersea

Maldon

EAST ANGLIA

There is not much doubt where the main emphasis for the region lies: with the fishing industry. Grimsby has been one of the greatest fishing ports of the world, sending out deep-sea trawlers as far as the Arctic Circle. Great Yarmouth and Lowestoft were equally important in their day, as home ports to immense fleets of herring drifters. The great days when hundreds of vessels could be seen coming back to harbour, their holds full of fish, are now gone as a result of over-fishing. Change has also overtaken the formerly busy coastal trade. Spritsail barges were regular visitors to many of the small ports

along the coast, and many of the preserved craft still call in and gather for the regular barge matches. They were by no means the only sailing barges to be seen along this coast, and there are some magnificent survivors, each with its own distinctive personality, from the fine lined wherries of the Norfolk Broads to the sturdy keels and sloops of the Humber. There are reminders, too, of just how long a maritime history there is to be unearthed – literally – in the region, from the prehistoric boats found in the mud of the Humber to the Saxon burial ship of Sutton Hoo.

MALDON

Maldon has been an important port for 'Thames' barges since at least the 1830s, when records show a 'spreety', called rather ambivalently *Rogue in Grain*, being built. Today you are likely to find more barges here at any one time than anywhere else in Britain. The port is also home to one of the major barge charterers, who are also in the process of setting up a visitor centre in a historic shipyard.

Topsail Charters

Prices vary with different charters; Cook's Yard, The Hythe; Tel: 01621 85767; Website: www.top-sail.co.uk and www.sailingbarge.co.uk

There are four barges in the fleet: *Hydrogen*, *Reminder*, *Repertor* and *Thistle*. *Hydrogen* is the only one built with a wooden hull, the other three being steel. *Thistle* is the oldest and most unusual, originally built on the Clyde at Port Glasgow in 1895. The company offers a variety of trips, from day outings to short holidays, for individuals and groups. There is also a chance to go along for one of the barge matches and join the race.

WEST MERSEA
Mersea Island Museum

£; Wednesday to Sunday afternoons; High Street; Tel: 01206 385191

The museum was set up in a brand new building in 1976, with the aim of covering all aspects of life in the area. There is a fisherman's cottage, and displays and models relating to the local fishing

A Thames sailing barge with its traditional red sails. This is *Thistle*, one of the barges preserved and run by Topsail Charters.

industry, including a rare model of the local fishing method, known as 'stowboating'. Another activity rarely shown in museums appears here: wildfowling. A locally made punt of 1919 still has its original built-in gun, which to the uninitiated looks rather more like a small cannon than a shotgun or rifle.

BRIGHTLINGSEA

The town once had great significance as a port, being a limb of the Cinque Ports. Fishing was a vital part of the life of the area, and from the eighteenth century on, the local smacks

used to have annual races. Later, Thames barges joined in the fun, and the races still continue. In 1971 The Colne Smack Preservation Society was formed to preserve and restore a number of these fine vessels; they can now be seen at the Aldous Heritage Dock when they are not out sailing.

Brightlingsea Museum

£; April to end of September Saturday all day, Monday and Thursday afternoons; Duke Street

A local history museum with a special emphasis on the Cinque Ports connection.

WALTON-ON-THE-NAZE

What appears to be a folly on the cliffs at The Naze is actually a tower built in 1720 as a landmark. The town boasts Britain's second longest pier, with a lifeboat station at the end.

Walton Maritime Museum

£; Easter and Spring Bank Holiday afternoons, July and September afternoons daily; East Terrace

Housed in an old lifeboat station, there are a number of exhibits relating to maritime history, with the main emphasis on the lifeboat service. The story goes back as far as 1884, but the most important exhibit is the *James Stevens No.14*, the oldest surviving motorized lifeboat in the world. It is currently being restored to sea-worthy condition.

HARWICH

Harwich is a delight, and quite the best introduction is to take a walk around the Maritime Heritage Trail, which also takes you past most of the individual sites listed below. In the past, the port was also a naval base, and it was from here that Edward III led his ships to attack the French fleet at Sluys, in the first sea battle of the Hundred Years War. One unique survivor from the naval past is the two-man treadwheel crane of 1667. The two separate wheels inside the housing produced a balanced action. The two lighthouses off Marine Parade are curious devices, rising out of the waves at high tide on spindly legs. The other, earlier lighthouses have found new uses, described below. Other features include The Redoubt, the fortress built in 1808 to protect the harbour. One other attraction, which is certainly not maritime but should not be missed, is the Electric Palace, a cinema almost unchanged since it was built in 1911.

Maritime Museum

£; April and September Sunday, May to August daily;
Tel: 01225 503429

The building itself is extraordinary, originally the Low Lighthouse, built in 1818 and designed by John Rennie. The ground floor looks like a cottage with a veranda, on to which someone has stuck a squat tower. Inside are displays on both the Navy and the Merchant Marine in Harwich.

Wireless Museum

£; Opening times are irregular

This is a privately owned museum, so if the owner isn't there, the museum doesn't open. It is interesting, and the building itself is certainly worth a visit. This is Rennie's High Lighthouse and is almost as strange as the Low, a ten-sided brick tower. Low and High Lights worked as a pair: anyone approaching Harwich had only to align the two, one above the other, and he was sure of his course into harbour.

Lifeboat Museum

£; May to September Tuesday to Sunday; Wellington Road; Tel: 01255 503429

It looks like a garage with a tower on top, but this is the original lifeboat house of 1876. There are exhibits on local lifeboats and a 1968 example that visitors can board.

Ha'penny Pier Visitor Centre

Free; May to September

These rather exotic little buildings were the ticket office and waiting room for the paddle steamers using the pier. There is an exhibition on the *Mayflower*, a Harwich vessel, and the master, Christopher Jones, who took the Pilgrim Fathers to America, was a local man. His old home, 21 Kings Head Street, still stands, though it was much altered in the seventeenth century.

The Harwich Maritime Museum building looks more like a seaside folly than what it really was, the old Low Lighthouse.

Ships still call in at Ipswich Docks, but these days they seem almost insignificant against the background of tall office blocks.

IPSWICH
Maritime Trails

Open Access; Brochures from Tourist Information Centre, St Stephen's Church; Tel: 01473 258070

The dock was created in 1842, by cutting off the river and diverting it into a new channel, the New Cut. The old bend of the river now formed the basis for a new dock, open at one end via a lock and closed at the other. It brought new life to the ancient port and a brand new Custom House was built. This is the start of the tour, which takes in not only the nineteenth-century developments, but also earlier commercial expansion along the river frontage, dating back to the Tudors.

WOODBRIDGE
Sutton Hoo

NT; ££; Mid-March to end of May and October Wednesday to Sunday, June to September daily, November to February weekends; Tel: 01394 389700

The landscape is characterized by a number of low humps: burial mounds from the Saxon period. It was here in 1913 that the famous Sutton Hoo burial ship was uncovered with its immensely rich hoard. In the new exhibition hall, opened in 2002, there are replicas of some of the beautifully crafted objects – even the warrior's helmet is a masterpiece of ornate decoration. If not so obviously glamorous, the burial ship itself was of first rate importance, all its details preserved as a ghostly image in the sand after the timbers had decayed. A reconstruction of this ship is on display.

Woodbridge Museum

£; April to November all day Thursday to Saturday and Sunday afternoons, School holidays Monday and Tuesday; Market Hill; Tel: 01394 380502

This small local history museum also has information on Sutton Hoo and displays on the shipbuilders of Woodbridge.

ORFORD

The sea gave Orford its importance and the sea took it away again. The Norman port was guarded by a great castle, whose splendid polygonal keep still dominates the town, and the wealth of the area is reflected in the equally grand church. Then the sea brought in the shingle that piled up to form Orford Ness, leaving a long, tortuous channel to the open water. All that remains of the old harbour is a grassy depression alongside the main street leading down to the modern quay.

Dunwich Underwater Exploration Exhibition

£; Daily; Front Street; Tel: 01394 450678

The exhibits show work in progress in studying the former settlements and wrecks that vanished beneath the sea along this section of coast, combined with a thorough study of the patterns of erosion. It is a continuing story, so the displays themselves change as new information appears and more artefacts are recovered.

ALDEBURGH
Moot Hall Museum

£; April to May and September to October weekend afternoons, June daily afternoons, July and August daily;
Tel: 01728 452730

George Crabbe the poet was born in Aldeburgh, while Benjamin Britten the composer and tenor Peter Pears made their home here. All three are connected to the Moot Hall, a fine timber-framed building of the sixteenth century. Crabbe wrote *Peter Grimes*, and Britten turned it into an opera with Pears in the title role for its first production. The climactic trial scene is set in the Moot Hall. The museum tells the story of the coast, the fishing village that became a resort and of another Saxon burial ship discovered at nearby Snape.

One of England's many Martello Towers, built as defences against France in the nineteenth century, stands on the shore and is now let as a unique, if rather forbidding, holiday home by the Landmark Trust.

DUNWICH
Dunwich Museum

Free; March weekend afternoons, April to November daily; St James Street;
Tel: 01728 648796

Here is an even more devastating example of the power of the sea than was seen at Orford. Dunwich was a Roman fort, capital of a Saxon kingdom and one of the great ports of Norman England. At one time it featured among the ten largest towns in the country. Then the sea rushed in and gradually covered almost the whole town, until all that was left is the present modest village. The centrepiece of the museum is a detailed model of Dunwich in its prime in the twelfth century, while other exhibits include artefacts from the different historic periods.

SOUTHWOLD

The town is as elegant as any in East Anglia, and it owes much of its sense of spaciousness to a disaster. The town was devastated by fire in 1659, and the rebuilding was based on a

Fishing boats are still part of the East Anglian scene: these are seen on the River Blyth at Walberswick.

series of greens. Beside one of these is the very traditional Adnams Brewery, and the church where angels stare down from the roof on the exotic creatures carved into the choir stalls. Overlooking both of these is the sparkling white tower of the lighthouse. The town is a place of contrasts: there are still fishing boats in the harbour, while the long beach is lined with brightly coloured beach huts. There are many places to visit that give a feeling for the working life of the port and insights into the past, starting with two lifeboat museums.

Alfred Corry Museum

Free; April to end October daily except Wednesday, November to March weekends but only in fine weather;
Ferry Road;
Tel: 01502 723200

Here is a historic boat in a historic building. The *Alfred Corry* went into service as Southwold No.1 Lifeboat in 1893, a typical East Anglian sailing and pulling boat. She is currently being restored on site. The lifeboat shed originally stood on the end of Cromer pier and was rebuilt beside Southwold harbour in 1998.

Southwold Lifeboat Museum

Free; June to September afternoons; Gun Hill;
Tel: 01502 722422

The story of Southwold's lifeboats told through models and photographs.

Sailors Reading Room

Free; Daily; East Cliff

This is a lovely place to visit. The name needs no explanation but the Reading Room has real atmosphere. There is a small museum where visitors can browse through old newspapers and cuttings describing all kinds of events connected with Southwold and the sea. It is the sort of place you pop into for a minute and finish up staying for an hour.

Southwold Museum

Free; Easter to July, September, October afternoons, August all day; Victoria Street;
Tel: 01502 723374

It is very much a general local history museum, but there is a good section on the Battle of Sole Bay, fought off the coast here in 1672 when the Dutch caught the English unawares. More peaceful Dutch influences can be seen in the building itself, more or less contemporary with the battle, which has typical shaped gables.

LOWESTOFT

Lowestoft & East Suffolk Maritime Museum

£; May to October daily; Sparrow's Nest Park, Whapload Road; Tel: 01502 561963

The museum is overlooked by the lighthouse, built in 1874, but standing on the site of the very first lighthouse to be built by Trinity House in 1609. The main emphasis is on the fishing fleet, from the days of sail, through the later generation of steam herring drifters and on to the modern diesel trawlers. Among the exhibits is the reconstruction of the aft cabin of a steam drifter. Sadly, the last surviving steam drifter, *Lydia Eva*, is currently languishing at anchor in the river, awaiting essential repairs to the hull before she can again be opened to the public.

Royal Naval Patrol Service Association Museum

Free; Monday, Wednesday and Friday, mid-May to mid-October plus Sunday afternoons; Sparrow's Nest; Tel: 01502 586250

The story of the minesweepers and anti-submarine vessels of World War II, told through photographs and models.

Mincarlo

Free; Based in Lowestoft Easter to July open daily; in Great Yarmouth July and August. Days for the latter vary, but are available from local Tourist Board; Tel: 01493 846347

The herring drifters were replaced in the latter part of the twentieth century by trawlers. *Mincarlo* was launched in 1962 and is open to the public as part of a floating museum of the local fishing industry – the other half being the temporarily absent *Lydia Eva*. The slight vagueness about opening days is due to the reliance on volunteers – and there never seem to be quite enough!

The modern trawler *Mincarlo* (top) and the old steam drifter *Lydia Eva*.

THE THAMES BARGE

Of all the rich variety of craft that have carried on the coastal trade of Britain, none has survived in such large numbers as the Thames barge. One reason is that they are good sized vessels, suitable not just for conversion into house boats for leisure, but big enough to be made into permanent homes. And once preserved, there is always the chance to re-rig the barge and take it to sea again. One owner never intended to take his barge from its moorings, but somehow enthusiasm took over and his new home was under sail. So what exactly is a Thames barge? There is no clear answer, as the barges come in different sizes and with variations in their rigging, and they are not – and never were – limited to the Thames. They do, however, form an easily recognizable class of vessel, which has emerged from a long period of development to become the biggest sailing barges to be handled by a crew of two. Indeed, not so very long ago, when they were still trading under sail, it was not unknown for a barge to be managed by just one man.

The first barges to appear on the Thames were dumb barges and lighters, mainly employed in loading and unloading the ships in the Pool of London. They worked the tides, but could also be rowed with long sweeps. The next obvious step was to add a simple mast and square sail. Early illustrations show vessels such as this, either under sail or being hauled along by teams of men on the towpath. The first barges were little more than boxes with rounded ends, yet in time more graceful lines were provided. Bow and stern were still more or less square, but now had a pronounced slope down towards the waterline. The overhanging ends were known as 'swims' and the

The diagonal sprit extending the main sail, which gives the spritsail barge its name, can be clearly seen in this picture.

barges became 'swimmies'. The big change came when a new type of rig appeared in British waters. The Dutch presented Charles II with a yacht, rigged with a spritsail. This was the rig that became the main characteristic of the Thames barge. The sail was still square, but now it was set fore and aft, the peak extended by the sprit, a wooden spar which ran from the foot of the mast, diagonally across to the upper corner of the sail. As in a gaff-rigged sail, the lower corner of the sail was controlled through sheets that could be adjusted from the steering position. The upper end of the sprit, however, was managed through two extra lines, the vangs. The bottom of the sprit sat in the 'snotter', a rope collar round the mast, and could be raised and lowered by means of a standing lift, a rope running up to the masthead and down again. It sounds complex, but in practice is easily handled. Unlike the gaff rig, the mainsail does not have to be laboriously raised and lowered. Instead, it is brailed into the sprit and mast, so that setting sail involves no more than releasing it to fall into place.

Over the years there were many improvements. The lines of the hull became more refined and steering was made easier by the change from the tiller to the steering wheel. A topsail was added above the mainsail, and a triangular staysail added forward of the mast. A short mizzen was placed right at the stern, with the boom attached to the rudder. This helps with manoeuvrability. In the larger vessels a bowsprit was included, carrying up to three jibs.

Because these were river barges, they were built with flat bottoms. However, with the improvement in rigging, they were able to make long coastal voyages as

Changing times: a scene from the early twentieth century, a steam tug towing a spritsail barge, with a large lighter also being towed in the background.

well. Most sea-going vessels maintain stability by means of a keel at the bottom of the hull, but that was no solution for a river barge. So another device was added, the leeboard, which prevents the barge making leeway, sliding sideways across the water. These are heavy wooden boards, one on each side of the barge, only one of which is in use at any one time. When a barge comes about, the leeboard on one side is dropped into the water, and the one on the opposite side winched up – heavy work, so it is as well that barges seldom indulged in a lot of tacking in their working days.

In 1863 a Mr Henry Dodds inaugurated the first of the Annual Barge Sailing Matches. This was not just so that owners and crews could have a bit of fun. He hoped that builders would rise to the challenge and vie with each other to produce faster boats without sacrificing any of the essential cargo-carrying qualities. He also felt that they would add to the prestige of the skippers and would become a showcase for their seamanship and skills. They were a huge success, and from a single annual event the matches have grown into a series of races held around the coast of south east England and up into East Anglia. Looking back at an old race programme, I see there were twenty-three barges racing that day, the oldest of which was built in 1892 and the youngster of the fleet in 1926. To see so many sailing barges out on the water at the same time is one of the great sights of maritime Britain, and to this, admittedly somewhat prejudiced writer, beats anything on view at Cannes. The greatest thrill is to take part as one of the crew, and somehow, although it is great to win, the day is just as splendid sailing on one of the also-rans. Because many of the surviving barges are chartered with a skipper, it is possible to go along for the day, either helping out or simply as a spectator. Then, at every race, there is a small flotilla of yachts and dinghies coming along for the fun. But even those who only watch from the shore can still enjoy a splendid spectacle, and as most races follow triangular courses, they can be there for the start and the finish. Individual barges can also be seen at a number of ports, either permanent residents or just visiting, and the sailing barges have their own museum in Sittingbourne.

GREAT YARMOUTH

Today a busy, boisterous seaside resort, the port has a long and distinguished history. In the thirteenth century it was entirely circled by walls, with fifteen defensive towers. Everything was crammed inside, right up to the nineteenth century. As well as being a busy fishing port, it was also a naval base to which the local hero, Nelson, returned after two of his great victories. A monument was built in 1819, and there was a time when visitors could climb the 217 steps to admire the view from the top, but sadly no more. It remains, however, an impressive site. The past is remembered in a number of museums, and Great Yarmouth shares in playing host to *Lydia Eva* and *Mincarlo* (see p.81 for details).

Maritime Museum

£; Monday to Friday, June to September plus weekend afternoons; Marine Parade; Tel: 01493 842267

This is one of those modest museums that turn out to be full of interest, starting with the building itself. It was constructed in 1861 as a sailors' club and refuge for shipwrecked mariners. The sailors left behind objects they had picked up on their travels and, even more interestingly, things they had made themselves. There are a number of charming, rather naive toys carved in the men's spare time. Shipwreck features strongly, largely because of the importance of Captain George Manby and his various life-saving devices. His own working model of the breeches buoy appears, complete with little carved sailors. Paintings and models deal with the story of the fishing industry.

Elizabethan House Museum

£; Monday to Friday, April to November plus weekend afternoons; 4 South Quay; Tel: 01493 855746

A sumptuous sixteenth-century merchant's house, it gives a good notion of the wealth generated by the trading port of the time. One real gem is a stained glass window of 1612, showing one of the large Dutch fishing vessels, or busses, at work in the North Sea.

A Dutch pinnace portrayed in a seventeenth-century stained glass, now installed in a window at the Elizabethan House in Great Yarmouth.

Tolhouse Museum

£; Monday to Friday, July to October plus weekend afternoons; Tolhouse Street; Tel: 01493 858900

The Tolhouse was built in the thirteenth century and later served as the town court and gaol. The great hall was the Heighening Chamber, where the Corporation met to fix the price of herring – 'heighening' means raising, so no one expected them to start bringing prices down, especially as the Corporation took its share of the profits. Now it tells the history of the town.

LUDHAM

Albion

Available for long and short charter with skipper and mate; Tel: 01493 740140, or write: Charter Secretary, Victoria House, 49 White Street, Martham, Great Yarmouth, NR2 4PQ

Albion, built in 1898, is the last of the Norfolk wherries still to be seen under sail. She is a wonderful example of a vessel ideally suited to the working environment. The lines are fine, the draught shallow, a mere 4ft fully loaded. The single tall mast forward of the hatches can be dropped to go under bridges. Contrary to what one might expect, the mast is wound down by a windlass but springs back up thanks to a counterweight. This is a gaff rig, with the huge single sail controlled by the steerer through sheet blocks. The wherries mostly traded on The Broads, and when the wind failed to blow they were quanted, pushed along by poles – as *Albion* still is today. Today instead of carrying cargo she carries passengers in the adapted hold – the crew occupy the one small cabin. To sail on *Albion* is a memorable experience: you can start the day in a dead calm and work up a sweat on the quant poles, then the breeze gets up and by the end you can be flying along in grand style. When not out on charter, the wherry can be seen at her berth at Womack, Ludham.

Because the wherries were so successful as cargo vessels, they were later adapted for pleasure boating, and the wherry yacht was born. A number of these elegant craft are also available for charter in the area.

One of the truly great sites of the Norfolk Broads: the traditional wherry *Albion*. This was a working barge, but the basic design was also copied for the wherry yacht.

Plain and tiny, the former coastguard station at Mundesley can at least boast a splendid sea view.

MUNDESLEY
Maritime Museum

£; May to October daily; Beach Road; Tel: 01263 720879

It claims to be Britain's smallest museum and it might well be. It is housed in a former coastguard lookout, and the first floor has been restored as it might have been in the 1930s. Downstairs is a more conventional small museum, dealing with different aspects of the maritime history of the area.

CROMER
Cromer Museum

£; Monday to Saturday plus Sunday afternoons; Tucker Street; Tel: 01263 513543; Website: www.norfolk.gov.uk/tourism/museums

Housed in former fishermen's cottages, the first thing you see on walking into the yard is a crabber, a small, clinker built boat. One of the cottages has been refurbished as a typical, cramped one-down two-up. Apart from the general history, there are some wonderful photographs of the days of the sailing colliers, a model of the Cromer lifeboat specially made for the Great Exhibition, and a lighthouse display, including the very first ornate example, built in 1719. This is a little museum big on charm.

RNLI Henry Blogg Museum

Free; Easter to end of October daily; The Gangway; Tel: 01263 511294

Here in the old lifeboat station is the story of a man and a boat. Henry G. Blogg joined the Cromer lifeboat in 1894 and finally retired in 1947, having been coxswain for almost thirty-eight of those years. The boat is *H.F. Bailey* – with the lucky number ON777. It was lucky for the 520 lives saved by Blogg, his crew and this boat between 1935 and 1945. There are grander museums but few that tell a more heart-warming story of voluntary endeavour and bravery spread over half a century.

SHERINGHAM
Boat Collection

Free; Wednesdays; The Mo

This is a temporary arrangement while work goes on in developing a permanent site for this important collection. There are a number of boat collections around the country, but none so closely tied to one place. Sheringham still has four of its lifeboats, which between them represent a continuous service from 1894 to 1990; three are preserved here. The oldest is a pulling and sailing

Henry G. Blogg, the famous lifeboatman, who was awarded three RNLI gold medals and four silver medals for gallantry.

The lifeboat *J.C. Madge* on its original carriage and ready for launching at Old Hythe.

lifeboat, *J.C. Madge*; the next a traditional motorized vessel, *Foresters Centenary*; and the last offshore lifeboat, *Manchester Unity of Oddfellows*. The last name might seem peculiar, but the Oddfellows Hall just behind the present site is the original lifeboat station of the 1860s. There are also three fishing boats, each of which was both built and used at Sheringham.

KING'S LYNN

Here is a port which has known great days and immense prosperity, and fortunately a large number of old buildings survive from those times, many of which have a story to tell. Council offices are generally mundane places, but not here. The buildings started off as warehouses built for the Hanseatic League in 1475. The League was formed to serve a powerful combination of mainly German cities that traded throughout the Baltic and North Sea. A house in Bridge Street, built in 1605, was a rope maker's home, and is now a home and offices again today, but in between was an inn, The Greenland Fishery. Old houses still line Pilot Street, and the chapel favoured by the fishing community, St Nicholas, boasts a gloriously ornate porch. It is well worth walking around the town and the quays along the bank of the Great Ouse before going to any museum. A leaflet is available from the Tourist Office, but there are also guided walks between May and October: tickets can be bought at the Tales of the Old Gaol Museum, Saturday Market Place (£).

Custom House

Free; Daily; Tel: 01553 763044; Website: www.west-norfolk.gov.uk

The very grand Jacobean building was a merchant's exchange before becoming the Custom House in 1718. It is now home to the Tourist Information Centre, and maritime history displays can be seen in rooms restored in a Georgian style.

The elegant eighteenth-century Custom House at King's Lynn.

True's Yard Fishing Heritage Museum

£; Daily; North Street; Tel: 01553 770479

Here is where you find out about the people who created the wealth so apparent in the rest of the town. This was the quarter where the fishermen and their families lived, squeezed into tiny cottages. Most of the houses were swept away as slums in the 1930s, but there are survivors. One cottage is fitted out as it would have been in the 1850s, the other in the style of the 1920s. Memorabilia of the fishing community complete the picture. Even sanitized for visitors, this is still a picture of a grim existence.

The Green Quay

£; Daily; Tel: 01553 818500; Website: www.thegreenquay.co.uk

As part of a major restoration programme along the waterfront, the sixteenth-century warehouse has been transformed into a discovery centre and exhibition space. The emphasis here is on the natural history of The Wash.

The wheel house of the trawler *Ross Tiger*, a mixture of the traditional and the modern: the shiny brass of the ship's telegraph in the background contrasting with the modern navigation aids in the foreground.

GRIMSBY

In its day, this was one of the great fishing ports of the world, and although still active, the fleet has greatly reduced in recent years. Much of the development came with the arrival of the railways, able to move fish rapidly around the country. The port's most famous landmark was, in fact, built by the Manchester, Sheffield & Lincolnshire Railway in the early 1850s. The tower rising nearly 100m above the dock entrance, designed like an Italian campanile, is no folly. It was an accumulator tower. Water was pumped up by a steam engine to a tank at the top to provide the pressure to work hydraulic machinery.

National Fishing Heritage Centre

££; Easter to end of October daily; Alexandra Dock; Tel: 01472 323345

The centre is based on two trawlers. The first has been built inside the centre, where all kinds of modern techniques are used to give an idea of the life of the community and the conditions under which the fishermen work. Interactive displays give the visitors a chance to try their hand at skippering a fishing vessel, plotting a course to the fishing grounds. After leaving 'the ship', visitors can walk the reconstructed streets of old Grimsby. The second trawler is the real thing, the *Ross Tiger*, built in the 1950s and now permanently moored at the quay. The conducted tours on board gain enormously from having a former trawlerman on hand.

The Humber sloop *Amy Howson* has a similar hull to her sister ship, the keel *Comrade* (p.61), but carries a fore and aft instead of a square rig.

SOUTH FERRIBY
Comrade and *Amy Howson*

Sailing dates from Humber Keel and Sloop Preservation Society:
Comrade, *Tel: 01482 703947;* Amy Howson, *Tel: 01652 635288*

Both these vessels are Humber ships, built to very precise specifications. In their working days they not only sailed the Humber, but also travelled far inland on the canals of the Sheffield and South Yorkshire Navigation system. They had to fit in the locks, so to maximize cargo space they had blunt bows and rounded sterns. *Comrade*, built in 1923, is a keel, square-rigged with a large mainsail and smaller topsail. This is a type of rig that any medieval sailor would recognize and feel quite at home in handling. Fred Schofield, a keel man all his life, was the owner and he passed her over to the Preservation Society because she was the last of her kind and he was anxious to see her preserved. He also passed on something of his own knowledge and skills gained in sailing *Comrade* for so many years, so that the Society has been able to keep her out on the water She can usually be seen under sail on about ten weekends a year. The second ship has a fore and aft rig, thus *Amy Howson* qualifies as a sloop rather than a keel. She, too, has been fully restored and joins *Comrade* for sailing weekends. Unfortunately, trips on the ships are limited to members, friends and societies who have a special interest, but they are well worth looking out for.

See Also
Pin Mill

A single street leads down to the quay on the Orwell, and apart from being a delightful spot, this is home to a number of Thames barges. It is also the start and finishing point for one of the annual barge matches.

WELLS-NEXT-THE-SEA Maritime Museum

£; Easter to autumn all day weekends, Tuesday to Friday afternoons (times are variable, so check for details); The Quay; Tel: 01328 711646

Housed in the former lifeboat house, it tells the story of the lifeboat and coastguard services through models and pictures, plus dealing with more general maritime history.

Immingham Museum

Free; Monday to Friday afternoons; Margaret Street; Tel: 01469 577066

The story of the port created by the Great Central Railway is featured here, from the cutting of the first sod in 1906, illustrated by a series of historic photographs and memorabilia.

The port of Immingham was built by Britain's last mainline railway, the Great Central, completed in 1899. This photograph of its construction shows a tipping wagon.

THE WOODEN SHIP

The story of wooden shipbuilding is one of slow, steady development over many centuries. There were no abrupt changes until the end of the eighteenth century, with the appearance of the first iron hulls and the steam engine. The earliest vessels were all clinker built, a system in which the planks that make up the hull overlap each other. This provides the main strength of the boat, which is then reinforced by internal frames. Perhaps the grandest of all the ships built in this was Henry V's *Henri Grâce à Dieu*, known rather more familiarly to sailors of the day as *Great Harry*. She was a warship of about 1400 tons, with a hull built up from three layers of planking, held together by wooden pegs known as trenails. Seams were reinforced by iron bolts. This system was later replaced by ships that were carvel built, where the planks of the hull abut each other to create a smooth hull, which decreases water resistance. In these ships the skeleton is created and the planking added afterwards. This was soon the standard for most larger vessels.

The first stage was design, the work of the Master Shipwright. In early days these men worked in their own mysterious ways, and even as late as the end of the nineteenth century a shipbuilder such as James

Goss of Calstock sketched out plans on a bit of wooden board propped up against his kitchen wall. The system obviously worked, for one of his vessels, the ketch *Garlandstone*, still survives and can be seen at Morwellham Quay. The man who first changed the old rule of thumb system of building to something altogether more organized was Henry VIII's principal designer, Matthew Baker. He developed a method of laying out a ship's lines on paper, setting out cross sections at various places along the hull, with curves based on arcs of circles. He also introduced a system of defining the size of a ship by the number of tunns or barrels of Bordeaux wine that could fit in the hold. This was formalized as tons, and has now gone on to the metric tonne. The method of laying out the lines eventually became formalized into three sets of planes at right angles to each other. It was common practice at this stage to make an accurate model, on the not unreasonable grounds that many owners were unable to interpret the drawings. It is thanks to this practice that, while comparatively few old vessels have survived, we have a very clear idea of how they looked from the many models still to be seen in a number of maritime museums.

The construction of a carvel-built ship followed a

A drawing from the collection of Henry VIII's shipwright Matthew Baker, showing a ship's lines being laid out with large compasses.

set pattern. First, suitable timber had to be ordered, including compass timber, which had a natural curve for frames; 'thick stuff', for planking 4 inches or thicker; and crooked timber for the right angled knees, which are in effect the brackets that were to support the beams. English oak was the most prized for shipbuilding, and a first rate man of war such as *Victory* would require the felling of perhaps as many as 2000 mature trees. As trees are not the easiest things to move, it made a great deal of sense to establish shipyards near a forest. One such eighteenth-century site is Buckler's Hard on the Beaulieu River, with an immensely wide main street, specially designed for big cartloads of timber. Visitors to the site today will perhaps be surprised to see few signs of the docks, covered slipways and sheds that are such a familiar part of a modern dockyard. But this is because most of the building went on in the open.

The first stage was to lay down the keel, which in a big ship would be made out of several timber sections scarfed together by overlapping joints. Above that was a similar structure, the keelson, which held the frame to the keel. To this the upright stem at the bows and sternpost were added. The skeleton was completed by the addition of the carefully shaped ribs that would define the outline of the hull. Templates had to be made from the drawings so that the ribs could be accurately shaped. The quintessential tool for the job was the adze, looking rather like an axe, except that the cutting edge is at right angles to the shaft. The planking was added to the inside and the outside of the hull. Further structural strength was supplied by

Shipbuilding at David Williams' yard, Porthmadog, in the 1900s; tools on show include an adze in the centre and a caulking mallet.

the beams, which also support the deck planking. To make everything watertight the planking was caulked. Oakum was forced into the gaps between the planks and then covered over with pitch. With the hull complete, the ship could be launched ready for fitting out: masts and rigging were added, rudder hung and steering gear attached, and everything made ready to receive the crew.

A medieval shipwright would have quickly adapted to work in an eighteenth-century yard and found his old skills just as useful as they had ever been. There were, however, some notable improvements. To fit the planking to the hull in the oldest vessels involved carving a plank to shape, but then it was realized that if wood was steamed, it became flexible and could be bent into position. A man of war might have had as many as 500 knees, each of which had to be carved out of specially selected timber. In order for the grain to run true, a section was cut out from the point where a sturdy branch grew out of the main trunk. The oak was particularly useful, as the branches tend to grow out straight. It was obvious that when iron became widely available, it offered a far cheaper alternative. Standardized knees could be used in place of the old wooden ones. There was to be one further advance in the early nineteenth century when Robert Seppings, the Surveyor of the Navy, recognized that he could build longer hulls by reinforcing them with iron strappings. The system can be seen in the hull of *Unicorn* in Dundee. The composite ship was the final stage reached before wood finally gave way to iron and steel for the big ships.

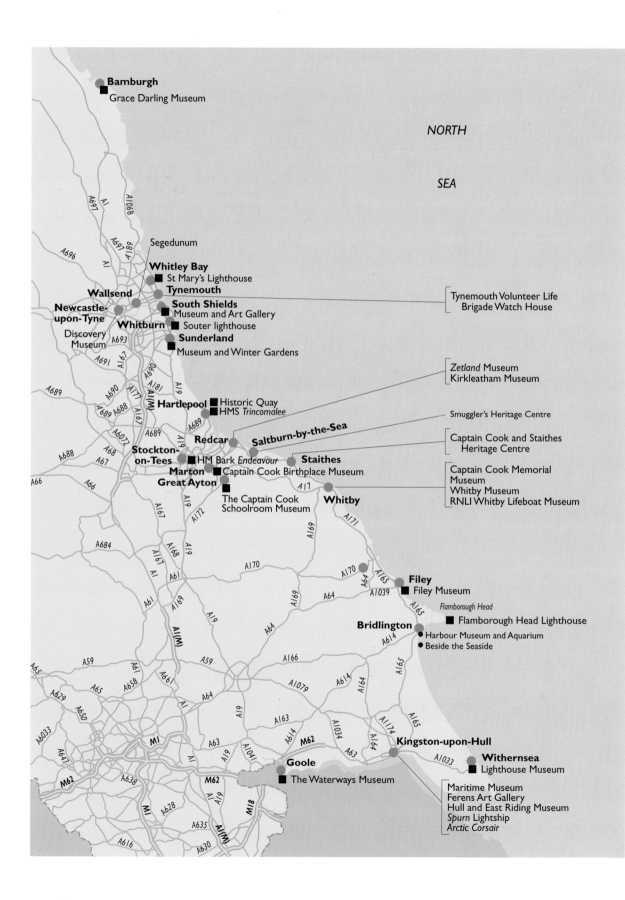

Bamburgh
Grace Darling Museum

NORTH

SEA

Segedunum
Whitley Bay
St Mary's Lighthouse
Tynemouth
Wallsend
South Shields
Newcastle-
upon-Tyne
Museum and Art Gallery
Whitburn
Souter lighthouse
Discovery
Museum
Sunderland
Museum and Winter Gardens

Tynemouth Volunteer Life
Brigade Watch House

Zetland Museum
Kirkleatham Museum

Hartlepool
Historic Quay
HMS *Trincomalee*

Smuggler's Heritage Centre

Redcar
Saltburn-by-the-Sea

Captain Cook and Staithes
Heritage Centre

Stockton-
on-Tees
HM Bark *Endeavour*
Staithes
Marton
Captain Cook Birthplace Museum
Great Ayton
The Captain Cook
Schoolroom Museum
Whitby

Captain Cook Memorial
Museum
Whitby Museum
RNLI Whitby Lifeboat Museum

Filey
Filey Museum

Flamborough Head
Flamborough Head Lighthouse
Bridlington
Harbour Museum and Aquarium
Beside the Seaside

Kingston-upon-Hull
Withernsea
Lighthouse Museum
Goole
The Waterways Museum

Maritime Museum
Ferens Art Gallery
Hull and East Riding Museum
Spurn Lightship
Arctic Corsair

NORTH EAST ENGLAND

Moving north brings one to an area typically associated with heavy industry. Shipbuilding has a long history in the region, but came to real prominence with the move from sail to steam, from wooden hull to iron and later steel. The range of work varied from that of the great yards, such as Swan Hunter on Tyneside, builders of the mighty *Mauretania*, to modest ships' boiler manufacturers, such as Riley Brothers of Stockton-on-Tees, one of whose boilers was supplied to the paddle steamer *Kingswear Castle*. There was a busy coastal trade, particularly in coal for London and the south east. Colliers were being sent out as early as 1305, when a document records that a merchant called Thomas Miggs shipped a consignment of coal from Newcastle to London on the *Welfare*. The colliers were sturdy vessels, and one of them, built at Whitby in 1764, the *Earl of Pembroke*, was destined to find fame when she was renamed the *Endeavour* and commanded by Captain Cook. The area also had an important part to play in the development of the lifeboat service. Fishing ports can be found all around Britain's coast. But the north-eastern ports sent out vessels to distant waters, often as far as the Arctic, and there was a long tradition of whaling in the region.

GOOLE
The Waterways Museum

£ (price does not include boat trips); All year Monday to Friday, Sunday and Bank Holiday afternoons Easter to October; Tel: 01405 768730;
Website: www.waterwaysmuseumandadventurecentre.co.uk

Goole was created as a nineteenth-century canal town by the Aire & Calder Navigation Company as the port for shipment of coal from South Yorkshire. It was a trans-shipment centre between the coal barges and the ships arriving up the tidal Ouse. The museum tells the story of the town and its trade, and an extension opened in 2002 provides interactive displays, where visitors can try a number of activities, from hoisting sails to handling the traditional tools of the boat builder. Outside on the water, a former grain barge has been turned into a floating art gallery. A former lightship, *Audrey*, has been converted to resemble a 'billy boy', a close cousin to the Humber keels and sloops, which came in a variety of different rigs; in this case a fore and aft gaff rig was selected. This offers river

The coal hoist at Goole Docks. Containers, tom puddings, were lifted up and inverted to fill a waiting collier.

and coastal trips. Canal trips, short and long, are available on a motorized keel, *Sobriety*, originally designed for use on the Sheffield & South Yorkshire Canal system. More modest trips are also available round the docks. These provide an opportunity to see a unique feature of Goole docks.

In 1862 the engineer William Bartholomew introduced compartment boats to the Aire & Calder. These were basic, square metal boxes that would be filled with coal, the shape earning them their popular name 'tom puddings'. Trains of these were hauled along the canal by tug, and once they reached the docks, they were lifted by mechanical hoists and upended into the hold of a waiting collier. Tom puddings can be seen beside the preserved Boat Hoist No.5.

The *Spurn* lightship at Princes Dock, Hull. The original dock was developed by the engineer Jesse Hartley, the man best known as the designer of Liverpool's Albert Dock. Sadly, little of Hartley's work can now be seen in Hull.

KINGSTON UPON HULL

This is a city with a long maritime history, first mentioned in 1193 when the Yorkshire monasteries sent wool to help pay the ransom of Richard I from the 'port of Hull'. There is still a great deal of the historic city to roam around and enjoy. The most interesting area of Georgian streets, including the delightfully named Land of Green Ginger, is to be found down by the River Hull. Here is Trinity House, with its elaborately carved pediment, built in 1787 to train boys for the Merchant Navy. The river itself is still busy with barges and coasters, and a notable feature is the tidal surge barrier, completed in 1980. Hull had an impressive array of enclosed docks with imposing warehouses, many of the buildings having

been designed by the engineer Jesse Hartley, who was responsible for so much splendid work in Liverpool. Sadly, very little has survived modernization: conversion into a marina for one part and concreting over for much else. There is, however, still a fine waterfront on the Humber, with the Pilot House of 1820 and the former booking office for the steamers of the Humber ferry service. They were made redundant with the building of the Humber Bridge.

There are a number of excellent museums to explore, and information covering them all is to be found on:
Tel: 01482 613902
Website: www.hull.gov.uk/museums

Maritime Museum

Free; Monday to Saturday and Sunday afternoons; Queen Victoria Square

The building is High Victorian, built in 1871 as the offices of the Hull Dock Company. The elaborate façade topped by three domes was intended to impress and still does. Inside, as well as the usual range of maritime exhibits, there are galleries devoted to the once important local industry of whaling and intriguing collections of scrimshaw – tusks and bones carved by sailors.

Ferens Art Gallery

Free; Monday to Saturday and Sunday afternoons; Queen Victoria Square

This is a good companion to the maritime museum, and it is not a bad idea to visit these two museums before starting any explorations. They give the city a context. The gallery has a general art collection, but in amongst the conventional old masters is a first rate collection of maritime paintings. What gives them a special interest is the large number devoted to local marine subjects – just look, for example, at the works of John Ward, a great recorder of Hull, the Humber and its ships.

Hull and East Riding Museum

Free; Monday to Saturday and Sunday afternoons; High Street

Another reused building, this time the old Corn Exchange of 1856, hence the various agricultural symbols carved on the façade. It is a general local history museum but home to one exhibit of outstanding importance: the Hasholme Boat, built in the Iron Age (see p.36-7).

Spurn Lightship

Free; Monday to Saturday and Sunday afternoons; Prince's Dock

Visitors can go aboard the lightship that guarded the entrance to the Humber for forty-eight years from 1927.

Arctic Corsair

£; On board tours April to October Wednesday, Saturday and Sunday; Tickets from Wilberforce House, High Street

The very last of Hull's fleet of sidewinder trawlers can be explored with expert guides. The entrance is via the house where William Wilberforce, the famous anti-slavery campaigner, lived.

The bridge of the 1960 trawler *Arctic Corsair*. She is the very last of what was once an extensive fleet of deep-sea trawlers working out of the port.

WHITBY AND CAPTAIN COOK

There are really two Whitbys: the modern seaside resort with its hotels, sandy beaches and amusement arcades; and the old port, with houses packed together above a narrow inlet. The harbour was once a centre for shipbuilding and home to whalers – an arch made from a whale's jawbone still stands to the west of the estuary. Today the whalers have all gone, but not the fishing boats, nor the traditional smokeries where herring are turned into kippers. These are enticing places, which as a small boy on holiday I loved to visit, much to the annoyance of my parents – the smell lingers a very long time! There is a lot to see, starting with a museum to the man whose statue looks down on the town, Captain Cook.

This seventeenth-century house was home to ship owner John Walker, and would probably never have been preserved if Mr Walker had not taken on a young man called James Cook as an apprentice.

Captain Cook Memorial Museum

££; Easter to November daily; Grape Lane;
Tel: 01947 601900;
Website: www.cookmuseumwhitby.co.uk

The seventeenth-century house was home to Captain John Walker, owner of a collier who took the seventeen-year-old James Cook on as an apprentice in 1746 and taught him his trade. The house itself has been restored, and there are original illustrations and artefacts from Cook's voyages. There is also a portrait of a man who served with Cook and who went on to a dubious fame of his own, Captain William Bligh of the *Bounty*.

Whitby Museum

£; May to September Monday to Saturday and Sunday afternoon, October to April Wednesday to Saturday and Sunday afternoon; Pannett Park; Tel: 01947 602908

The first museums were known as 'cabinets of curiosity', which is a fair description of this museum. Alongside such serious items as part of Cook's original journal and lifeboat models are more bizarre exhibits, including a murderer's hand used as a candleholder.

RNLI Whitby Lifeboat Museum

Free; Easter to October daily; Tel: 01947 602001

The main exhibit is the 1918 lifeboat *Robert & Ellen Robson*, built in 1918. This was a pulling lifeboat with ten oarsmen out of a crew of thirteen, the very last of its kind when it was taken out of service in 1957.

Ship models are commonplace in maritime museums, but this man of war from Whitby Museum is really special. The detail is superbly executed, not in wood but ivory.

GREAT AYTON

The Captain Cook Schoolroom Museum

£; April to June, September, October afternoons, July and August all day; Tel: 01642 724296;
Website: www.captaincookschoolroommuseum.co.uk

The Charity School was founded here in the shadow of shapely Roseberry Topping in 1704. James Cook was a pupil from 1736 to 1740, an unlikely starting place for one of Britain's greatest sailors and navigators. The eighteenth-century schoolroom has been recreated. In the village there is an obelisk marking the site of the Cook family home and a memorial in the Norman church.

MARTON

Captain Cook Birthplace Museum

£; Tuesday to Sunday; Stewart Park; Tel: 01642 311211;
Website: www.middlesbrough.gov.uk

Marton is now a suburb of Middlesbrough, but the museum is housed in an attractive park. It has recently been given an update, with lots of interactive displays, special effects and film, as well as more conventional exhibits. The emphasis is on Cook's early years before joining the Navy.

STAITHES

Captain Cook and Staithes Heritage Centre

£; February to December daily, January weekends; High Street; Tel: 01947 841454

Staithes would be a place worth visiting even without the museum. Snuggled up to the cliff face, the village crowds together. A narrow, cobbled street leads down to the harbour, with entrances to little courtyards and alleys leading off to the side. The museum is housed in a former Methodist Chapel, and among the other exhibits is a collection of the famous Webber engravings, made from the original paintings of scenes from Cook's voyages.

JAMES COOK

This is an extraordinary story of a man who rose to fame as one of the greatest naval officers of all time after making his way through the ranks. His father was an agricultural labourer in the village of Marton, just south of Middlesbrough, and his birthplace now has a museum devoted to his life and exploits. He went to school at Great Ayton for a short time, where another museum has been set up, and was then apprenticed to a shopkeeper in the delightful fishing village of Staithes, home to museum number three. Shopkeeping did not appeal, and he was apprenticed to a ship owner, Walker of Whitby – and here, not surprisingly, is a fourth Cook museum. In 1755, when war with France broke out, he was already mate on a coaster, even though he was still only fourteen years old. He at once volunteered for the Navy and joined the 60-gun *Eagle* under the command of Captain Hugh Palliser. It was a fortunate choice. Although Cook was only an able seaman, Palliser recognized his talents and the boy soon found himself on the road to promotion. In 1759 as master, or navigator, on the *Mercury*, he successfully found a deep-water channel up the St Lawrence. The British fleet was able to make its way right up to Quebec, a vital factor in the capture of the city from the French. His reward was the command of the *Northumberland*.

Palliser was now governor of Newfoundland, and in 1763 he arranged for Cook to be in charge of a marine survey of the Newfoundland coast. Cook was largely self taught, but the survey was carried out with remarkable accuracy and efficiency. It brought the young man to the attention of a number of important men in the Admiralty.

In 1768 he was given an opportunity to take charge of a mission which began the process that brought him lasting fame. The Royal Society was anxious to mount an expedition to the Pacific to observe the transit of Venus. His ship was the *Endeavour*, a barque built in Whitby as a collier in 1764, a modest vessel of 366 tons, a replica of which can be seen at Stockton-on-Tees. Cook and the scientists sailed away in 1768. They rounded Cape Horn and made their way to Tahiti for the astronomical work. That, however, was by no means the end of Cook's work. It was on the return voyage that Cook was required to show his navigational and surveying skills. He sailed round New Zealand, charting the coast, and then made his way down the east coast of Australia. He landed and claimed the country for Britain, naming the spot Stingrays Bay. He changed his mind, however, on the homeward voyage, and because one of the scientists, Joseph Banks, had discovered so many new flowers there, he renamed it Botany Bay. By the time they had returned to England in 1771 thirty men out of a crew of eighty-five had died of disease. This was something that greatly concerned Cook and which he set out to remedy on his next voyage.

Cook was now appointed to the rank of Commander, and in 1772 he was off again to the Pacific, this time on the *Resolution*. One of his tasks was to search for Terra Australis Incognita, the huge continent that was supposedly to be found in the southern hemisphere. Now he set out in the opposite

The portrait of Cook, after a painting by William Hodges who accompanied Cook on his travels. The face is that of a man of great determination.

direction, sailing round the Cape of Good Hope. He successfully circumnavigated Antarctica, in the process discovering New Caledonia and South Georgia – and proving that no vast, undiscovered, fertile continent existed. During the voyage, he took steps to improve the diet of the crew, including sauerkraut as a regular part of the diet. The sailors were not keen, and Cook had two men flogged because they refused to eat this novel food. Although the importance of the diet was not immediately recognized, Cook had discovered that by providing food containing Vitamin C he had the cure for the fatal disease scurvy. The result was that the terrible death toll of the first circumnavigation was not repeated. This time only one crew member died out of a complement of 118.

After a brief rest in England, he was sent out again to explore the North Pacific. The able seaman had now finally achieved the rank of Captain. He set sail in 1776 with two ships, *Resolution* and *Discovery*.

He was given a new, unrealizable objective, to find a sea route round the north of America. Cook was remarkable among the ranks of the great explorers in that he soon developed a real respect for the native people he met. He spoke highly of the courage and honesty of the Maoris, and when in 1779 he stopped off in Tahiti for a refit after being caught in a gale, everything seemed to go well with the local population. There were a few reported instances of petty theft, but otherwise it was trouble free. One of the locals, however, was seen stealing from one of the ships, and a boat went ashore to arrest him. A skirmish led to bloodshed, and soon the islanders were attacking the small English force. In the sudden upsurge of violence Cook was killed.

In his three great voyages Cook had transformed European knowledge of the world, but perhaps even more importantly, he had at the same time reduced the appalling loss of life from scurvy, a disease that had killed more seamen than warfare had ever done.

A 'cat' leaving Whitby harbour with the Abbey in the background, a scene that would have been very familiar to the young James Cook.

The stark angularity of Withernsea lighthouse rises high above the rooftops of the town.

WITHERNSEA

Lighthouse Museum

£; Mid-June to mid-September weekdays and weekend afternoons, March to mid-June and mid-September to October weekend afternoons; Tel: 01964 614834

The immense 127ft (39m) lighthouse rises above suburban rooftops behind the Promenade. There are exhibits on the lifeboat and coastguard services on the ground floor. A tiring 144 steps lead to the top and a panoramic view, improved by a mounted telescope – or you can cheat and see it all on screen at the bottom. Robert Drewery worked on the lighthouse construction in the 1890s and was a coxswain of the lifeboat. His granddaughter followed a very different career. Kay Kendall was a star of British films in the 1950s, and extracts from some of her films are shown.

FLAMBOROUGH

Flamborough Head Lighthouse

£; Easter to September Monday to Friday; Tel: 01262 850345

The old fishing village was built inland from a bay to the south by the site of a former beacon. The road out to the cliffs of Flamborough Head passes the tower of the first lighthouse, built in 1674, and then continues on to the 'modern' light of 1806.

FILEY

Filey Museum

£; All day Monday to Friday and Sunday, Easter to October Saturday afternoons; 8–10 Queen Street; Tel: 01723 515013

Filey has the air of a genteel Victorian resort, but here is a reminder that before that, it was a fishing port. The two cottages making up the museum were built in 1696, and exhibits concentrate on Filey the fishing port. A local salmon coble sits in the garden alongside a replica baiting shed of the 1950s.

REDCAR

RNLI *Zetland* Lifeboat Museum

Free; May to September afternoons; 5 King Street, Tel: 01642 485370

Zetland is the oldest surviving lifeboat in the world. Built in 1800, this was one of thirty-one vessels constructed to the original design of the local boat builder Henry Greathead. A basic craft with five pairs of oars and two steering oars at the stern, she had a highly successful career, remaining in service right up to her last rescue in 1880. In that time it has been estimated that *Zetland* saved 500 lives.

Kirkleatham Museum

Free; All day, closed Mondays; Tel: 01642 479500

The museum is housed in the Old Hall, not, as it might appear, a grand family house, but built in 1709 as the Free School by the local benefactors, the Turner family. It became a museum in 1981, covering all aspects of local history, including maritime. There are a number of displays, particularly relating to shipbuilding on the Tees. Three fishing boats have been preserved, including a 100-year-old sailing coble, and the Oakley Class lifeboat of 1963, *Sir James Knott*.

STOCKTON-ON-TEES

HM Bark *Endeavour*

££; Easter to end of October daily; Castlegate Quay; Tel: 01642 676844; Website: www.castlegatequay.co.uk

This is a full-scale replica of Captain Cook's ship the *Endeavour*. Visitors can either go on a guided tour or do their own audio tour. Cabins have been recreated much as they would have been in the eighteenth century, and there are displays telling the story of the first voyage to Australia. One mystery remains: how did ninety-four crew and scientists ever cram into such a comparatively small ship?

The replica of Captain Cook's ship, the *Endeavour*, at the quayside in Stockton-on-Tees.

HMS *Trincomalee*, an odd sounding name for a ship of the Royal Navy, but she was built in India and Trincomalee is a town in Sri Lanka, then part of British India.

HARTLEPOOL
Historic Quay

£££; Daily; Tel: 01429 860888; Website: www.thisishartlepool.com

This ambitious project has seen the recreation of an eighteenth-century port, with a whole variety of houses, shops, market and even a prison. There are displays on fighting ships, film shows and lots of activities which are part fun, part educational. In fact, in their search for realism, the creators of the fighting ship exhibit have felt it necessary to warn off visitors 'of a nervous disposition'. One would have to be very frail to faint away, so there is no real cause for concern. The Museum of Hartlepool has been incorporated into the complex, which is a more traditional museum, but inevitably it is mostly concerned with the town's industrial and maritime history. The café is actually one of the most interesting exhibits in its own right, on board the 1934 paddle steamer *Wingfield Castle*. Visitors can view the engine room, and the machinery is occasionally turned over for demonstration purposes, though no longer, alas, by steam.

HMS *Trincomalee*

££; Daily; Tel: 01429 223193;
Website: www.hms-trincomalee.co.uk

This venerable fighting ship has the honour of being the oldest British fighting ship still afloat. She was built in Bombay in 1817, as a frigate, a fifth rate ship of forty-six guns. She is very much in the wooden walls tradition, with three masts and the typical closed gallery at the stern. The latter consists of an area with rows of windows that look as if they've been borrowed from a country cottage. Later she was reduced to a sixth rater and served all over the world, from the Pacific to the Arctic Circle. In 1898 she was renamed *Foudroyant* and served as a training ship. Now fully restored under her original name, she is one of the finest examples of the ships of the Royal Navy when sail still commanded the seas.

Sail and steam jostle together in this picture by J.W. Carmichael of the opening of the new docks in Sunderland in June 1850.

SUNDERLAND
Museum and Winter Gardens

Free; Monday to Saturday, Sunday afternoons; Mowbray Gardens, Burdon Road; Tel: 0191 553 2323

This is a brand new complex, opened in 2001, set in the splendour of a restored Victorian park. The new buildings are uncompromisingly modern yet still have echoes of the nineteenth century. The glass rotunda, for example, is a close relation to the ornate hothouses of the nineteenth century. The new museum is an integral part of the scheme, and one gallery is called 'Launched on Wearside'. The slogan 'Sunderland-built ships sail every sea' may no longer be true, but this gallery gives an idea of what ship-building meant to the town at the beginning of the twentieth century, when it employed a work force of over 10,000. There are reconstructions of shipbuilding from the days when hulls were put together from riveted metal plates, as well as models and photographs of the ships themselves. The Art Gallery in the same building has some spectacular maritime paintings.

WHITBURN
Souter lighthouse

NT; £; April to November daily except Friday; Tel: 0191 529 3161

Enjoying a magnificent situation above the high limestone cliffs of Marsden Bay, the striking red and white lighthouse is of considerable historic interest. The year it was opened, 1871, was also the year that Frederick Holmes perfected his new generator to supply an alternating electric current. One machine was installed here but has now gone, though an example of the Holmes machine can be seen in the Science Museum, London. The engine room itself has changed little since Holmes' day and among the more modern machines is an impressive compressor to provide the blast for the foghorn. There are a number of artefacts in the museum, including a clockwork mechanism similar to the one that once turned the optic here. Altogether this is an excellent lighthouse to visit, and those unable to manage the stairs can still enjoy the view from the top on closed circuit TV.

SOUTH SHIELDS
Museum and Art Gallery

Free; Easter to September Monday to Saturday and Sunday afternoon, October to Easter Monday to Saturday; Ocean Road; Tel: 0191 456 8740

South Shields has a very special place in maritime history. Following the sinking of the *Adventurer* with all hands while in sight of land, a reward was offered for the design of a lifeboat that could cope with the roughest seas. The successful first design came from the South Shields parish clerk William Wouldhave. It was developed into a practical boat by Henry Greathead, and the whole story is told in the museum. A locally built lifeboat of 1833, the *Tyne*, a development of the Greathead design, is on display at an open-air site near the bus terminus in Ocean Road. There is also a memorial plaque to Wouldhave in the parish church.

WALLSEND

Segedunum

££; Daily; Buddle Street;
Tel: 0191 295 5757;
Website: www.hadrians-wall.org

A Roman fort might seem an odd place to go to look at the story of the maritime history of Tyneside, but if it does nothing else, it gives a notion of the importance of the area over a long period of time. The fort stands at the eastern end of Hadrian's Wall, has been fully excavated and a new museum created on the site. The museum also looks at more recent history. There is a whole section devoted to the coal industry, which for many centuries provided the main cargo for ships of the Tyne. And there is also a section on the shipbuilding industry, which concentrates on the famous company Swan Hunter, builders of the *Mauretania*. The company is still there, right next door, and a panorama tower above the museum provides a splendid view of Swan Hunter, Newcastle and the Tyne.

The experimental steam yacht *Turbinia* was built to try out Charles Parsons' new turbine engines. The vessel promptly broke all existing speed records and now has a place of honour in the new Discovery Museum.

Souter lighthouse goes to work in the early evening, and lights come on in the Keeper's Cottage.

NEWCASTLE UPON TYNE

After enjoying the bird's eye view from Segedunum, the other good way to get a feel for the history of Newcastle is to walk along the river bank, upstream from the new Millennium Bridge, the already famous 'blinking eye' footbridge that lifts to allow ships to pass. Two nineteenth-century solutions to the problem of passing ships are the High Level Bridge and the Swing Bridge. There are still reminders of the busy days of the port, in warehouses and granaries, and after passing under the procession of bridges packed close together you reach a number of interesting buildings, including the nineteenth-century fish market with its rather incongruous carved relief of Neptune watching herring gutters. Further on, across the water, are the pier-like coal staithes along which trucks would run to tip the coal into waiting colliers. At Elswick there are reminders of the great Armstrong Works, where warships were fitted out with their guns.

Discovery Museum

Free; Monday to Saturday, Sunday
afternoon; Blandford Square;
Tel: 0191 232 6789

This is a museum in the process of development, but already there are some real four-star attractions. Heading the list has to be the pioneering vessel in which Parsons first tried out the marine turbine, *Turbinia*. Sleek, purposeful, clearly built for speed, it is astonishing to think that this very modern-looking craft first took to the water in the 1890s. Just a few years later and the engines had been scaled up to power the mighty *Mauretania*. There is a huge, and hugely impressive, model of this ship that held the Blue Riband of the Atlantic for twenty-two years. There are other ship models in the collection, but one of the biggest models of them all, at around 20m long, shows the Tyne and all its shipyards as it was in 1928. At the time of writing, work is going ahead in preparing for the opening of the new Tyne Galleries.

TYNEMOUTH

Tynemouth Volunteer Life Brigade Watch House

Tuesday to Saturday, Sunday afternoon; Spanish Battery; Tel: 0191 257 2057

This is a watch house with a fascinating history. In 1864 a steamer foundered in the mouth of the Tyne and, watched by the people of the town, the ship broke up on the rocks, with the loss of twenty-seven lives. The mayor proposed setting up a volunteer force to help the coastguards. The idea was enthusiastically received and the watch house was built in 1866. The idea caught on and within half a century there were around 400 Volunteer Life Brigades spread around the coast, but this is where it all began. The building itself with its two turrets could almost be mistaken for a seaside hotel, and the volunteer members preserve it as a memorial to a great and useful institution. Inside is a rich array of material on all aspects of life-saving at sea.

WHITLEY BAY

St Mary's Lighthouse

£; Times vary with tides; April to October daily, November to March weekends; Tel: 0191 200 8650

The lighthouse on St Mary's Island is reached by causeway, which emerges from the waves at low water, hence opening times are entirely dependant on the tides. Built in 1898, the tower rises 37m above the sea, so visitors who want to enjoy the view have 137 steps to climb – or they can stay at the bottom and watch the TV relay. During construction, builders discovered the site had once been the burial ground for monks from Tynemouth Priory.

An artist's impression of Grace Darling and her father rowing out to the grounded paddle steamer *Forfarshire*, 7 September 1838.

BAMBURGH

RNLI Grace Darling Museum

Free; Easter to October Monday to Saturday, Sunday afternoon; 2 Radcliffe Road; Tel: 01668 214465

Grace Darling achieved fame when she went with her father, the keeper of the Longstone lighthouse, to rescue passengers and crew from the steamer *Forfarshire* in 1838. She was twenty-three years old, and willingly set out with her father in an open coble through immense sea whipped up by gale force winds, to the rocks where the survivors were huddled. They brought back four men and a woman, and two of the men returned with William Darling to continue the rescue. Within three years Grace herself had died of consumption, and she was always said to have been astonished by the public adulation. She was simply responding to an emergency, but as she wrote in her school copybook, now in the museum, 'Friends in adversity are not often found.'

See Also

BRIDLINGTON
Harbour Museum and Aquarium

£; Easter to September daily; Harbour Road;
Tel: 01262 670148

A modest museum, but one that provides an insight into the life of the harbour, as opposed to the popular seaside resort.

Beside the Seaside

£; Easter to October daily; Queen Street; Tel: 01262 608890

The other side of the picture: this is all about the resort. Not strictly maritime, perhaps, but immense fun. There are displays on local lifeboats and fishing cobles.

SALTBURN-BY-THE-SEA
Smugglers Heritage Centre

£; April to September; Tel: 01287 625252

Housed in old cottages overlooking the beach, the museum is not just about smuggling in general, but tells the story of one highly successful eighteenth-century gentleman, John Andrew, landlord of The Ship Inn.

A sniff of contraband tobacco, perhaps: an exhibit at the Smugglers Heritage Centre.

IRON SHIPS

One of the key elements in the Industrial Revolution that took place in Britain in the nineteenth century was the improvement in iron manufacture. It began when Abraham Darby discovered how to smelt iron ore using coke, and continued when Henry Cort invented a new method of producing wrought iron in large quantities. Among those who contributed to the new technology was the Shropshire iron master John Wilkinson, and in June 1787 he watched the launch of a new barge, built to his own design and appropriately called *The Trial*. Made out of iron, Wilkinson noted with delight that 'it had convinced the unbelievers, who were 999 in a thousand'. Contrary to what most people thought, iron could be made to float.

A number of small iron vessels were built over the following few years, but the next important event, the building of a sea-going iron ship, began in the unlikely setting of Tipton in the Black Country. In 1822 Charles Manby designed an iron paddle steamer, which he named after his father, the *Aaron Manby*. The vessel was built in sections and sent down to London, assembled and set off on her maiden voyage to France. The first iron steamship had taken to the seas.

It was a modest beginning but it soon led to greater things. Among the pioneers was a Scotsman, William Laird, who decided to create a shipyard that would concentrate entirely on iron steamships. He established his works beside the Mersey at Birkenhead, around which he built a new model town of wide streets, lit by gas, where the workers' houses were provided with such rare amenities as pumped water. The works prospered and eventually became one of the biggest shipbuilders in Britain, Cammell Laird. One of Laird's vessels, the *Rainbow*, steamed into Bristol in October 1838. It was here that Isambard Brunel was beginning work on his

A young rivet boy. He is pumping the bellows with his foot to heat the rivets, which he will then throw to a catcher to set in place for the riveter.

second steamship for the Atlantic crossing, the *City of New York*. The local press recorded that 'a large cargo of African oak timber has been purchased for this and further ships'. It was never to be used. Brunel was already interested in the use of iron for ships, and his associate Captain Christopher Claxton went on board the Laird ship for a number of voyages to assess her performance. He came back a convert, noting that the use of iron allowed more space for cargo and provided 'a more compact framework and greater strength, than wood can under any circumstances'. Plans for the wooden *City of New York* were abandoned and in its place the iron *Great Britain* was born.

In the wooden ship, strength was supplied by the framework of ribs and beams rising above the keel, all held together by planking. The iron ship was to be far larger than anything ever built before and a new system had to be introduced to ensure rigidity. The solution owed little to conventional shipbuilding ideas. Instead of the usual keel, there were ten girders running from bow to stern, covered by iron decking. Above this rose five transverse and two longitudinal bulkheads, creating a series of boxes. The structure had immense strength. The hull was formed out of iron plates, but here the new technology was somewhat inadequate, for the largest sheets that could be rolled at the time were no more than two metres long. So the hull of the ship was built up out of a huge number of overlapping plates riveted together. When Brunel replaced the paddle wheels of the original design with a screw propeller, he had created the forerunner of a generation of ocean liners. The return of this famous ship to her home port of Bristol and gradual restoration has been one of the great stories of maritime conservation.

The construction of an iron ship began, as with all ships, with the design. The plans were taken to the mould loft where they were eventually converted into wooden templates. The individual iron frame members were hammered into shape to fit the templates. Once the frame was complete, the iron plates for the hull and decks could be added. In general, plates were butted together and riveted to the frame. In the early days all riveting was done by hand. The rivets were heated in a portable stove by the rivet boy. The hot rivet was thrown to the holder-up, who caught it and held it in place with a heavy hammer. Two riveters, striking alternately, hammered over the end. The work had to be quick, completed before the rivet cooled. The sound of gangs of men hammering away inside a metal box was described by one shipyard worker as like walking into a wall of noise. Eventually, the pneumatic riveter took over, a machine which squeezed both ends of the rivet, and that in time gave way to welding, as steel took over from wrought iron.

The most extraordinary feature of the story of the iron ship is the speed of development. Just eighty-one years after work began on the little *Aaron Manby*, plans were laid for two mighty new ocean liners, one of which, the *Mauretania*, was to hold the Atlantic speed record for many years. Built at Swan Hunter on the Tyne, she was an immense vessel, capable of carrying 2335 passengers, with a crew of over 800. Everything was on a gargantuan scale, with three thicknesses of steel plates, hydraulically riveted with an astonishing 400 million mild steel rivets heated in a brand new oil furnace. The days of such great ships being built in Britain are now over, though Swan Hunter is still at work; ironically, the best view of the modern works is from the observation tower designed for viewing the adjoining Roman fort. As a footnote to this story, it is worth commenting that it was not just steamships that were constructed of iron and steel. An outstanding example is the *Glenlee*, built on the Clyde, now restored and back in Glasgow Harbour.

A painting by Fred Jay Girling showing work at Alexander Stephen's yard at Linthouse on the Clyde in the 1950s; the technology has scarcely changed since the 1930s.

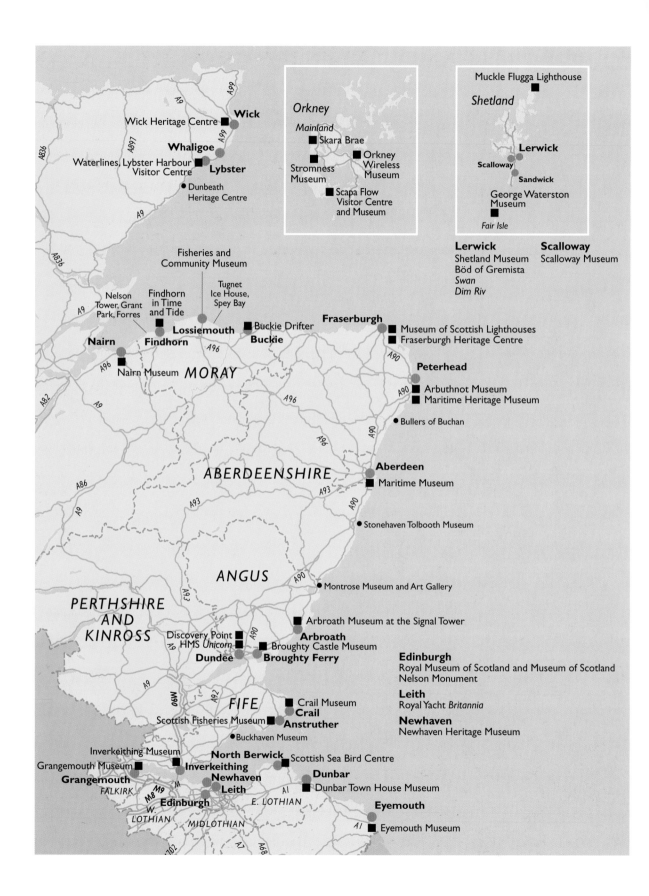

Wick Heritage Centre ■ **Wick**

Whaligoe

Waterlines, Lybster Harbour
Visitor Centre ■ **Lybster**

● Dunbeath
Heritage Centre

Orkney

Mainland
■ Skara Brae
■ Orkney
Stromness ■ Wireless
Museum Museum
■ Scapa Flow
Visitor Centre
and Museum

Muckle Flugga Lighthouse ■

Shetland

Lerwick
Scalloway ● ● **Sandwick**

George Waterston
Museum
■
Fair Isle

Lerwick   **Scalloway**
Shetland Museum   Scalloway Museum
Böd of Gremista
Swan
Dim Riv

Fisheries and
Community Museum

Tugnet
Ice House,
Spey Bay

Nelson   Findhorn
Tower, Grant in Time
Park, Forres and Tide   ■ Buckie Drifter   **Fraserburgh**

Lossiemouth   **Buckie**   ■ Museum of Scottish Lighthouses
Nairn   **Findhorn**   ■ Fraserburgh Heritage Centre

■ Nairn Museum   **MORAY**   **Peterhead**
                                          ■ Arbuthnot Museum
                                          ■ Maritime Heritage Museum

                              ● Bullers of Buchan

ABERDEENSHIRE   ● **Aberdeen**
                         ■ Maritime Museum

                   ● Stonehaven Tolbooth Museum

ANGUS   ● Montrose Museum and Art Gallery

**PERTHSHIRE
AND
KINROSS**   ■ Arbroath Museum at the Signal Tower

          Discovery Point ■   **Arbroath**
          HMS *Unicorn* ■ ● Broughty Castle Museum
          Dundee   **Broughty Ferry**

                                                        Edinburgh
                                                        Royal Museum of Scotland and Museum of Scotland
                                                        Nelson Monument

                                                        Leith
                                                        Royal Yacht *Britannia*

          FIFE   ● Crail Museum
                        Crail
          Scottish Fisheries Museum ■ **Anstruther**   **Newhaven**
                                                        Newhaven Heritage Museum
          ● Buckhaven Museum

Inverkeithing Museum   **North Berwick**
                       ● Scottish Sea Bird Centre
Grangemouth Museum ■ ● **Inverkeithing**
Grangemouth **Newhaven** **Dunbar**
FALKIRK   ● **Leith** ■ Dunbar Town House Museum
         Edinburgh   *E. LOTHIAN*   **Eyemouth**
*W.
LOTHIAN* *MIDLOTHIAN*   ■ Eyemouth Museum

EAST SCOTLAND, ORKNEY AND SHETLAND

Historically, fishing has been one of the most important activities along Scotland's east coast. The fishing communities were, and are, immensely varied. On the one hand, there are the tiniest harbours, some beautiful, neat and tidy, such as Crail, others luridly dramatic, like Whaligoe. Then there are the major ports, such as Arbroath, which for those who have tasted the local produce will forever be associated with the Arbroath smokie. This is not the whole story. There are also important harbours. Dundee had a brisk trade with the Baltic, and later became an important shipbuilding centre. Now the most famous ship ever built in the city has come home, Captain Scott's exploration ship *Discovery*. Aberdeen enjoyed a modest success as a trading port, but found new importance in the twentieth century, when the city became the capital of the North Sea oil industry. This is an area of contrasts, and the contrasts appear just as strongly in the ranks of preserved vessels, which range from sturdy, no-nonsense fishing boats to the Royal Yacht *Britannia*.

EYEMOUTH
Eyemouth Museum

£; April to September Monday to Saturday and Sunday afternoon, October closed Sundays; Auld Kirk, Manse Road; Tel: 01890 750768

This is an unusual, and moving, museum devoted to perpetuating the memory of what is known locally as Black Friday. On 14 October 1881 the fishing fleet set out from Eyemouth on a calm day, but the pressure was falling and a huge storm swept in suddenly and ferociously. A few vessels made it back to port but others were lost literally within sight of the harbour and the watching crowds. In all, 189 east coast fishermen were killed. The setting for this museum is, appropriately enough, a former church built in the classical style of 1812. Inside are exhibits telling the story of Eyemouth from the thirteenth century to the present day, but pride of place goes to an exquisite and imaginative tapestry made by the local people to commemorate the Great Disaster.

DUNBAR

The harbour is an area of considerable interest. The earliest part is a simple basin formed by one curved pier and a short straight pier. A wharf for coal imports was added in 1761 and then, in 1842, a new harbour was created, with little respect for Dunbar's history. In building Victoria Harbour much of the old castle was destroyed. Around this complex are a number of eighteenth- and nineteenth-century warehouses, some later converted into maltings. The latter supplied the old Bellhaven Brewery, still happily brewing in the 'new' brewery of 1814.

Dunbar Town House Museum

Free; April to October daily; High Street; Tel: 01368 863734

Housed in a handsome sixteenth-century house, the museum covers every aspect of local history.

NORTH BERWICK
Scottish Sea Bird Centre

££; Daily; Tel: 01620 890202; Website: www.seabird.org

The main attraction of the centre is the opportunity it provides for viewing the huge colonies of sea birds on the nearby islands. Images are sent by remote cameras, which provide a chance to see the lighthouses on Bass Rock and the Fidra Islands, too. There is also an opportunity to take a boat trip to Bass Rock and get a closer look at the lighthouse, though as the island is also home to an estimated 150,000 nesting birds, the conditions are a little unsavoury – not perhaps the place for sandals.

Part of the tapestry sewn by Eyemouth women to commemorate the centenary of the Great Fishing Disaster of 1881.

The building housing the Royal Museum of Scotland is arguably the finest exhibit of them all.

EDINBURGH

Royal Museum of Scotland and Museum of Scotland

Free; Daily; Tel: 0131 225 7534; Chambers Street; Website: www.nms.ac.uk

These two adjoining museums together aim to present the story of Scotland, with the Royal Museum having international as well as national exhibits. The older of the two buildings is worth a visit for itself alone, a glorious example of the Victorian use of iron and glass to create an immense light space for exhibitions – Edinburgh's very own Crystal Palace. Inside, in the technology section, is a wide range of exhibits dealing with maritime history and ship-building.

Nelson Monument

£; Monday to Saturday; Calton Hill; Tel: 0131 556 2716; Website: www.cac.org.uk

Designed like an overgrown telescope, this monument to Admiral Nelson also had a practical purpose. A time ball at the top drops at 1 p.m., which allowed ships in Leith docks to adjust their chronometers. Energetic visitors can climb to the top for a view of the city.

LEITH

Royal Yacht *Britannia*

£££; Daily; Ocean Drive; Tel: 0131 555 5566; Website: www.tryb.co.uk

The last in a long line of Royal Yachts which began when Charles II was presented with the *Mary* in 1660 – 'yacht' is indeed a Dutch word meaning 'hunt', suggesting the speed of the chase. George V had a *Britannia*, a sailing yacht he regularly raced. This is a very different vessel, a 5769-ton ship, which had a crew of 270 officers and men. In over forty years of service the ship carried the royal family on visits around the world, covering more than a million miles. Now decommissioned, she has been given a permanent berth at Leith, and visitors can get a chance to tour the whole ship, from the State Dining Room to the immaculate, highly polished engine room.

Leith itself is a very interesting place, which began as quays at the mouth of Water of Leith and was extended by dock development throughout the nineteenth century. Much of the old waterfront has been restored and old buildings given new uses.

When the Royal Yacht *Britannia* was retired from official duties, she was given a permanent berth at the Ocean Terminal, Leith.

The portrait of Admiral Samuel Greig painted in 1773 by Ivan Petrovitch Arunov hangs in Inverkeithing Museum.

NEWHAVEN
Newhaven Heritage Museum

Free; Daily; 24 Pier Place;
Tel: 0131 551 4165;
Website: www.cac.org.uk

The dockside museum is set in what was the old fishmarket, so not surprisingly many of the displays are concerned with the local fishing industry. Newhaven was also, for a time, a naval dockyard, and was the birthplace of one of the biggest warships of the age, the *Great Michael*, launched from here in 1511.

GRANGEMOUTH
Grangemouth Museum

Free; Monday to Saturday afternoons;
Victoria Library, Bo'ness Road;
Tel: 01324 504699

Grangemouth developed as the port at the eastern end of the Forth & Clyde Canal. Begun under an Act of 1768, most of the work was carried out under the direction of the great engineer John Smeaton. Shipbuilding facilities also developed at the end of the eighteenth century. It has one real claim to fame: it was here that the pio-

neering steamship *Charlotte Dundas* was built by William Symington and given a trial on the canal. This is one of the tales told in this museum, which deals with the story of the canal and the docks. The canal itself has recently been restored to navigation.

INVERKEITHING
Inverkeithing Museum

Free; Thursday to Sunday afternoons; The Friary, Queen Street; Tel: 01383 313838

Inverkeithing is an ancient royal burgh that received its charter in the twelfth century, and the museum is housed in part of the fourteenth-century friary – though it is a very heavily-restored building. The region still has considerable maritime interest, with the Rosyth naval base as a next door neighbour. The museum reopened after a major refurbishment in 2002, and now has an exhibition space that changes every year. One part, however, remains as a permanent fixture: the display on Admiral Samuel Greig, who founded the Russian navy for Catherine the Great.

CRAIL
Crail Museum

Free; June to September Monday to Saturday and Sunday afternoon;
62–64 Marketgate;
Tel: 01333 450869

This is a typical local history museum which, given its situation, includes sections on fishing and artefacts from wrecks. There is, however, one special area of interest, for Crail in World War II was home to the Fleet Air Arm station HMS *Jackdaw*.

The other major attraction is Crail itself and particularly its snug little harbour, begun back in the sixteenth century and completed in the nineteenth by Robert Stevenson & Son, the famous lighthouse builders.

A fisherman and his family depicted outside their cottage at the Newhaven Heritage Museum.

ANSTRUTHER
Scottish Fisheries Museum

££ (accompanied children free); Daily; Harbourhead; Tel: 01333 310628; Website: www.scottish-fisheries-museum.org

Here is a museum where everything comes together to make a most satisfying whole, a place where the buildings and exhibits blend together and contribute to the historical story. One reason why this is such an appropriate place for a national fisheries museum is that Anstruther itself has such a long history. The land on which the museum stands was given to the Cistercian Abbey of Balmerino in what was then the Kingdom of Fife in 1318. The abbey then granted local fishermen the right to build booths and dry their nets here, in exchange for a levy of 100 salt fish out of every barrel of herring. Part of a fifteenth-century chapel is still incorporated into the present buildings. The group that forms the museum also includes an eighteenth-century merchant's house, a nineteenth-century storehouse and cottages from the eighteenth and nineteenth century. Even before one goes inside, there is a sense of historical continuity.

Inside there are displays covering the whole story, from the days when local fishermen went out in open rowing boats, through the age of steam, to the modern world of the diesel-powered trawlers. There are displays on whaling and boat building and the human element is never forgotten. The story ends where it should end – at the fishmonger. The boat collection here is of national importance, most of

The fifie *Reaper* at the quayside, Anstruther. This hundred-year-old fishing boat is a survivor of what were once thousands of similar craft that pursued the herring.

them preserved under cover. One special area holds the *Research*, a Zulu drifter, a class of vessel which owes its curious name to the fact that the very first was built in 1879 at the time of the Zulu Wars.

One of the grandest of all the craft is the fifie *Reaper*. She, together with the smaller baldie *White Wing*, can be seen in the harbour, are regularly sailed and attend festivals all around the coast. Details are available from the museum. *Reaper* is a classic herring drifter built in 1901. She is 70ft long, 20ft beam with a towering 65ft main mast and an only slightly smaller mizzen. She is rigged with a dipping lugsail on the main and a standing lug on the mizzen. This is a vessel that can get to fishing grounds fast and make an equally speedy return with the catch. An innovation that came in late in the nineteenth century was the steam capstan that could be used to haul in the warp from which the drift nets were hung – seventy of them on *Reaper* with a total area of 40,000 square yards. Sailing on *Reaper* is made even more interesting than usual by the fact that this class of boat is decked but has only a very low rail, easy for fishing but alarming to the inexperienced sailor. This is a fine vessel, providing the finishing touch to an excellent museum.

DUNDEE

Discovery Point

£££; Daily; Tel: 01382 201245;
Website: www.rrsdiscovery.com

The star of the show is the restored Royal Research Ship *Discovery.* Here is an extraordinary mixture of the old and the new. She was one of the very last three-masted wooden ships to be built in Britain, but as the funnel clearly shows, she was also fitted with a steam engine. At the same time she was the very first ship to be built specifically for scientific research. The ship was commissioned by the British National Antarctic Expedition, who raised half the money, the government supplying the rest. Dundee was a natural place to come, for the Dundee Shipbuilders Company had a long experience of building whalers for use in the Polar seas. She was launched in 1901 and was soon off for the first Antarctic voyage, under the command of Captain Robert Falcon Scott. After that the ship had a distinctly varied career, doing everything from carrying arms to Russia in World War I to acting as a store ship for the Hudson Bay Company. In 1986 she came home to Dundee for a complete restoration to her original condition as she was in Scott's day.

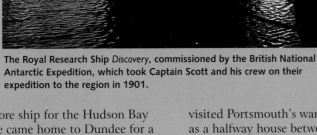

The Royal Research Ship *Discovery*, commissioned by the British National Antarctic Expedition, which took Captain Scott and his crew on their expedition to the region in 1901.

HMS *Unicorn*

££; April to October Wednesday to Monday, November to March Wednesday to Sunday; Victoria Dock;
Tel: 01382 200893; Website: www.frigateunicorn.org

Here is a real curiosity, one of the oldest British warships afloat – but one that was never completed. She was built at Chatham in 1824 as a frigate, but Britain was at peace and work stopped when the hull was completed. A roof was built over the deck for protection and the ship was eventually towed up to Dundee in 1873 by a paddle steamer for use as a drill ship. So one of the best preserved sailing warships in the world has never actually had sails at all, let alone been to war. But this is a most interesting vessel, one step away from the traditional wooden ship. The technology of the Industrial Revolution is just beginning to put in an appearance, with iron knees joining the hull to the beams and iron strapping on the hull itself for greater strength. The interior has been fitted out in the style of the period. Between decks the space is limited, and this visitor got a stiff neck from walking around bent over like Groucho Marx. The captain's cabin looks cosy, positively chintzy, but if *Unicorn* had ever gone to war, everything would have been cleared for action stations, with guns replacing comfortable chairs. Anyone who has already visited Portsmouth's warships will recognize this ship as a halfway house between *Victory* and *Warrior.*

Victoria Dock is also home to the North Carr Light vessel, built in Glasgow in 1933.

Few maritime museums can boast a more commanding home than this at Broughty Castle.

BROUGHTY FERRY

Broughty Castle Museum

Free; April to September Monday to Saturday and Sunday afternoon, October to March closed Monday;
Tel: 01382 436916;
Website: www.dundeecity.gov.uk

This is certainly a mightily impressive building and unmistakably Scottish. The original castle was built on its rocky promontory in 1496 to defend the entrance to the Tay. It was restored and added to in the nineteenth century but its defensive role has long since ended. Now it looks out over the houses built by wealthy Victorians, eager to get away from the industries of Dundee where their wealth was created. The Castle Museum tells, in its own words, the story of 'Life on sea and shore'. It has gone through a major refurbishment in 2002, but the maritime displays still concentrate on the themes of whaling and shipbuilding.

ARBROATH

Arbroath Museum at the Signal Tower

Free; All year Monday to Saturday, July and August plus Sunday afternoon;
Ladyloan; Tel: 01241 875598

The buildings are of considerable historic interest. Robert Stevenson completed work on the lighthouse on the infamous Bell Rock that threatened shipping approaching the mouth of the Tay in 1811. He then set about building the shore station for the keepers and their families, and it is this group of buildings overlooking the harbour that holds the museum. The story of the incredibly difficult task of building a lighthouse on the distant wave-swept rock is told in full, as is the story of the local fishing industry. The Arbroath Smokies get the attention they deserve as a famous local delicacy. There are also displays on Arbroath's textile and engineering history.

ABERDEEN

Maritime Museum

Free; Monday to Saturday and Sunday afternoon; Shiprow;
Tel: 01224 337700;
Website: www.aagm.co.uk

This is an imaginatively designed museum, incorporating the sixteenth-century Provost Ross's House, linked by a modern glazed structure to Trinity Church. Inside there is a mixture of displays. The collection of paintings, ship models and shipbuilders' drawings is outstanding. There are modern displays, including an immense 8.5m high model of an oil platform. One area of special local interest is Aberdeen Harbour, associated with two great engineers. Work began in the 1780s under John Smeaton and was extended in the 1810s by Thomas Telford, with more developments following in the latter half of the nineteenth century. It is interesting to come to the museum, look over the models and drawings and then go down to the harbour to see the real thing.

PETERHEAD

Arbuthnot Museum

Free, Monday, Tuesday, Thursday to Saturday and Wednesday morning;
St Peter Street;
Tel: 01771 477778;
Website: www.aberdeenshire.gov.uk/heritage

A long established museum, which has taken its themes from the voyages of local whalers into the Arctic. As well as the exhibits on the fishing industry, there is also an excellent collection of Inuit carvings and artefacts.

Maritime Heritage Museum

£; April to October Monday to Saturday and Sunday afternoons, phone for winter openings;
The Lido, South Road;
Tel: 01779 473000;
Website: www.aberdeenshire.gov.uk/heritage

This is a new museum in a new building on Shore Bay, which tells the story of local maritime history using the full range of modern interactive and audio-visual displays.

FRASERBURGH
Museum of Scottish Lighthouses

HS; ££; Monday to Saturday and Sunday afternoon; Kinnaird Head; Tel: 01346 511022; Website: www.lighthousemuseum.co.uk

There is a whole section of this museum devoted to the Stevenson family, and it is certainly an appropriate place to have one. Robert Stevenson built the first light, which he incorporated into the fabric of the sixteenth-century castle on Kinnaird Head. It was improved by his son Alan in 1851, who also worked on designing the cottages, and there was a final round of improvements by the third generation, David A. Stevenson. When it was decommissioned in 1991, this was the last Scottish lighthouse to still retain the mechanism that served it in the days when paraffin lamps provided the illumination. There are displays on other lighthouses and a tour to the top of the light.

Fraserburgh Heritage Centre

£; April to October Monday to Saturday and Sunday afternoon; Quarry Road; Tel: 01346 512888

A local history museum with a good deal of material on the fishing port.

BUCKIE
Buckie Drifter

£; Easter to October Monday to Saturday and Sunday afternoon; Freuchny Road; Tel: 01542 834646; Website: www.moray.org/area/bdrifter

This is a new museum designed to tell the story of the herring drifters that worked out of the local port. At the heart of the display is a recreation of a 1920s street scene, complete with a replica drifter. The theme is amplified by an exhibition of paintings by the marine artist Peter Anson, and an excellent selection of documentary films from the 1930s and 40s. There is also a display on lifeboats, and visitors can board an Orkney Class boat, *The Doctors*, that was brought here after ending its working life at Anstruther.

LOSSIEMOUTH
Fisheries and Community Museum

£; Easter to October Monday to Saturday; Pitgaveny Quay; Tel: 01343 813772

The title says almost everything one needs to know, except that there are also displays on the life of the town's most famous son, the first Labour prime minister, Ramsay MacDonald.

FINDHORN
Findhorn in Time and Tide

£; Wednesday to Monday afternoons Easter, June to August, weekend afternoons May, September; Northshore; Tel: 01309 690659

The main building is an ice house, built around 1810. Salmon exports to England were a vital part of the local economy. To preserve the fish for the journey they were parboiled and packed in ice. Ice was collected in winter and stored in well-insulated stone buildings, such as this at Findhorn. Two salmon fishers' huts are also preserved, one laid out as a bothy, the other having local history displays.

Scotland's oldest lighthouse stands at Kinnaird Head, begun by Robert Stevenson, founder of a dynasty of lighthouse engineers.

LIGHTHOUSES

The lighthouses of the ancient world, like the Roman pharos at Dover, were not built to warn of dangerous rocks and reefs, but as navigation lights to guide ships safely into harbour. The first lighthouses in the modern sense seem to have appeared in Britain in medieval times. These were simple towers, designed to take a fire at the top. One remarkable example can still be seen on St Catherine's Down on the Isle of Wight. Said to have been built by Walter de Godyton in 1323 as the Chantry Lighthouse, it is now known either as St Catherine's Oratory or, more popularly, the Pepperpot. What it actually looks like is a stone rocket: the tower has a pointed roof, and is supported by four fin-like buttresses.

The building of lighthouses was carried on in a somewhat random fashion for centuries, and the early structures, mostly of timber, have not survived. In England the system was formalized in 1514 with the formation of the Most Glorious and Undivided Trinity of St Clement in the Parish of Deptford Strood in the County of Kent, a cumbersome title that was soon reduced to the more manageable Trinity House. At first they did little more than allow individuals to build lighthouses, for which they were permitted to extract payment from shipowners. The results were not always satisfactory. Lighthouse design was slow to develop and there were many mistakes and tragedies before really effective solutions began to emerge. The history is best illustrated by the story of the famous Eddystone lighthouse.

One of the greatest hazards facing shipping approaching Plymouth is the Eddystone reef, 14 miles off

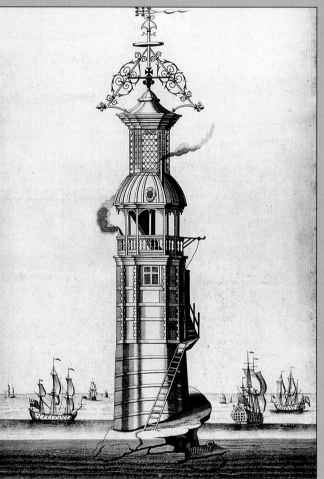

Probably the most bizarre lighthouse ever built, Henry Winstanley's original Eddystone lighthouse. It looks and proved fragile, lasting a mere five years.

shore. The rocks protrude no more than a metre above the waves at high tide, which makes them all but invisible until a ship is too close to take evasive action. Trinity House was approached in 1664, but declared that it was impossible to build an offshore light in such a hazardous position. It was only when a Plymouth man offered to build a light at his own expense that they finally gave permission in the 1690s. The work of building went to the splendidly eccentric Henry Winstanley, who had no qualifications whatsoever for the work, but who had a personal interest, as a ship that he owned had been wrecked on the reef. The light he constructed was extraordinary, more like a garden folly than a working beacon. It was built of iron, wood and brick, with balcony, cupola and a vast ornate wrought iron weathervane. It would, Winstanley declared, last for ever. It failed to survive a decade. The lantern was lit for the first time in 1698, and Winstanley set about adding yet more ornamentation. Then in 1703 a great storm swept it away and all the men in it, including Winstanley himself, were drowned. The next builder, John Rudyerd, began work on the successor, a simpler affair altogether, using a mixture of timber and stone. As a result of a fire in the lantern room, it too was destroyed, though not until it had done good service for nearly half a century. With the arrival of a third engineer, bringing fresh ideas, lighthouse construction entered a new age.

John Smeaton has been described as Britain's first great civil engineer. He was a man of prodigious talents, whose work ranged from a scientific investigation of windmill sails to canal construction. He realized that he needed to overcome the dangers from both gales and fire. His tower was designed on the basis of the shape of the resilient English oak tree, with a broad base, narrowing in a gentle curve. It also needed to have sufficient mass to withstand the waves. He built in stone. The lower courses consisted of solid discs of stone, each stone dovetailed to its neighbour and held by hydraulic mortar. The different courses were further held together by oak pegs set in drilled holes. On this solid foundation the hollow upper part of the tower was constructed, approached from the rock by a ladder. The lantern at the top contained the twenty-four candles, which were the only source of light. Completed in 1759, it stood for over 100 years, and in the end it was not the tower that failed. The sea ate away the rock beneath the lighthouse, and in 1882 it was finally replaced. The tower was brought back and re-erected on Plymouth Hoe as a memorial to a great lighthouse engineer.

This old postcard shows the new Eddystone lighthouse and the stump of Smeaton's, which has now been re-erected on Plymouth Hoe.

In Scotland the Northern Lighthouse Board was established in 1786, and almost from the start, right through into the mid-twentieth century, work was dominated by just one family: the Stevensons. To the general public, the best known member of the family was nothing at all to do with engineering – the author Robert Louis Stevenson – but to those who sailed in Scottish waters they were simply the Lighthouse Stevensons. Between them they designed and built ninety-seven lighthouses, including some in the most difficult situations imaginable. Robert Stevenson, the first of the dynasty, was responsible for the Bell Rock of 1811, built on even less promising ground than the Eddystone. His son Alan constructed the still more difficult Skerryvore, but it was Alan's brother David who was given the job of constructing what many thought was the impossible lighthouse. It was built on Muckle Flugga, a vast rock pinnacle set in the wild ocean between Shetland and the Arctic Circle.

Lighthouse construction was an arduous and dangerous occupation, and the tall towers are much admired. It is easy to forget that some of the greatest advances were not made in the construction of the towers themselves, but in the all-important lights at the top of them. In the early years the open fire was replaced by candles protected by glass. Robert Stevenson Senior was one of the pioneers in the introduction of oil lamps, their beams concentrated by the use of reflectors, and in 1806 he introduced a clockwork mechanism to turn the lantern, producing the characteristic flashing beam. It was an Englishman, Frederick Hale Holmes, who persuaded Trinity House to experiment with his electromagnetic generator to power electric lights. Full-scale trials were carried out at South Foreland in 1858, and the arc lamp proved a great success. The days of the oil lamp had come to an end.

Not all lights were housed in solid towers. As early as 1732 a lightship was permanently moored in the Nore, and by the end of the eighteenth century there were permanent lightships on the Goodwin Sands. Today the ships have been replaced by beacons and buoys and the lighthouses of Britain have been automated. But the lighthouses themselves survive, many of them open to the public, imposing memorials to the skill and daring of nineteenth-century engineers.

NAIRN

Nairn Museum

£; All year Monday to Saturday; Viewfield House, Viewfield Drive;
Tel: 01667 456791

The very grand Georgian house has actually been a museum since 1858, and one whole section has been set aside as 'Fishertown'. The name is self-explanatory, and there are models, photographs and a recreated cottage interior.

LYBSTER

Waterlines, Lybster Harbour Visitor Centre

£; May to September; Lybster Harbour;
Tel: 01593 721520

The centre tells the story of the harbour, originally built for fishing boats in 1849 and entirely rebuilt in 1882, with the Duke of Portland paying for all the work. It is an unusual complex with four basins and a small lighthouse at the entrance. There are also displays on wooden shipbuilding, and a CCTV system gives a close-up view of seabirds on the cliffs.

WHALIGOE

Free; Open Access

If ever one wanted a demonstration of just how important the herring fishing industry was by the late eighteenth century then this is the place to come. The tiny village stands high on the cliffs and the shoreline seems to offer few places where boats could land. This did not deter the locals. They built a tiny quay and joined it to the village by constructing over 300 steps that wind their way down the cliff face. For those who take the precipitous route today, it is worth thinking about what it must have been like not just to climb up the steps, but to do so carrying the day's catch.

WICK

Wick Heritage Centre

£; Monday to Saturday; 20 Bank Row;
Tel: 01955 605393

There is a great deal of heritage to deal with here, as the town's name suggests, being derived from the Norse word *vik* for a sheltered bay. Even now one can still see how the town has developed around the formal street grid of the medieval port. Like so many places on this coast, herring fishing was of huge importance and the museum buildings down by the harbour include a kippering shed. Among the conventional exhibits is a reconstructed nineteenth-century lighthouse.

See Also

Buckhaven Museum

Free; Monday afternoon and evening, Tuesday, morning and afternoon, Thursday, morning, afternoon and evening, Friday afternoon, Saturday morning; College Street;
Tel: 01592 412860

The museum probably deserves a prize for the most complicated set of opening times in the country! It is a local history museum with the emphasis on the fishing industry.

Montrose Museum and Art Gallery

Free; Monday to Saturday; Panmure Place;
Tel: 01674 673232;
Website: www.angus.gov.uk

A first-rate general museum of regional history, built in 1842 in an architectural style proclaiming it to be a 'temple of learning'. Displays include material on whaling.

Stonehaven Tolbooth Museum

Free; May to September Wednesday to Monday afternoons; The Harbour; Tel: 01771 622906

The sixteenth-century building was the district Tolbooth from 1600 to 1767. It now houses a local history museum.

Bullers of Buchan

Free; Open access; North of Cruden Bay: Map ref: 30/1038

A former fishing hamlet, where boats were kept in the now scarcely accessible natural bowl where the sea seethes, overlooked by almost sheer cliffs. The astonishing thing is that anyone ever thought this a safe haven.

Tugnet Ice House, Spey Bay

Free; May to September daily; Tel: 01309 673701

The ice house, dated 1630, consists of three vaulted bays covered with thatch, where ice was stored, having been collected in winter. The salmon were parboiled in a 1783 boiler and sent on their way packed in ice.

Nelson Tower, Grant Park, Forres

Free; May to September Tuesday to Sunday afternoon;
Tel: 01309 673701

Built on Cluny Hill to the east of the town, the monument was erected in 1806 by the Trafalgar Club to celebrate that victory. The climb to the top brings wide views over the Moray Firth.

Dunbeath Heritage Centre

£; Easter to September daily; Tel: 01593 731233

A local history museum housed in an old school, which covers a whole spectrum of subjects, including fishing. There is also a local heritage trail available from the museum.

The southern lighthouse on Fair Isle, just one of the many lights constructed throughout Scotland by the Stevenson family. It enjoys a spectacular wild and rugged location that is typical of much of the coastline of this beautiful island.

FAIR ISLE
George Waterston Museum

Free (by donation); May to September Monday, Friday afternoon and Wednesday morning; Tel: 01595 760244

Housed in the Auld Schule, or old school to those from southern Britain, this is the museum that covers all aspects of the history of this remote island sat halfway between Orkney and Shetland. Maritime history is mainly concerned with fishing and shipwrecks. The North and South Lighthouses at the ends of the island were the work of D. Alan Stevenson, and were completed in 1892.

ORKNEY

Stromness Museum, Mainland

£; April to September daily; 52 Alfred Street;
Tel: 01856 850025

Stromness itself is a wonderful place to explore, with its harbour and little cobbled alleyways leading down to private jetties often equipped with simple jib cranes. A variety of vessels call in and one might even be fortunate enough to see one of the few remaining Orkney yoles, a two-masted fishing boat used for long-line fishing offshore. I certainly cannot guarantee you will be as fortunate as I was on my first visit when two fully rigged ships called in and sailed, not motored, off the quay. The museum is one of those delightful places that seem to reflect the enthusiasm and magpie instincts of the true collector. In among fossils, butterflies and stuffed birds are ship models, sea chests and all kinds of memorabilia, even including drinking mugs with naval insignia from ships of the German fleet scuttled at Scapa Flow in 1918.

Orkney Wireless Museum, Kirkwall, Mainland

£; Easter to September Monday to Saturday and Sunday afternoon; Kiln Corner;
Tel: 01856 871400

This is another museum born out of one man's enthusiasm, the late Jim MacDonald, who set it up in 1983. The maritime connection comes with the wartime displays, showing the complex radio and telephone communication system that was set up for the protection of the Home Fleet at Scapa Flow. Original equipment has been installed, as well as charts of the defences. This is only a part of the story of this collection, which also contains a huge number of domestic sets.

Scapa Flow Visitor Centre and Museum, Lyness, Hoy

Free; All year Monday to Friday, May to October plus weekends; Tel: 01856 791300; Website: www.visitorkney.com

Scapa Flow is a site of major importance in twentieth-century naval history. It was the base for the British Home Fleet in both world wars and it was here that the German fleet was brought after the surrender of 1918. In 1939 a German U-boat penetrated the anchorage and sank HMS *Royal Oak*. In later years Scapa Flow became a tanker terminal for North Sea oil. The museum is based on the pumphouse used for refuelling the fleet, and the pumps themselves form the most spectacular exhibit.

Remains of some of the German

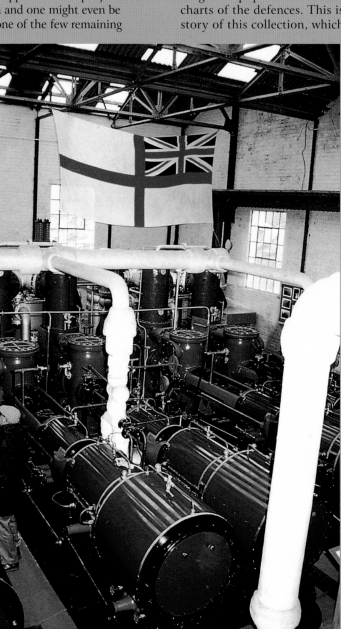
The pump room at Scapa Flow. The Worthington oil pumps were used to supply fuel to the British Home Fleet during World War I and II.

Fleet, poking their superstructure above water, can be seen from the Churchill Barriers, built to protect the anchorage and now used as a causeway linking Mainland to South Ronaldsay. A number of charter boats offer a chance to dive down to the wrecks. A list of authorized boats operated by the Orkney Dive Boat Operators Association can be obtained from the Orkney Tourist Office.

Right **Stromness is Orkney's main harbour, but each alleyway ends, it seems, in a slipway or jetty.**

SANDWICK, MAINLAND
Skara Brae

HS; ££; April to September daily, October to March Monday to Saturday and Sunday afternoon; Tel: 01856 841815; Map ref: 6/231188.

This is certainly the oldest surviving fishing village in Britain, for it was occupied some 4500 years ago by seven or eight families. The remains of fish and shellfish shows that they got much of their food from the sea, and there are stone tanks probably used for soaking limpets for bait. The stone houses, still with their original stone furniture, have survived, making this one of the most remarkable archaeological sites in the country (see p.29).

Below **The extraordinary neolithic village of Skara Brae. The stone houses come complete with stone furniture. Grouped round the central hearth are beds which would have been filled with fern or bracken, and a stone 'dresser' graces one wall.**

SHETLAND

LERWICK

Shetland Museum

Free; Monday to Saturday; Lower Hillhead;
Tel: 01595 695057;
Website: www.shetland-museum.org.uk

This is a general museum, covering over 5000 years of Shetland history. There is a large section devoted to Shetland and the sea, dealing with both the local fishing industry, whaling and the Merchant Navy. There is a good collection of model boats and the current enthusiasm for interactive displays here comes in a rather more practical way than usual: visitors get a chance to learn a few useful mariners' knots. Altogether it makes a very useful introduction to the rest of Lerwick, its historic buildings and its boats.

The harbour was built in the 1880s and the quayside buildings include an ice factory and houses with their own quays as at Stromness.

Böd of Gremista

Free; May to October Wednesday to Sunday;
Tel: 01595 694386;
Website: www.shetland-museum.org.uk

Dim Riv is a replica of a Viking longship, and visitors can enjoy a sail – without the rape and pillage.

The name alone tells you that this is a very Shetland place, and the official description reinforces the impression, inviting you to view the 'kishies' and learn about the 'haf'. The Böd itself is an eighteenth-century fishing booth, acting both as a home and a working store for fish drying and curing. It was also the birthplace of Arthur Anderson, who went on to become one of the founders of P & O, or as it was more grandly called in those days, the Peninsular and Oriental Steam Navigation Company. All these elements come together in this atmospheric museum, which tells the story of fishing from the earliest times and explores the work involved in salting and curing fish, as well as providing an insight into the development of P & O.

Swan, Lerwick

Prices vary; Tel: 01595 880667/697406;
Website: www.swantrust.org.uk

Swan is a fifie, similar to the one at Anstruther (p.112) built in Shetland in 1900, the biggest ever built here, 67ft overall and 20ft beam, with a steam capstan to help with working the nets. In her later working life she was smack rigged and an engine was added in 1935. Working life over, she was bought and restored by the Swan Trust and sails again much as she did in 1900. The only difference is that now she carries passengers in the converted hold,

The fifie *Swan* sailing past a colony of gannets on Noss cliffs. The typical lugsail rig of the fifie has been replaced by a smack rig, which requires fewer hands to manage.

not herring. There are short cruises around Shetland and further afield, and among the delights on offer are a malt whisky cruise and trips as far away as Norway. When not off on her travels, *Swan* can be seen in Lerwick harbour.

Dim Riv, Lerwick

££; June to August Mondays; Book at Tourist Information Centre; Tel: 01595 693097

The Norse tradition remains strong in Shetland, not surprisingly as the country was Norse until 1469 when Shetland joined Scotland as part of a royal wedding dowry. Each year in January a Viking longship is burned in the ceremony of Up Helly Aa. Fortunately one replica longship does not go to the flames, but has a permanent berth in Lerwick harbour. From here passengers can enjoy a trip round the harbour in the full-sized replica ship.

SCALLOWAY
Scalloway Museum

Free; May to September Monday to Saturday; Tel: 01595 880783/880666

Scalloway was once the capital of Shetland but in later years has been a prosperous fishing port. Fishing features in the museum, yet the unique story concerns 'The Shetland Bus'. In World War II there was a renewal of old contacts with Norway, and a small fleet of fishing boats ran a shuttle service taking refugees out and taking arms and freedom fighters in.

Muckle Flugga Lighthouse

£££; May to September Wednesday boat trip; Tel: 01950 422493

Boats leave from Mid Yell, Unst, Britain's most northerly island, and the lighthouse is even further north than that. In 1853 David Stevenson took on the seemingly impossible task of building the light on the rock that rises like a miniature mountain from the wild seas. The gales were so fierce that during construction the only way the workmen could get about on the worst days was on their hands and knees to avoid being blown away. But in 1857 the job was done. The boat trip gives visitors a chance to admire the lighthouse and wonder at the workers' stamina, as well as enjoy views of the wild life and the spectacular cliffs of Unst.

IRONCLADS

The story begins in 1824 when a French artillery officer, Henry-Joseph Paixhams, gave a demonstration of the destructive power of guns firing shells: one salvo blew an old 80-gun ship of the line out of the water. The search was on for a defence against the new weapons. In Britain, Lairds of Birkenhead proposed building iron battleships for the Admiralty, but their Lordships declined. So Lairds built two armoured paddle steamers for the East India Company and an iron frigate for Mexico. For once the Admiralty's conservatism was justified. Tests were carried out and the iron hull proved worse than useless: 'The number and destructive nature of the splinters produced by the breaking up of the shot would cause a few well directed shot to clear away whole guns' crews.' Meanwhile one of Lairds' iron steamers took part in an action in the first of the Opium Wars of 1839 with devastating results, but as the opposition consisted entirely of wooden Chinese sailing junks, it was not much of a contest. Floating gun batteries were used during the Crimean War, ponderous vessels of shallow draught, with wrought iron plates backed by timber. Though scarcely ships at all, they were perhaps the first true ironclads.

Real change began in 1859. Britain had just launched a new warship, HMS *Victoria*. With its wooden hull and rows of cannon poking out of gunports, there was nothing to distinguish it from the ships of Trafalgar apart from stubby funnels in among the masts and rigging. The captain could at least turn to steam power if he found himself becalmed. The same year a very different vessel was launched in France. Designed by Depuy de Lôme, the *Gloire* was a warship fitted with heavy armour plating outside a conventional wooden hull. It was, in effect, an old style frigate in a suit of armour, but it stirred the admiralty into action. A new design was prepared by Isaac Watts, Chief Constructor to the Navy, and John Scott Russell, one of the new generation of shipbuilders who had worked with Brunel on the *Great Eastern*. The heart of the vessel was the 'citadel', an armoured box, occupying the space between clipper bows and a rounded stern. The armour plating consisted of a sandwich. First came the thick iron hull, then a backing of teak and on the outside the second layer of iron. She can be described as the first true, modern warship and has now been fully restored. The vessel *Warrior* is described in more detail on p.50.

One of the most remarkable examples of restoration in modern times has seen Britain's first armour-clad warship *Warrior* transformed from a hulk to its current splendid condition. The same care that can be seen in the exterior has been extended to every detail below decks as well.

The next stage of development was a contest between engineers designing ever more powerful guns, while others tried to find a defence against them. John Brown, the Sheffield steel maker, had managed to get a sneak look at the *Gloire* and found the iron cladding was made up of thick plates, 1.5m long by 0.6m wide, shaped by hammering. Brown was sure he could do better by rolling the hot metal from the furnaces. He produced a giant slab, 9m by 1.2m and over half a metre thick, which could be reduced in thickness by further rolling. No one now doubted that a new generation of iron battleships was here to stay. A ship of the line, the *Colossus*, still in perfect condition and never having seen a battle, had been built in 1848 for £100,000, a shining example of the Navy's finest efforts. The best price the Admiralty could get when they tried to sell her little more than a decade later was just over £6,000. At the forefront of the improvement in armament was William Armstrong, owner of an engineering works on Tyneside. It was well known that guns could be fired more accurately using a rifled barrel, one with a spiral groove on the inside that imparted spin to the shell. The process of cutting grooves weakened cast iron, but Armstrong used wrought iron. Bars of hot iron were coiled into a spiral, then hammered together to make a tube. A number of tubes were welded together and an extra tube welded to the outside for strength. He tested his new eighteen-pounder against a conventional cast iron gun: his shells went twice as far and with greater accuracy. There was one other change that was to lead to the development of the warships of the twentieth century. Even *Warrior* was still basically a frigate, with guns lined up along the sides of the ship to fire broadsides. The trouble with such a system is that only half the ship's guns can be used at any one time. The answer was the rotating turret, first tried in America. There were experiments in Britain in the 1860s, which culminated in the appropriately named two-turret warship *Devastation*. By the early twentieth century a new class of warship was being developed – huge armour-plated battleships with immense guns mounted on turrets. The *Dreadnought* that provided the name for the new ships was built in 1906, with a main armament of ten 12-inch guns in five turrets. There were refinements and improvements, ships getting faster, guns more powerful, armament stronger. Yet it is still possible to walk on board the World War II cruiser HMS *Belfast* in London or the destroyer *Cavalier* at Chatham and see a continuous line of development that stretches all the way back to *Warrior*.

Rolling armour plating at Charles Cammell's Atlas steel works in Sheffield in 1861. By this date steel had replaced the heavy wrought iron sheets used on the first British armoured warship, *Warrior*.

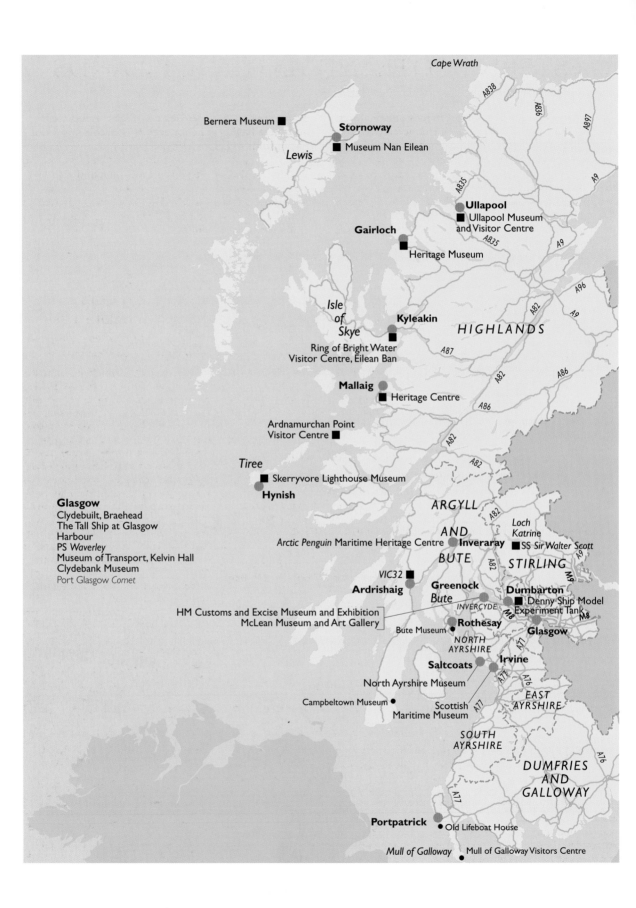

Cape Wrath

Bernera Museum ■

Stornoway
■ Museum Nan Eilean

Lewis

Ullapool
■ Ullapool Museum
and Visitor Centre

Gairloch
■
Heritage Museum

*Isle
of
Skye*

Kyleakin
■
Ring of Bright Water
Visitor Centre, Eilean Ban

HIGHLANDS

Mallaig
■ Heritage Centre

Ardnamurchan Point
Visitor Centre ■

Tiree
■ Skerryvore Lighthouse Museum
Hynish

Glasgow
Clydebuilt, Braehead
The Tall Ship at Glasgow
Harbour
PS *Waverley*
Museum of Transport, Kelvin Hall
Clydebank Museum
Port Glasgow *Comet*

*ARGYLL
AND
BUTE*

*Loch
Katrine*
■ SS *Sir Walter Scott*

Arctic Penguin Maritime Heritage Centre **Inveraray**

STIRLING

VIC32 ■
Ardrishaig

Greenock
Bute

Dumbarton
■ Denny Ship Model
Experiment Tank

HM Customs and Excise Museum and Exhibition
McLean Museum and Art Gallery

INVERCLYDE

Bute Museum ● **Rothesay**

Glasgow

*NORTH
AYRSHIRE*

Saltcoats
Irvine

North Ayrshire Museum

*EAST
AYRSHIRE*

Campbeltown Museum ●

Scottish
Maritime Museum

*SOUTH
AYRSHIRE*

*DUMFRIES
AND
GALLOWAY*

Portpatrick
● Old Lifeboat House

Mull of Galloway   Mull of Galloway Visitors Centre

WESTERN SCOTLAND AND THE ISLANDS

This is a region with two very different personalities. The northern part is Highland in character: even the islands are rugged and mountainous. Communities tend to be small and maritime activity has historically been concentrated on fishing. Further south, however, there is a dramatic change. The area around the Clyde developed heavy industries, with shipbuilding one of the most important of them all. Even now, when the industry has shrunk, there is still a working presence, despite the great days when the mighty liners were built here having gone for ever. It is in this area, too, where some of Britain's major maritime museums have found a home. Another long tradition survives in the region, that of the pleasure steamer, and visitors have a choice: doing as generations of Glaswegians have done by taking a trip doon th'water by paddle steamer or enjoying an equally enjoyable cruise to enjoy the peace of a loch.

CAPE WRATH

Free; Open access Ferry; Tel: 01971 511376; Minibus; Tel: 01971 511287/511343

It is something of an adventure getting to this, the north-west tip of Scotland. The very enthusiastic can walk there, though it is a long trek. A short cut can be taken by means of the passenger ferry across the Kyle of Durness, and in summer life becomes much easier with a minibus service. The effort is well worth while. The cliffs are spectacular, rising nearly 1000ft above the sea, and right at the end is the lighthouse, built in 1828 under the direction of Robert Stevenson.

ULLAPOOL
Ullapool Museum and Visitor Centre

££; November to February Thursday and Saturday, March to October Monday to Saturday; 7–8 West Argyle Street; Tel: 01854 612987

As part of a programme of regeneration of the Highland economy, the British Fisheries Societies established a number of new ports in the late eighteenth century. Ullapool was one of these and the engineer Thomas Telford also designed a church for the new communities, which now houses the museum. This is a general local history museum with a number of maritime exhibits. One of these is a model of the *Hector*, which in 1773 became the first ship to sail from Scotland with emigrants for Nova Scotia. It was this emigration that did much to spur the authorities into action to provide employment for the Highlanders.

LEWIS
Bernera Museum

£; May to September Tuesday to Saturday; Tel: 01851 612331

A local history museum, this covers a wide range of subjects, from archaeology, including the nearby Iron Age house, to historic photographs of island life. The fishing industry is included, with a special exhibition on lobster fishing.

Museum Nan Eilean, Stornoway

Free; April to October Monday to Saturday, October to March Tuesday to Friday and Saturday morning; Francis Street; Tel: 01851 703773; Website: www.cne-siar.gov.uk

This local history museum is housed in an old secondary school, the Nicolson Institute of 1898. It tells the story of 9000 years of life in the Western Isles, with areas devoted to fishing and the island ferries.

GAIRLOCH
Heritage Museum

£; April to September Monday to Saturday, October Monday to Friday mornings; Achtercairn; Tel: 01445 712287; Website: www.GairlochHeritageMuseum.org.uk

The museum, based on old farm buildings, covers a variety of subjects, and is particularly good on maritime interest. There are wooden boats, built and sailed locally, and the most imposing exhibit of all is a lighthouse lantern, containing one of the largest lenses ever made for a Scottish lighthouse.

KYLEAKIN, SKYE
Ring of Bright Water Visitor Centre, Eilean Ban

£££; Mondays; Tel: 01599 530040/ 530087; Website: www.eileanban.com

The island of Eilean Ban lies in the shadow of the new bridge linking Skye to the mainland, and one side effect of the bridge's construction was to make the lighthouse on the island redundant. The island itself is being developed as a nature reserve, and it has its own claim to fame. One of the lighthouse cottages was home to Gavin Maxwell, whose famous book about otters gives the visitor centre its name. It has been refurnished as it was in his day. The boat trips from Kyleakin give visitors 1½ hours to explore the island and its lighthouse.

Rainbow over the Kyle of Durness, the crossing to Cape Wrath.

Colourfully painted fishing boats in the harbour at Mallaig, still a very active port.

MALLAIG
Heritage Centre

£; July to September Monday to Saturday plus Sunday afternoon, April to June, October, winter Wednesday to Saturday afternoon; Station Road; Tel: 01687 462085; Website: www.mallaigheritage.org.uk

Mallaig was, and still is, one of the more important fishing ports on the west coast, nowadays specializing in shellfish. The maritime story is taken right back to the days of the Highland Galleys of medieval times. These were close relations to Viking long ships, with the same high-swept prow and a square sail on a single mast. At the opposite extreme are exhibits on the Highland steamers that plied between the mainland and the islands. There are also archive films.

ARDNAMURCHAN POINT
Ardnamurchan Point Visitor Centre

£; April to November daily; Kilchoan, Acharacle; Tel: 01972 510210; Website: www.ardnamurchan.u-net.com

This is just one of ten lighthouses designed and built by Alan Stevenson between 1844 and 1854, and the only one in the whole of Scotland to be built in the Egyptian style. Completed in 1849 and built of granite quarried on Mull, it rises over the rocky peninsula to a height of 36m. It is an entirely appropriate place to have a centre which tells the story of the Stevenson family and their dominant role in lighthouse building in Scotland. The 152 steps to the top provide magnificent views, and this is a good place to watch for dolphins and whales. Those with a taste for the wild scenery of the peninsula can prolong the experience by renting one of the keepers' cottages.

HYNISH, ISLE OF TIREE
Skerryvore Lighthouse Museum

Admission by donation; All year in daylight; Tel: 01865 311468

The museum is housed in the old signal tower for the distant lighthouse, 12 miles to the south on a rocky islet. When it was completed in 1842 it had taken seven years to build, during which time almost 60,000 tons of granite had been brought across to the tiny island to create the 137ft (42m) tower. The museum tells the story of this heroic task and itself stands by the harbour specially built for the work by the lighthouse engineer Alan Stevenson.

ARDRISHAIG
VIC32

Information on cruises from Highland Steamboat Holidays, The Change House, Crinan Ferry, Lochgilphead, PA31 8QH Tel: 01546 510232; Website: www.highlandsteamboat.com

VIC32 is a Clyde Puffer, one of a long line of sturdy coastal steamers that served the west coast of Scotland and the islands for about a century. Few ships have earned themselves more affection, largely thanks to the fictional Puffer *Vital Spark* of the Para Handy Tales by Neil Munro. This particular vessel was built as a Victualling Inshore Coaster (hence the name) in World War II, but is identical with the purely civilian craft. She is powered as she always has been by a compound steam engine and the boiler is still fed with coal. I have to confess a deep prejudice in favour of this little ship. I fell in love when I first saw her gently simmering by the quay at Tarbert and since then I have spent many weeks on board, doing my share of steering and having shovelled what feels like several tons of coal into the old vertical boiler – an interesting exercise in the confined engine room. Today she has been converted to take twelve passengers on week-long holidays – and those who

The foghorn at Ardnamurchan lighthouse.

The Clyde puffer *VIC32* on the Crinan Canal.

come along can do nothing at all and just watch the world go by or join in with any aspect of the work on board. When not out on the water, she is regularly berthed at Ardrishaig at the eastern end of the Crinan Canal.

INVERARY

Arctic Penguin Maritime Heritage Centre

££; All year daily; The Pier;
Tel: 01499 302213

The main exhibit is the museum itself, the *Arctic Penguin*, a former lightship built in 1911. The ship is historically interesting, being one of the last to be constructed with an iron hull before steel took over. Visitors can see the engine room, though these are not the original engines, the ship having been converted into a schooner between lightship duties and its present role. The captain's cabin has been restored and the main exhibition area is in the hold. Much of the display space is taken up with the infamous stories of the Highland Clearances and the conditions of the emigrants forced out of their homeland. A less grim picture is provided by archive film of Scottish shipping, largely on the Clyde.

LOCH KATRINE

SS *Sir Walter Scott*

££; Morning cruises daily except
Wednesday; afternoon cruises daily April
to October; Trossachs Pier, by Callander;
Tel: 01877 376316

It could be argued that this cannot strictly be called maritime, as Loch Katrine is landlocked, but anyone who cares for the glorious days of steam passenger ships will not want to miss this. The loch is a famous beauty spot, even if its main function is the mundane one of supplying Glasgow with water. The steamer was built in 1900 by the Denny yard in Dumbarton and was carried overland in sections to be assembled at the loch. For over a century she has delighted passengers by offering views of the 9-mile long loch which inspired Sir Walter Scott's poem 'Lady of the Lake', and has provided equal joy to all steam enthusiasts.

The former lightship *Arctic Penguin* built in 1911, now rerigged as a schooner.

The Denny Experiment Tank. Ship models are still tested here to see just how the real thing will perform out at sea.

DUMBARTON
Denny Ship Model Experiment Tank

£; All year Monday to Saturday; Castle Street; Tel: 01389 743093; Website: www.scottishmaritimemuseum.org

This is the world's first-ever commercial tank specially designed for testing the performance of ships' hulls and propellers. The idea is simple and logical: try out a new design on a model before spending a fortune building the real thing. There had been various attempts to work with model ships in the eighteenth century, but it was the engineer William Froude who first approached the problem scientifically and eventually constructed an experimental tank for the Admiralty. Wiliam Denny, a shipbuilder on the Clyde, at once saw the importance of Froude's work and began building a tank of his own in 1881. It is 100m long and 2.5m deep and continued in commercial use right up to 1984. Among the hulls tested out in the latter days was the P & O liner *Canberra*. All kinds of sea conditions can be created by the wave machine and the scale models are moved by an electric carriage. One of the most fascinating objects to be seen here is the machine used to translate the lines drawn on a plan by a designer to movements of a cutter, delicately slicing away at a block of wax. The result is an accurate three-dimensional model. The advantage of using wax is that adjustments can easily be made where needed. Although the tank is now run by the Scottish Maritime Museum, it is still in use for testing.

GREENOCK

HM Customs and Excise Museum and Exhibition

Free; Monday to Friday; Tel: 01475 726331

If you want to know just how important Greenock was as a port then here is the evidence. The Custom House was designed by William Burn in 1818 and was given the full classical treatment with two Doric porticoes. It is all very stylish, and inside displays tell the story of the two services in the area.

Ship models at Greenock: these are not models of existing ships, but were specially made to show owners how their new ships would look.

McLean Museum and Art Gallery

Free; Monday to Saturday; 15 Kelly Street; Tel: 01475 715624; Website: www.inverclyde.gov.uk/museum/index.htm

This is one of those delightful museums where everything seems to have been assembled for the love of the things themselves rather than to fit any predetermined pattern. Certainly there is plenty of material on local history, but why big game and Egyptology? It really doesn't matter why, it makes for most satisfactory browsing. There are, however, two areas that win it a place in this book. Shipbuilding is well represented, and there are a number of good models and some excellent paintings, many of which throw a clear light on the local scene of earlier years. There is also an area devoted to James Watt, the great pioneer steam engineer who was responsible for turning a simple pumping engine into a powerful driving force that would ultimately find its place in the world's ships.

PORTS AND HARBOURS

This is a story of slow evolution. In the earliest days of seafaring, vessels were simply run up on a beach or sought out a sheltered cove or estuary. Some of these natural havens were to develop into major ports. This was particularly true of the great ports on tidal rivers, such as London, Bristol, Newcastle, Liverpool and Glasgow. Vessels could make their way many miles inland until progress was stopped at a river crossing or until they reached shallow water. This was often a factor in the development of cities. The river Ouse could be reached from the Humber and followed inland to a marshy area crossed by a natural causeway. The Romans came here and built a fort, with wharves for seagoing ships. It was to become the City of York.

The next stage of development came when men began to add artificial barriers to provide extra protection from the sea. There are examples all round the coast, from tiny fishing harbours to substantial ports. Mousehole in Cornwall, for example, was noted as a fishing village in King John's reign. A stone quay was built in the 1390s and extended in the eighteenth century. A hundred years later the second pier was added. Even quite tiny harbours show a pattern of development spreading across the centuries. One of the most charming of all fishing ports can be found at Crail on the Fife coast. The small natural cove was first protected by a stone pier in the sixteenth century and the second pier added by the famous lighthouse builders Robert Stevenson & Son in the 1820s. The result is a snug little anchorage with only the narrowest of entrances.

Harbours were later improved by the construction of breakwaters, harbour walls and wharves, and the use of dredgers to improve access and prevent the build-up of silt. Up to this point, ships were still subject to the rise and fall of the tides, which limited the time available for loading and unloading. The answer was the enclosed dock where water levels could be kept constant. Liverpool is as good a place as any to see how the system began and later developed. The city grew from a little village on the edge of the Pool, a broad

The little fishing port at Crail in Fife represents harbour building at its simplest, just two stone jetties and a narrow entrance.

shallow creek. The shoreline was then much further back than it is today, its memory preserved in the name of Strand Street, which was then at the water's edge. Work on building an enclosed dock began in 1708. Instead of excavating dry land, the dock was created within the tidal area of the Pool. It was rectangular, enclosing roughly 1.5 hectares of water. The entrance was closed off by lock gates, beyond which was a small tidal basin, open to the river. A graving dock was also added that could be pumped out to allow for work on a ship's hull. These early developments were swallowed up in later improvements, for this was just the start of a long process of expansion in which more and more of the Mersey shoreline was enclosed to create docks. The best known of the older docks was authorized in 1841, the Albert Dock. This was an enclosed dock built to a similar pattern to that used in London for St Katharine's Dock, and indeed the dock engineer Jesse Hartley consulted Philip Hardwick who had designed the London warehouses. The dock was not approached directly from the river but from the Canning Half-Tide Basin. Five storey warehouses are carried over the quay on colonnades of cast iron columns. There is another, not so obvious use of iron. Anyone who gets a chance to climb up on the roof will find that it consists of undulating waves of wrought iron covered by galvanized iron plates riveted together. The dock was only a part of the new scheme, for Hartley was also commissioned to construct a river wall, with 'a parade for the recreation of the public'. He was always on the lookout for new ideas, and in 1847 he went to Newcastle to inspect the new hydraulic cranes invented by Sir William Armstrong. He was so impressed he at once ordered two hoists for Liverpool. By the end of the nineteenth century hydraulic power was in use throughout the dock area. The Albert Dock now provides a splendid setting for the Liverpool Maritime Museum. As trade increased and ships grew bigger, with sail gradually giving way to steam, more and more docks were added, until eventually they were to stretch for 7 miles along the bank of the Mersey. As

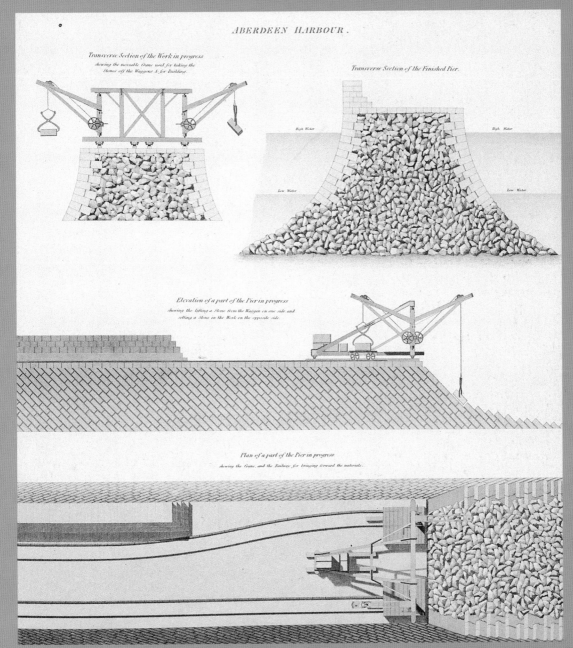

ABERDEEN HARBOUR.

Transverse Section of the Work in progress
shewing the moveable Crane used for taking the
Stones off the Waggons & for Building.

Transverse Section of the Finished Pier.

High Water

High Water

Low Water

Low Water

Elevation of a part of the Pier in progress
shewing the lifting a Stone from the Waggon on one side and
setting a Stone in the Work on the opposite side.

Plan of a part of the Pier in progress
shewing the Crane, and the Railway for bringing forward the materials.

Thomas Telford's own drawings of the construction of the pier and breakwater for Aberdeen harbour.

recently as the 1950s, passengers were still arriving at Liverpool to board liners for Atlantic crossings.

Ports also developed specialized equipment to deal with special needs. Goole, for example, was built at the junction of the Ouse and the Aire and Calder Navigation specifically for the use of coastal colliers that would be filled with coal from the South Yorkshire coalfields. In 1862 the engineer William Bartholomew introduced a new type of vessel onto the canal, known as a tom pudding. It is easy to see where the name came from, as they looked just like oversized pudding tins. They were designed to be towed by steam tugs in trains of up to fifteen vessels. At Goole the individual tom puddings were plucked out of the water by a hoist, carried aloft and upended over the hold of the waiting coaster. The trade has ended but the hoists survive. One of the great fascinations of Britain's ports and harbours lies in their immense variety, for no two are ever quite the same.

Glasgow

Scotland's foremost port and once one of the great shipbuilding centres of the world, Glasgow grew and developed alongside what was originally the shallow, shoal-filled River Clyde. It was only in the eighteenth century that the long process of developing the river really began. Work began under John Golborne in 1771 and was continued by Thomas Telford and later engineers, who between them transformed the wayward river into what was virtually a canal. The result was that vast ships such as *Aquitania* and *Queen Mary* could float where a century or so earlier it was possible to walk across the river at low tide. Much of the old prosperity can be seen in ornate buildings like the Clydeport offices in Robertston Street. Ships are still built on the Clyde, though the industry has shrunk, and today many of the old docks and yards lie derelict. Fortunately, enough remains to hint at what was once so grand such a short time ago.

Clydebuilt, Braehead

££; Daily; Tel: 0141 561 4242;
Website: www.scottishmaritimemuseum.org

On the bank of the Clyde, close to the King George V dock, the museum is modern and like most new museums makes maximum use of interactive displays and video presentations. The full range of local industries is covered, but much of the emphasis is on shipbuilding. Out on the water is the venerable coastal steamer *Kyles*, built by John Fullerton of Paisley as long ago as 1872, so that surprisingly she is actually older than the preserved sailing ship in the centre of Glasgow. Inside, visitors are invited to try their skills at anything from loading a cargo to steering a ship through shoals and sand banks to a safe harbour. Displays provide a chance to follow the processes of building a ship, from the first plans through to launch, and spectacular exhibits include a mighty triple expansion marine engine.

The Clyde Room at Glasgow's Museum of Transport has a wealth of magnificent ship models, covering the full range of vessels built on the river.

The last seagoing paddle steamer in the world, the *Waverley*, on one of her regular runs along the Scottish west coast, here seen approaching Largs.

The Tall Ship at Glasgow Harbour

££; March to November daily; Clyde Maritime Museum, 100 Stobcross Road; Tel: 0141 222 2513; Website: www.thetallship.com

The three-masted ship *Glenlee* was built at Port Glasgow in 1896, one of the last of the great sailing cargo ships that made round the world voyages, notably in the wool trade with Australia. The steamers were handicapped by the lack of coaling stations on long voyages. After four circumnavigations she found a new role as a training ship for the Spanish navy. She has now been restored to her original condition. There are also exhibitions on the Clyde and its shipping in the former hydraulic pumphouse on the dockside.

PS *Waverley*

Prices and times vary; Anderston Quay; Tel: 0141 221 8152; Booking hotline: 0845 130 4647 Website: www.waverleyexcursions.co.uk

Waverley is the last sea-going paddle steamer in the world, and there could scarcely be a grander ship to hold that proud title. She was built on the Clyde by A. and J. Inglis in 1947, the fourth to bear her name, *Waverley III* having been sunk in the Dunkirk evacuation of 1940. Like her predecessors, she was designed as a pleasure steamer, taking the citizens of Glasgow for excursions down the Clyde. She still does, and Glasgow remains the home port, but now she also embarks on an annual journey around the British coast, calling in at many different ports and offering a varied range of cruises. Some things, happily, have not changed. She is still powered by a quite magnificent triple expansion engine, and it is not tucked away out of sight below decks. At the beginning of the twentieth century the Caledonian Company decided that passengers would enjoy watching the engine at work, so they built an open engine room with walkways down the sides. It was a huge success, and other pleasure steamer companies followed the lead. Some passengers are so enthralled at watching the giant at work that they forget all about the scenery.

Museum of Transport, Kelvin Hall

Free; Daily; Bunhouse Road; Tel: 0141 287 2720

The museum covers a wide range of material, from horse-drawn carriages to railway locomotives, and does the job of displaying its wares with a minimum of fuss. When the exhibits are as interesting as these, they need no extra embellishments, though some are given a context with recreations of a street scene and an underground station. The maritime exhibits are concentrated in the Clyde Room, which is a feast of absolutely magnificent ship models.

Clydebank Museum

Free; Monday, Wednesday to Friday afternoons, all day Tuesday and Saturday; Town Hall, Dumbarton Road, Clydebank; Tel: 01389 738702

A community museum that includes displays on shipbuilding.

The former Brixham trawler *Provident* shows just why there has been such enthusiasm for saving this magnificent class of vessels.

THE FISHING FLEETS

Going to sea to catch fish is an activity that dates back far beyond the world of written records. In history, however, we do know that one fish dominated all others for British fishermen: the herring. Yarmouth, for example, was described as a major fishing port in the Domesday Book, and William I laid down an annual tribute of 60,000 herring to be paid by the town to the Abbey at St Edmund. It is no wonder that the Bishop of Norwich built a chapel in Yarmouth and appointed a minister specifically to pray for the success of the herring fleet. Fishing was so important that a special 'Statute of Herrings' was passed in 1357 to regulate the trade. At first, fishing vessels were all quite small, but by the seventeenth century the Dutch were fishing the North Sea in vessels called 'busses', with a crew of up to fifteen. Britain was slow to respond: as late as 1809 the government had to offer a bounty to anyone building a vessel of not less than 60 tons to fish off Britain's coast. The age of the large fishing vessel had finally arrived.

Originally, the herring fleets used baited lines, but in time these were almost entirely replaced by drifters. A vessel would sail out to the fishing grounds and then release a big net, suspended by a series of buoys, which spread out like an underwater curtain to capture the fish caught by their gills. The fishing boats themselves were kept in position by a small sail on the mizzen mast. Many of these vessels were luggers, in which the main mast and sail could be lowered and stowed out of the way during fishing. *Barnabas* of Falmouth is an excellent example of this type of fishing boat. A good place to see a varied collection of herring boats is the Scottish Fisheries Museum at Anstruther. These range from the tiny single-masted lugger, *Light*, which looks almost too delicate to go to sea and too small to hold much fish, to the more impressive two-masted fifie and zulu. The fifie has vertical stem- and stern-posts; the zulu has somewhat finer lines, with a steep rake to the stern. The latter owes its odd name to the fact that the first of its class, the *Nonsuch*, was built in 1879 at the time of the Zulu Wars. Herring drifters worked far out into the North Sea and needed to be sturdy vessels. Having sailed on a drifter built at St Ives in Cornwall in 1884, I was aware of how responsive the vessel was, and the crew were to have good reason to give thanks for her seaworthiness. She later went out to the Azores and on her return was caught in a severe gale and had no option but to run before the wind. One huge wave hit her and the very top of the tall main mast touched the water – but she came back upright, and if she had not, I would probably never have heard the tale.

Anstruther's fifie was built in 1901 and had one concession to the twentieth century: a steam capstan to help with handling the nets. It was inevitable that, in time, the steam engine would take over from sail. A particularly fine Yarmouth drifter has survived, the *Lydia Eva*, built in 1930 with a magnificent triple expansion engine. It is difficult now to imagine what the great herring ports were like in their heyday. The best year ever for the east coast herring fleets was 1913. The fleet followed the herring in their migration round the coast and 1006 vessels crammed into Yarmouth harbour, of which 246 were local. They landed 150,000 tons of herring and another 80,000 tons at nearby Lowestoft. Warning voices were raised but went unheeded. Fishing on such a scale was unsustainable and the unthinkable happened: catches dwindled as the great shoals disappeared for ever from British waters.

A new method of fishing was introduced to British waters some time in the eighteenth century: trawling. Instead of setting out a stationary net and waiting for the fish to swim into it, the nets are dragged along the seabed. There are a number of claims to the invention of this type of fishing, but as good as any is that of the Devon fishing port of Brixham. Certainly the Brixham trawler has become famous as epitomizing the best of the sailing trawlers. At first they were cutter-rigged, but later a ketch rig was used. These two-masted vessels carried an impressive spread of sail, gaff-rigged with topsails on both masts, with jibs flying from a big bowsprit. These were big vessels, broad in the beam and up to almost 80ft long but with fine lines and a deep keel for stability. They were fast boats and the sail pattern gave them great power, so that they were able to haul their trawls whatever the weather. The quality of these fine boats ensured their survival, often converted into yachts, quite capable of sailing to far-off seas. Happily, there are still examples of these splendid craft sailing out of their home port of Brixham.

So far, we have been looking at fleets fishing in local waters, but even in Tudor times British fishing boats were making far longer voyages. They were off searching for cod on the Grand Banks of Newfoundland or heading into the freezing waters of Iceland and Norway. Boats were away for weeks at a time and endured some of the most arduous conditions faced at sea. The fishing fleets developed all kinds of craft to suit different conditions, and a century ago fishing was a huge industry. It was estimated that Britain had 22,000 merchantmen but 30,000 fishing vessels. There were 100,000 men and boys crewing the boats and another 100,000 working on shore in various related trades. We shall never see such vast fleets again, partly because the modern trawlers and other craft can each catch and hold far more fish than their predecessors, but also, far more worryingly for the future, the fish stocks have fallen drastically. We are fortunate that so many vessels from the days of the fishing fleets have survived, for they are some of the finest old craft still to be seen under sail, and some of the most invigorating in which to put to sea.

A large fleet of Scottish fishing vessels, a mixture of fifies and zulus, putting to sea in search of the herring shoals.

The former engine shop from Alexander Stephen's yard has been rebuilt at the Scottish Maritime Museum, and is now home to some very impressive machinery.

SALTCOATS

North Ayrshire Museum

Free; Monday, Tuesday, Thursday to Saturday; Manse Street; Tel: 01294 464174

Saltcoats did once have a maritime museum down by the harbour, but a little too near, as it was flooded more than once. Now the collection has joined the other museum exhibits housed in a 1744 church. There are collections of ships' bells, models and paintings and a model of Ardrossan harbour. One of the most interesting sections deals with a lady who I, for one, had never heard of: Betsy Miller. She was the very first woman to be registered as a sea captain, right back in 1847.

IRVINE

Scottish Maritime Museum

£; Daily; Harbourside; Tel: 01294 278283; Website: www.scottishmaritimemuseum.org

This is a major museum currently in the process of redevelopment. The main museum building is the former Linthouse Engine Works. This was built in 1872 for the shipbuilder Alexander Stephen who had established a site on the former Linthouse country estate on the Clyde. It is itself a quite magnificent example of a Victorian iron frame industrial building. Before this building was acquired and re-erected on the present site, much of the museum collection was in storage. In a sense it still is, but it is now an 'open store' where visitors can wander around and see machines set up for display and others waiting, and all

kinds of things in view but not yet in order. It may not have the neat, logical order beloved of so many curators, but it does have a wonderful element of surprise. What will turn up next? But make no mistake, this is a major collection in spite of its present, rather random, appearance. No doubt, in the time between these words being written and the book being read, many changes will have been made.

There are other elements to the museum. A shipyard worker's tenement flat has been reconstructed, and there are three very different ships at the museum. *Spartan* is a Clyde Puffer, while *Carola* is an elegant steam yacht of 1898, and both are open to visitors. The third, the clipper *City of Adelaide*, is currently awaiting restoration but it is hoped will one day be back to her original condition.

See Also
Campbeltown Museum

Free; Tuesday to Saturday; Hall Street; Tel: 01586 552366;
Website: www.abc-museums.demon.co.uk

The museum building of 1898 is by one of Scotland's leading architects, J.J. Burnet, and features a carved relief of fishermen on the façade. Although much of the emphasis is on the natural history of the region, there are a number of maritime displays.

Bute Museum, Rothesay, Isle of Bute

£; April to September Monday to Saturday and Sunday afternoon, October to March Tuesday to Saturday afternoon; Stuart Street; Tel: 01700 505067

The full title is the Buteshire Natural History Museum, which indicates where the main emphasis lies. Nevertheless, the island has for many years been a popular holiday area, in the past served by fleets of Clyde steamers. The museum has an impressive collection of eighty-eight models of these elegant craft, plus other ship models.

Another splendid example of the work of the Stevenson family, this is Robert Stevenson's lighthouse at the tip of the Mull of Galloway.

Port Glasgow

A replica of Henry Bell's pioneering 1812 paddle steamer *Comet* can be seen in the town centre.

Old Lifeboat House, Portpatrick

June to September daily, April to May and October weekends; Tel: 01776 810855

There are displays of various classes of lifeboat. Portpatrick itself has a modest harbour now, but was once the main embarkation point for ferries to Ireland before the terminus moved to Stranraer.

Mull of Galloway Visitors Centre

Free; April to October daily; Tel: 01776 830682; Website: www.mull-of-galloway.co.uk

The imposing lighthouse stands at the southernmost tip of the peninsula, rising above cliffs that are home to a large and noisy population of seabirds. The centre occupies the barracks erected for the men who built the light under the direction of Robert Stevenson in the early nineteenth century.

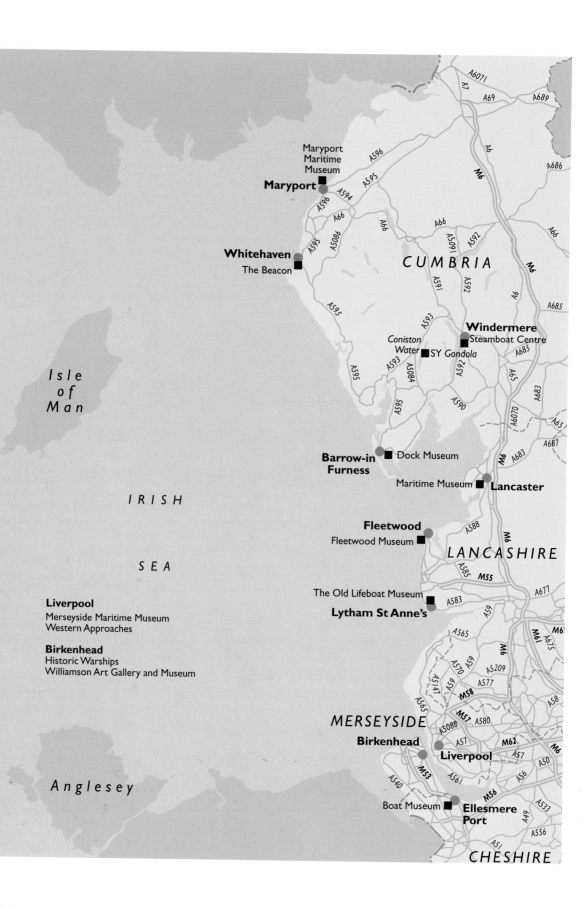

A6071
A7
A69
A689

A596

Maryport
Maritime
Museum
Maryport
A596
A595
A594
A596
A66
A66
A6
A686

CUMBRIA

A66
A66

Whitehaven
The Beacon
A595
A5086
A66
A5091
A592
A66

A595
A591
A593
A592
A6
A685

Windermere
Steamboat Centre
A685

Coniston
Water
SY Gondola
A593
A5084
A592
A65
A683

A595
A590
A6070
A65
A687

Barrow-in
Furness
Dock Museum
M6
A683

Maritime Museum
Lancaster

IRISH

Fleetwood
Fleetwood Museum
A588
M6

SEA

LANCASHIRE

A585
M55
A677

The Old Lifeboat Museum
Lytham St Anne's
A583
A59

Isle
of
Man

A565
M65
M61
A675

A565
A570
A59
A5209
A577
A58

A5141
A59

M58

Liverpool
Merseyside Maritime Museum
Western Approaches

Birkenhead
Historic Warships
Williamson Art Gallery and Museum

MERSEYSIDE
A5088
M57
A580

Birkenhead
A57
M62
M6

Liverpool
A57
A50

M53
A561
A56

Anglesey

A540
Boat Museum
Ellesmere
Port
M56
A49
A533

A51
A556

CHESHIRE

NORTH WEST ENGLAND

The journey round the coast has arrived at one of the most important industrial areas of Britain. An immense trade developed in both raw materials and finished products, passing through the major ports. Liverpool, in particular, became the main port for trade with America, feeding the insatiable demand for cotton from the Lancashire mills and exporting yarn and cloth. There were other, less savoury, trades, and local museums have not shied away from depicting the horrors of the slave ships. Shipbuilding has also been an important part of the history of both Cumbria and Lancashire, extending from the days of wooden ships to the age of the giant liners. The area is not all heavy industry. Relief from the harshness of the working world was available either in the bright and cheerful seaside resorts, such as Blackpool and Morecambe, or among the more peaceful mountains of the Lake District. The lakes themselves have been home to many craft, and there are still survivors from the golden age of steam.

MARYPORT

Maryport Maritime Museum

Free; Monday to Saturday and Sunday afternoon; 1 Senhouse Street;
Tel: 01900 813738;
Website: www.allerdale.gov.uk

This is instantly recognizable as a local museum, with almost everything in it coming from the personal collection of its founder, Miss Annie Robinson. It is housed in what was the Queens Head Public House. There are exhibits relating to two very different local men. Fletcher Christian owes his fame to his role as the leader of the *Bounty* mutineers, which does not seem to have been held against him in Maryport, as the citizens named Christian Street in his honour. The other is Thomas Ismay, the great shipping magnate, who is unfortunately best known as the owner of the *Titanic*. The port itself was developed by Humphrey Senhouse in the eighteenth century and named after his wife.

WHITEHAVEN

The Beacon

££; Tuesday to Monday; West Strand;
Tel: 01946 592302;
Website: www.copelandbc.gov.uk

The Beacon is a new museum standing right on the harbourside, and a very interesting harbour it is. You can almost read the story of the town in its stones. The oldest quay was built in the seventeenth century, and more and more were added over the next 200 years to create a complex of docks and harbours. The museum itself has a suitably nautical appearance, much like a small lighthouse. Inside, the story of the development of the harbour is told, and there are memories of the days when Whitehaven sat at one corner of a triangular trade route. Goods were sent out from here, sold in Africa to purchase slaves, which were then sold on to the American plantations and the profits either used to buy more goods or simply brought home. One interesting feature is the Weather Gallery run in conjunction with the Met Office, where visitors can join in tracking weather systems by satellite.

A tall ship calling in on a visit to Whitehaven is moored close to the new purpose-built museum known simply as The Beacon.

CONISTON
SY *Gondola*

NT; ££; 45-minute round trip from Coniston; Tel: 015394 41288

Once again, as at Loch Katrine, we have ventured inland, and once again without apology. *Gondola* is the epitome of Victorian opulence, a pleasure steamer that first puffed its way around the lake in 1860. She was built for the Furness Railway Company, whose line was built to serve local mines and quarries, but soon found a lucrative trade carrying tourists round the lake. Everything about her is designed to attract the eye, from the gilded serpent rearing up above the prow to the lushly upholstered saloon. She kept working right up to 1936 when her life was prolonged as a houseboat. She then fell into a state of dereliction until rescued by the National Trust. Now fully restored and back in steam, she sails the lake again.

The gilded opulence of the pleasure steamer *Gondola* takes passengers for trips on Lake Coniston, as she first did in 1860.

WINDERMERE
Steamboat Centre

*££; March to November daily; Rayrigg Road; Tel: 015394 45565;
Website: www.steamboat.co.uk*

No one needs an excuse to visit this collection of supremely elegant steam launches from the Victorian and Edwardian era. The museum offers an opportunity to see the craft at close quarters, and there are also regular trips out on the Lake, where the wonders of the Windermere steam kettle are revealed – enough to say it makes the fastest cup of tea ever. But there is a good deal more to this museum than just nostalgia. *Dolly,* built *c.*1850, for example, is the oldest surviving working steamboat in the world and also one of the first to use what was then a very novel device, the screw propeller. By Windermere standards she is a rather plain lady, unlike *Branksome* of 1896, built for luxury with the finest woods, teak and walnut, and embossed leather upholstery. We have also moved up the technological ladder. Where little *Dolly* has a simple, single-cylinder engine and a speed of around 5mph, *Branksome* boasts a compound engine and can hustle along at an impressive 14mph.

Swallow, a classic Windermere steamboat of 1911, all glowing teak and brass.

Note, by the way, that these domestic boats ignore the nautical 'knots' and stick to a landsman's miles per hour. One of the best known boats in the collection is the *Esperance* of 1869, known to generations of children as Captain Flint's houseboat in Arthur Ransome's *Swallows and Amazons.*

BARROW-IN-FURNESS
Dock Museum

Free; April to October Tuesday to Sunday, November to March Wednesday to Sunday; North Road;
Tel: 01229 894444; Website: www.dockmuseum.org.uk

This is an interesting project in that the museum itself is uncompromisingly modern but has been built over a Victorian dock. It covers a wide range of topics relating to the area, but the main focus here is on the shipbuilding exhibits. In practice, this means Vickers, who are particularly associated with submarines, having been built here since 1886. This is an odd story, as the Admiralty tended to regard submarines as rather sneaky, so the first orders came from abroad and were exported as 'merchant vessels' to get past military restrictions. The Vickers story is told in full and includes the magnificent photographic archive.

A schooner provides an old world foil to the very modern building of the new museum.

The small boat *Hannah* takes centre stage, but has a very impressive and appropriate setting in one of the old quayside warehouses.

LANCASTER
Maritime Museum

£; Easter to October daily, November to Easter afternoons; St George's Quay; Tel: 01524 64637

The museum has a splendid situation on St George's Quay beside the River Lune. The scene typifies an eighteenth-century port, where vessels still rise and fall with the tide. Rows of old warehouses stand with their gable ends facing the water, displaying a regular pattern of loading bays and hoists. One of the more lucrative trades was the import of hardwood from America to feed Robert Gillow's furniture business. It was so prosperous that Robert's son Richard Gillow was able to pay for the handsome Custom House of 1764, built like a small Palladian villa. This houses the main museum collection, which contains displays on the history of the port and the local fishing industry. An adjoining warehouse looks at Morecambe Bay and the Lancaster Canal. While visiting Lancaster it is worth taking a short walk to see John Rennie's elegant canal aqueduct over the Lune.

FLEETWOOD
Fleetwood Museum

£; Easter to November Monday to Saturday and Sunday afternoon; Queen's Terrace; Tel: 01253 876621; Website: www.nettingthebay.org.uk

As at Lancaster, this is a museum housed in a former Custom House, built in 1838 and although somewhat plainer than Lancaster, it has the distinction of having been designed by Decimus Burton. One area of interest deals with inshore fishing, and especially Morecambe Bay, famous for its shallow waters and the cockles, mussels and shrimps that have been harvested there for centuries – not to mention the end product, the famous potted shrimps. The Bay is immense, yet at low water it can be crossed on foot – an exercise only to be attempted with competent guides. The coastal and deep-sea fishing galleries offer more familiar sights. The prize exhibit is the last surviving north-west fishing smack *Harriet*, over a century old and currently being restored.

Coasters, barges and narrow boats intermingle in the basin at the Boat Museum at Ellesmere Port.

LYTHAM ST ANNE'S
The Old Lifeboat Museum

Free; End May to end September Tuesday, Thursday, Saturday and Sunday afternoons, plus July and August Wednesday; East Beach; Tel: 01253 725610

The museum is easy to find, for it stands right next to the windmill on Lytham Green. The lifeboat museum has a familiar story to tell of the development of the local service, but one with a peculiarly melancholy tinge. In December 1866 lifeboats from Southport, Lytham and St Anne's set out to rescue the crew of the barque *Mexico*. All of the crew was saved, but in the rescue twenty-seven lifeboatmen lost their lives, the greatest disaster in the long history of the service.

ELLESMERE PORT
Boat Museum

£££; Summer all day, winter closed Thursday and Friday; South Pier Road; Tel: 0151 355 5017; Website: www.boatmuseum.org.co.uk

This is a museum primarily concerned with canals and inland waterways, being based on the old warehouse complex created by Thomas Telford at the junction

An interesting pair of neighbours, the lifeboat museum and windmill at Lytham St Anne's.

of the Ellesmere Canal and the Mersey. It does this job excellently, and includes boat trips round the dock complex as part of the attractions. At the end of the nineteenth century, however, Ellesmere Port enjoyed a new importance with the arrival of the Manchester Ship Canal. This is reflected in the museum, which includes a number of bigger vessels in the collection, notably the 1902 Clyde Puffer *Basuto* and two tugs.

THE STEAMER

In the eighteenth century Britain led the way in the development of steam engines, but the idea of using such devices on the water was first tried across the Channel in France. The obvious starting point was the paddle wheel, which had been used for centuries: there is a fourth-century manuscript describing a Roman warship, with three paddle wheels, each driven by a pair of oxen. There were to be numerous attempts to devise practical paddle ships, powered by everything from men to horses, but all failed for lack of sustainable power. In 1775 J.C. Périer installed a small steam engine in a boat on the Seine – too small as it turned out. Three years later the splendidly named Marquis Claude de Jouffroy d'Abbans designed the world's first successful paddle steamer, the 182-ton *Pyroscaphe*, which had a successful trial on the Saône. There now followed a period of experimentation in a number of countries, especially in America and Britain.

Patrick Miller was the British pioneer. He began by experimenting with various designs of paddle and hull, using men to turn a capstan. The only result of that was an exhausted crew, so he turned to steam. The engine was built by William Symington in 1788 and the trials took place on a tiny loch at Dalswinton in Scotland. Robert Burns was on board, but although moved by steam, he was not moved to verse. Symington was then commissioned to make an engine for a steam tug that would work on the Forth and Clyde Canal. Although successful, the authorities were afraid that the wash would damage the bank, and the vessel, the *Charlotte Dundas*, was withdrawn from service. The trials were, however, seen by the American Robert Fulton, who in 1807 introduced the first regular paddle steamer service, between New York and Albany. Britain's first commercial steamer, *Comet*, was ordered in 1812 by Henry Bell for service on the Clyde. At her trials in August 1812 she steamed from Greenock to Glasgow, a distance of 20 miles in three-and-a-half hours. A replica of the craft can be seen at Port Glasgow, and the engine itself is preserved at the Science Museum in London. It

The steam pressure gauges on the compound engine of the Clyde Puffer *VIC32*. They show pressure in the two cylinders and vacuum pressure in the condenser.

is a small engine, with a 12.5-inch diameter vertical cylinder, worked at low pressure. Unusually, the paddle wheels are inside the hull.

Bell began a tradition that continues to this day of paddle steamers running excursions on the Clyde. The heyday of the Clyde steamers came at the end of the nineteenth century, when there was a large fleet, offering such grand entertainment as the 'Berliner Philarmonisches Blas-Orchester' on the *Duchess of York* – though passengers on other vessels might get no more than a penny whistle and a cracked violin. The traditions of the Clyde steamer are continued by *Waverley*. The great barrier to development of paddle steamers for long voyages was the need to carry enough coal for the boilers. Scientists of the day had 'proved' that there was no point in making bigger ships, because all the extra space would have to be filled with fuel to provide more power to move the larger ship. It was Brunel who pointed out the fallacy in the argument. Water resistance relates to the area of the hull, not its volume: if you take a box with, say, one-metre sides, then double the length of each size, you get four times the surface area but eight times the volume. So in 1836 he set out to build the *Great Western*, specifically designed for the Atlantic route between Britain and New York. She was beaten on the crossing by the tiny *Sirius*, which had started earlier, but the big ship made the faster crossing, and where *Sirius* ended the voyage with bunkers empty, Brunel's ship still had 200 tons of coal to spare. The case for the trans-Atlantic steamship had been made. Brunel was to continue to advance design when he replaced the paddle wheels with the screw propeller in the *Great Britain*.

Visiting the *Great Britain* in Bristol today, one is inevitably struck by the immense size of the engine. It needed to be big, for it worked at the very low pressure of little more than 5 p.s.i. (pounds per square inch) and this was almost forty years after Richard Trevithick had demonstrated the advantage of high-pressure steam at up to 50 p.s.i. The engine had four 88-inch diameter cylinders, set in a triangle, turning an 18ft diameter drum. Chains wrapped round the drum turned a smaller wheel on the propeller shaft. It was, it has to be said, a cumbersome arrangement. Producing steam had its own problems, as the boilers had to be fed with seawater and during the voyage salt deposits must have reduced efficiency. Improvements in engine design followed throughout the nineteenth century. Steam pressure became ever higher and economies were made by compounding. The simplest compound was the double. Steam passed from the high-pressure to the low-pressure cylinder before being exhausted. A further refinement was to lead the exhaust steam into a condenser, providing a source of fresh water for the boiler. Just such an arrangement can be seen in the Clyde Puffer *VIC32*. The ultimate development was the triple expansion engine. One can see a whole range of these engines on a small scale at

the Windermere Steamboat Museum. The tiny *Dolly*, built around 1850, has a simple, single-cylinder engine, while the supremely elegant *Swallow* of 1911 has a triple expansion engine, giving the launch a speed of 12 knots.

The final stage of steam development began when Sir Charles Parsons built the experimental *Turbinia* in the 1890s. What a change there had been since the early days of the paddle steamer. Now the boiler was delivering steam at a pressure of 210 p.s.i., which instead of driving pistons going up and down in cylinders, drove the rotor blades of the turbine engine. At the Spithead review of 1897 *Turbinia* made a grand entrance racing across the anchored fleet at the previously undreamed of speed of 34 knots. Seeing her today at her permanent home in Newcastle's Discovery Museum, this is still an amazingly impressive vessel which announces in every line that a new age of power and speed had arrived.

The paddles of *Kingswear Castle* churn the waters while passengers relax on deck enjoying the Medway scenery. She is a traditional, coal-fired steamer.

LIVERPOOL AND BIRKENHEAD

LIVERPOOL

Merseyside Maritime Museum

Free; Daily; Albert Dock; Tel: 0151 478 4499;
Website: www.nmgm.org.uk/maritime

This is a great museum in a spectacular setting. The riverfront positively shouts the message of prosperity through the pomp of its commercial architecture, elaborately decorated with pillars, domes and spires. Grandest of them all are the Liver building and its near neighbour built for Cunard. Beside these the Albert Dock seems restrained, but is none the less majestic, and it provides a most appropriate home for the maritime museum. There is a huge amount to see even without setting foot inside the building, with preserved craft out in the adjoining Canning Dock, notably the three-masted schooner *De Wadden*, the very last sailing-ship to trade regularly on the Mersey, and the former Liverpool pilot boat *Edmund Gardner*. They have been joined by other former working boats to create a truly lively dockland scene. It seems incredible now, but not so very long ago there was a proposal to fill in Albert Dock and turn it into a car park!

Inside the museum there are the displays that one expects and hopes to find in an absolutely first-rate maritime museum, including an immense collection of ship models, covering merchant shipping of the nineteenth and early twentieth century. There are artefacts ranging in size from a deckchair off the *Lusitania* to the engine from a steam yacht. To its credit, the museum has not turned away from the darker side of Liverpool history. Prosperity in the

Exhibits are to be found out on the water as well as in the former warehouses of Albert Dock.

eighteenth century was largely built on the slave trade, and a whole section is devoted to this story. This is a very powerful exhibition that sets out the unsavoury facts with commendable clarity and frankness. Another important social story fully dealt with is that of the emigrant ships which over the years took some 9 million people to a new life, most of them heading for America. A separate museum within the main museum deals with Customs and Excise and the ever-fascinating story of smugglers.

The Museum of Liverpool Life is part of the same Albert Dock complex, and the former Piermaster's House and offices have been refurbished as part of this local history museum.

Western Approaches

££; Monday to Thursday and Saturday; Rumford Street; Tel: 0151 227 2008; Website: www.waltongroup.co.uk (look in 'other exciting projects')

This quite ordinary street in Liverpool has its secrets. Beneath the paving stones are the offices from which the Battle of the Atlantic was controlled in the 1940s. Many of the old rooms have been restored to their wartime condition, including the operations room, the Admiral's office and the teleprinter station. One important area was the decoding room. Once the German Enigma code had been broken, messages could be intercepted and the fight against the U-boats turned in the Allies' favour.

The frigate HMS *Plymouth* built at Devonport entered service in 1961. She has a permanent berth at Birkenhead as a memorial to the seafarers who died in the Falklands War.

BIRKENHEAD
Historic Warships

£££; Daily; East Float, Dock Road; Tel: 0151 650 1573; Website: www.warships.freeserve.co.uk

History seems to be creeping ever closer to the present, as two of these ships saw action in the Falklands War: HMS *Plymouth*, a Type 12 frigate, and the submarine HMS *Onyx*. The latter is particularly interesting, being one of the last conventional, as opposed to nuclear, submarines in service. The other two craft take us back to World War II. LCT 7074 is a Landing Craft Tank, an amphibious vehicle used to unload tanks from ships anchored in deep water and carry them up onto the beach. This one was engaged in the D-Day landings. The quartet is completed by U534, a German U-boat sunk at the very end of the war, in 1945. She was finally brought up from the seabed in the 1990s. This is an impressive collection put together by the Warship Preservation Trust, and visitors can board the vessels for a complete tour. One further vessel has recently been added to the collection, HMS *Bronington*, a mine sweeper built in 1954. A considerable amount of restoration is needed, and work is underway, starting with the esssential task of making the deck watertight. As a result, there is only limited access to the vessel, and at weekends only at the time of writing. This will change as work proceeds, and information on progress can be checked by phone or on the website.

Williamson Art Gallery and Museum

Free; Daily; Slatey Road; Tel: 0151 652 4177

A general museum, dealing with many aspects of local life and the work of local artists. This being Birkenhead, much of the material has a maritime slant, and there are a number of ship models.

NAVIGATION

The earliest sailors probably never travelled out of sight of land where familiar landmarks could provide them with a position. For the medieval seaman the two most important tools of his trade were the magnetic compass and the lead. The compass is thought to have originated in China but is not mentioned in English writing until the twelfth century. The lead was essential when a vessel approached the coast. This was a weighted rope, marked off in fathoms (6ft lengths), which told the leadsman the depth of water. Pilotage books and charts appeared in time, showing bearings to landmarks to help keep on course. Quite different problems arose, however, once ships began to make voyages out of sight of land.

The early compass, which did no more than point north, was improved by the addition of the compass rose, so the steersman could be ordered to set a course south by south west, for example, or 202°. The navigator now needed to know the speed of the ship to fix a position at any one time by dead reckoning. This was done by throwing a 'log' over the stern, and no doubt an actual log was originally used. This was fastened to a knotted rope and the number of knots passing through the hands in a given length of time, measured by an hourglass, gave the speed. The standard of measurement was in nautical miles per hours, or knots, and the results were entered in the logbook. This was all very fine, but there were many sources of error. The compass does not point to geographical

The title page of Lucas Waghenaer's book of 1588. It shows sailors taking soundings with a lead and a variety of navigation instruments.

north but magnetic north, and the difference between the two poles varies from place to place on the earth. A far greater source of error lies with the measurements of direction. The steerer can point the bows on the right heading but it does not mean that the ship is actually going to travel the same way. Tide, wind and current can cause it to drift off the line. The further a ship travelled, the more the errors would multiply. It was not unknown for ships hoping to make landfall in some island to sail right past without ever seeing it at all. What was needed was a method of fixing a position accurately. Fortunately, there is a set of markers permanently available, the heavenly bodies.

It had long been known that north could be found by observation of the Pole Star, but it was not until the fifteenth century that methods were devised for determining latitude, the distance from the equator. It was recognized that the further south a ship sailed in the northern hemisphere, the lower the Pole Star appeared above the horizon. The first rough instrument was the quadrant, consisting of a plate graduated in 90 degrees, with a pair of pinholes for sighting, and a plumb line. Once aligned, the point where the plumb line crossed the scale gave the angle above the horizon – and thus the latitude. As time went on more sophisticated devices came into use, such as the astrolabe. These could be beautiful instruments, magnificently engraved. There are excellent examples in the National Maritime Museum. They were followed by more instruments for measuring angles, reaching near perfection with the sextant. Using a system of lenses and mirrors, the angle between the horizon and a variety of recognizable astronomical bodies could be made with a high degree of accuracy. Sailors could be confident of finding their latitude. Map making had improved over the years, so if a chart was available showing the latitude of an island, for example, the navigator had only to sail on to the correct latitude, then turn the ship in the right direction to reach the island. This was all very good providing the navigator knew whether he was east or west of his destination. To really fix a position, the longitude also has to be known. Because longitude is associated with the spinning of the earth and the passage from day to night, it can be determined quite simply if one can measure time. Once a fixed meridian has been agreed, and the line through Greenwich selected, the process is simple. If a clock is set for noon at Greenwich, and an observation of the sun shows that noon at your position differs by exactly an hour, then you are 1/24th of the way round the globe, or 15° away from the Greenwich meridian.

The only problem now was that the eighteenth-century mariner lacked an accurate timekeeper. Then in 1759 John Harrison perfected a clock that could be taken to sea and was assured of keeping accurate time. Man was no longer lost at sea.

Life became even easier after 1767 with the publication of *The Nautical Almanac*. This gave essential data, so that by measuring the angle above the horizon of a known star or planet, a position line could be drawn on the chart. The boat was somewhere along that line. By repeating the exercise for a different body, a second line could be drawn. Where the two met, with a small allowance being made for the ship having moved on, was the position at a specific time. Given a clear sky, a navigator could find a position with considerable accuracy. Today many go to sea with little or no knowledge of the old skills. Satellite navigation systems give an instant result with a high degree of exercise. Still, it is always a comfort to know that, armed with chronometer, sextant and almanac, some of us can still find our way when the electronics go on the blink.

An Admiralty chart of part of the Orkneys, showing soundings in fathoms and bearings to landmarks. The Wide Firth in particular has a number of shoals, with depths under two fathoms (12ft).

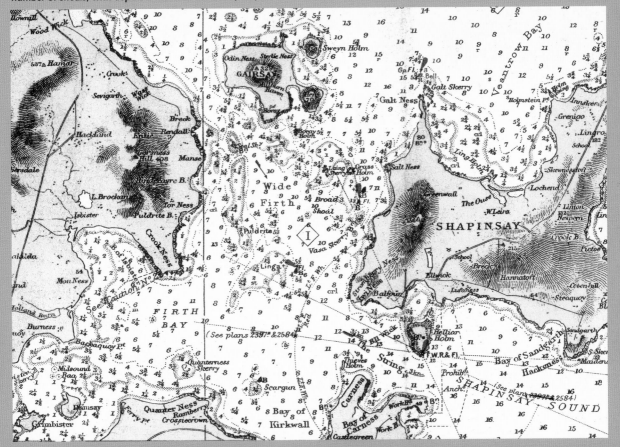

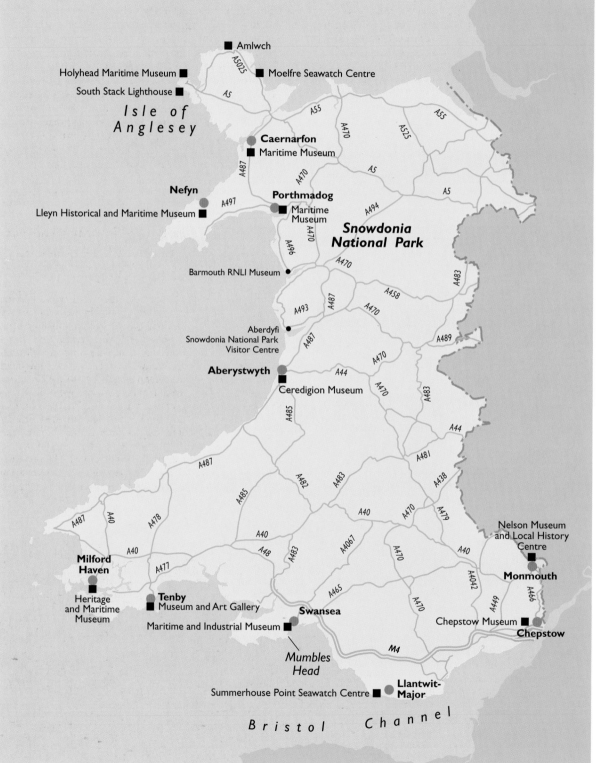

Irish Sea

■ Amlwch

Holyhead Maritime Museum ■

A5025

■ Moelfre Seawatch Centre

South Stack Lighthouse ■

A5

Isle of Anglesey

A55

A470

A525

A55

● **Caernarfon**
■ Maritime Museum

A487

A470

A5

Nefyn ●

A497

Porthmadog

A5

Lleyn Historical and Maritime Museum ■

● ■ Maritime Museum

A494

Snowdonia National Park

A470

A496

Barmouth RNLI Museum ●

A470

A483

A493

A487

A458

A470

Aberdyfi ●
Snowdonia National Park
Visitor Centre

A487

A489

Aberystwyth

A44

A470

■ Ceredigion Museum

A470

A483

A485

A44

A487

A481

A485

A482

A483

A438

A487

A40

A478

A40

A40

A4067

A40

A470

A479

Nelson Museum
and Local History
Centre ■

Milford Haven ●

A40

A48

A483

A470

A40

A4042

Monmouth

A477

A465

A449

A466

Heritage
and Maritime
Museum

● **Tenby**
■ Museum and Art Gallery

Swansea ●

A470

Chepstow Museum ■

Maritime and Industrial Museum ■

M4

Chepstow ■

Mumbles Head

Summerhouse Point Seawatch Centre ■ ● **Llantwit-Major**

Bristol   Channel

WALES

Wales can claim a speculative first in maritime history, in that it has been argued that stones from the Prescelly mountains were sent by sea to create the famous stone circle at Stonehenge. That was probably in the seventeenth century BC, which must make the stones the earliest known cargo to be shipped in Britain. Coming rather more up to date, there is a strong tradition of building wooden sailing ships along the west coast, mainly intended for the coastal trade. There were also, however, a number of larger vessels built, notably the big three-masted schooners, capable of long oceanic voyages. Welsh industry provided the cargoes. There was a busy trade associated with the mining and quarrying industries, leading to the construction of a number of small but, as far as local development was concerned, often very important ports. The main concentration of activity was the south coast, with Cardiff, Newport, Barry, Port Talbot and Swansea growing rapidly in the nineteenth century to meet the needs of the huge industrial development of the valleys. Although Wales is rich in museums and preserved sites dealing with the industries that created the cargoes, the actual maritime history is comparatively poorly represented. Fortunately, it is often of considerable interest.

A modern lifeboat at the Seawatch Centre at Moelfre.

ANGLESEY
Seawatch Centre, Moelfre

Free; Easter to October Tuesday to Saturday and Sunday afternoon;
Tel: 01248 410277

The main emphasis in this specially built centre is on shipwrecks and rescue, and an Oakley lifeboat, *Bird's Eye*, is on display. The shipwreck story is one of triumph and disaster. The first is represented by the brave rescue of the crew of the *Hinlea* in 1959, remembered now by her anchor mounted outside the museum. The disaster was the sinking of the clipper *Royal Charter*, bound for Liverpool from Australia in 1859 with a cargo of gold. Of the 450 on board, only a few survived, and a memorial now stands on the cliffs above the site of the accident.

Amlwch

Free; Open access

The harbour seems little more than a modest inlet but in its day it was as busy as any port in Wales. It was in the eighteenth century that copper ore was discovered in immense quantities at nearby Parys Mountain, and the port was created for shipment. It is hard to imagine now, but once upon a time schooners filled the harbour and many were even built here. An unusual feature is the dry dock, carved out of the natural rock.

Holyhead Maritime Museum

£; Easter to October afternoons but closed Monday; Newry Beach;
Tel: 01407 769745

The museum has a charming home in the mid-nineteenth-century lifeboat house. Where most lifeboat houses are rather plain and functional, this one has an end wall with an ornate, shaped gable. Holyhead has been used by shipping since Roman times, but the great period of expansion arrived with the completion of the new road under the direction of Thomas Telford and the development of the ferry route to Ireland. The museum looks out over the breakwater of 1873, stretching out to sea in an immense zigzag for over a mile.

The ornately gabled Maritime Museum at Holyhead.

Although permission to build a light on the Holyhead rocks was granted in 1665, the lighthouse was not actually built until 1809. It enjoys a superb position on a rocky island at the foot of the cliffs.

SOUTH STACK LIGHTHOUSE

£; Easter to September; Tel: 01248 724444

The lighthouse occupies a superb position, stuck on a rocky outcrop beneath tall cliffs that echo with the calls of huge colonies of seabirds. Today the birds, especially everyone's favourites, the puffins, are the main attraction for many visitors. The RSPB has established a centre here and installed a closed circuit television system, giving close-ups of the nesting birds. But the lighthouse itself is also of considerable interest. It was first lit in 1809, and in those days the only way to reach it from the cliffs was down slippery steps, then in a basket hauled along a cable. Given the roar of waves in the chasm between rock and cliffs it must have been a decidedly interesting experience. Now visitors enjoy the luxury of a bridge – but still have to cope with the 400 steps.

CAERNARFON
Maritime Museum

£; Spring Bank Holiday to September Sunday to Friday; Tel: 01248 752083

The museum stands beside the Victoria Dock, and nearby is the Slate Quay, which at least suggests one cargo that was regularly shipped from here. Indeed, Caernarfon was closely connected with the slate mines and quarries, and local foundries also built engines and locomotives for their use. So it was a busy place in the days of sail, and this is the basic story that the museum tells. Until recently, the steam dredger *Seiont II* was moored outside, but she has now been scrapped, though much of the machinery has been preserved and is on display. One result of the busy shipping trade at the port was that when Telford wanted to cross the Menai Straits with a bridge to carry the Holyhead Road, he was forced to allow enough room for the tallest masted ships to pass underneath. The result was the famous suspension bridge, standing high above the sea.

Various parts of the steam dredger *Seiont II*, ranging from the pressure gauges to the actual engine on display at Caernarfon Maritime Museum.

NEFYN
Lleyn Historical and Maritime Museum

Free; Beginning July to mid-September Monday to Saturday and Sunday afternoon; Old St Mary's Church, Church Street; Tel: 01758 720270

An easy museum to find, for this was once St Mary's Church and the weather vane on top of the tower comes in the form of a fully rigged ship. Inside, photographs, paintings and artefacts tell the story of the sea-going community. They built boats in the area in the nineteenth century, and the waters were busy with fishing boats and coasters.

PORTHMADOG
Maritime Museum

£; May Bank Holiday to end of September daily; Oakley Wharf; Tel: 01766 513736

Many visitors to Porthmadog are attracted by the famous narrow gauge railway that runs up to Blaenau Ffestiniog in the mountains. But without the port there would have been no railway. The museum is housed in a former slate shed, and slate holds the key to everything. It is an interesting story. It began when an English MP, William Madocks, hit on the idea of building a sea wall and embankment across the estuary and draining the marshy land behind. Work was completed in 1811, the new port was established and a railway built to bring down the slate, first using horses and later locomotives. Portmadoc, as it was then, prospered and soon became not just a busy port but a major shipbuilding centre, famous for its topsail schooners. Ships from here went all round the world, and I still remember my surprise at finding the remains of the 1874 Porthmadog brig *Fleetwing* doing service as a jetty in the Falkland Islands.

ABERYSTWYTH
Ceredigion Museum

Free; Monday to Saturday; Coliseum, Terrace Road; Tel: 01970 633088

A local history museum in the unlikely setting of a restored Edwardian theatre, there is a section devoted to the sea. There are pictures, charts and models, cannon and a reconstruction of a quayside scene.

MILFORD HAVEN
Heritage and Maritime Museum

£; Easter to November daily; Old Custom House, The Docks; Tel: 01646 694496

The museum is housed in the former Custom House and tells the interesting story of the town's vacillating fortunes. No less a person than Lord Nelson recognized the potential of this great natural harbour, and in the early nineteenth century the development of the port began as a shipyard for the Navy and as a whaling station. Brunel chose it as the coaling station for his immense steamship the *Great Eastern*, but it seemed that the port was doomed never to succeed. Expansion in the 1880s led to the establishment of a thriving fishing fleet; yet the real period of prosperity began in the 1960s with the development of the oil terminal. All these different facets are shown in the museum.

THE LIFEBOAT

Long before any purpose-built lifeboat had been designed, maritime communities were putting to sea to save lives – even if, on many occasions, the motive was as much the chance of profitable salvage as humanitarian concerns. The earliest records are those for the ports of Deal and Walmer in 1616, which tell of local boatmen going out to the notorious Goodwin Sands. The most famous rescue by ordinary boat was that of the crew of the steamer *Forfarshire* in 1838. The keeper of the Longstone lighthouse rowed out with his daughter, Grace Darling, for over a mile in an open boat to reach the ship, in the face of a ferocious gale. The Darlings never knew what the fuss was about when the public made Grace into a national heroine, the father declaring that for them it was just one rescue among many.

In 1721 Baron Crewe, Bishop of Durham, died, leaving instructions to set up a trust fund for establishing Britain's first specialist lifeboat station at Bamburgh. In 1786 a London coachbuilder, Lionel Lukin, designed what he called an 'unimmergible', an unsinkable lifeboat, which was sent up to Northumberland. It was simply an adaptation of the local fishing boat, the coble, given added buoyancy. Then, three years later, a Newcastle ship, the *Adventurer*, was wrecked in the mouth of the Tyne within sight of land. The watchers on the shore were unable to reach her and she broke up with the loss of all hands. A local society was formed and placed an advert in the Newcastle paper offering a reward of two guineas for the design of a boat able to carry twenty-four persons through a rough sea: 'The Inention of it being to preserve the Lives of Seamen, from Ships coming ashore, in hard Gales of Winds.' The winning design was produced by William Wouldhave of South Shields, but the committee felt it could be improved

Britain's oldest surviving lifeboat, the *Zetland*, is now preserved in a special museum at Redcar.

and only paid him half the money. The best features of this design were used by a local boat builder, Henry Greathead. In 1790 he launched the first true lifeboat, the *Original*, and was to go on to build another thirty-one, one of which, the *Zetland*, is preserved at Redcar (p.100). She is a 30ft-long clinker-built vessel, with a pronounced upward curve at bow and stern. She has cork fenders and buoyancy chambers, was rowed by five pairs of oars, with two steering oars at the stern. She was launched directly from the beach and remained in service for over sixty years, during which time she was used for rescues that saved some 500 lives.

In 1834 The Royal National Life-Boat Institution for the Preservation of Life from Shipwreck was formed, its cumbersome title eventually to be abbreviated to become the modern RNLI. Within a year enough money had been collected to build twelve boats and a further thirty-nine had been donated. The service was and still is run and manned by volunteers without government assistance. In 1893 the President of the Board of Trade wrote that 'no Government Department could ever evoke that generous sympathy with heroism which has characterized the work of the Institution'. This was never more vividly illustrated than in the rescue of the crew of *Forest Hall* in 1899. A distress call went out to the Lynmouth lifeboat crew but they were unable to launch from the local bay. With the help of horses borrowed from local farmers, they manhandled their boat up the 1000ft-high Countisbury Hill, across Exmoor and down into Porlock. It took them over ten hours, but they were still in time to help in the rescue. A similar lifeboat is now preserved in Lynmouth at the Exmoor National Park Visitor Centre.

There were several improvements made to boat design throughout the nineteenth century. As a result of a competition held in 1850, self-righting lifeboats were introduced. Not everyone thought this necessary, and in 1887 the yacht designer George L. Watson was one of those who argued that self-righting was not essential for big lifeboats, designing a 43ft sailing lifeboat instead. This was the first of the Watson class, which were standard for many years. Steam was introduced with the launch of the *Duke of Northumberland* in 1890, but the far more important development was the introduction of the internal combustion engine. At first, petrol engines were installed as auxiliaries, but with the launch of the first diesel lifeboat in 1932, the pattern for the future was set. Even so, the last of the old pulling lifeboats only went out of service in 1950. The long tradition of rescue continues, with the work shared between the RNLI and the coastguard service. Today there are some 200 lifeboat stations spread out around the British coast, many of which are open to the public. There are also a number of museums devoted to the lifeboat service, but only one dedicated to a single lifeboatman, Henry Blogg of Cromer, Suffolk. He joined the local crew in 1894 at the age of eighteen and only retired in 1947, having spent over thirty-seven of those years as coxswain. He went out 387 times, was awarded three Gold and four Silver RNLI medals for gallantry, the George Cross and the British Empire Medal. His life was a model of fearless effort in saving life at sea, but he is only one among the untold thousands who have risked their lives, and in many cases lost them, in the effort to save others.

This modern lifeboat is just one of a number of lifeboats from different periods collected together by the RNLI and on show at Chatham Historic Dockyard.

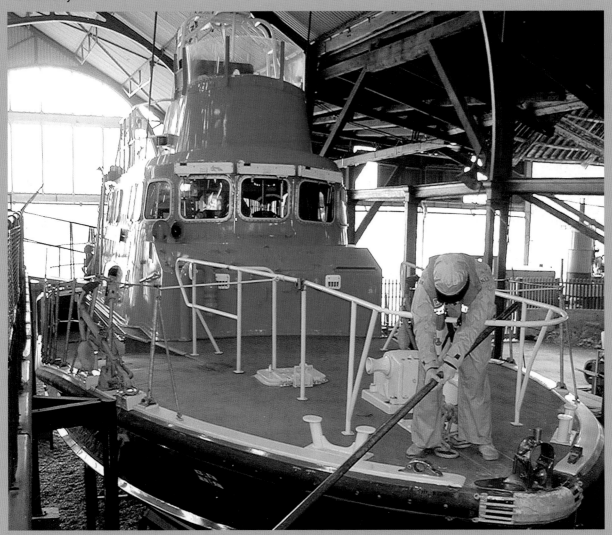

TENBY

Museum and Art Gallery

£; Easter to end of October daily; Castle Hill; Tel: 01834 842809

The museum is housed in an attractive building in a delightful setting. This was a school in the 1830s, but already established as the town museum by the 1870s, looking out over the picturesque bay. Tenby has a long history as a fishing port and was among the earliest towns to establish a lifeboat service; the museum tells the story of a century-and-a-half of rescue by sea.

SWANSEA

Maritime and Industrial Museum

Free; Tuesday to Sunday; Museum Square, Maritime Quarter; Tel: 01792 650351

This should be the biggest entry for any Welsh site, but there is a problem. The museum was to close its doors in 2002 for a major refurbishment and expansion. On completion it will have incorporated material formerly held in the big industrial and maritime museum in Cardiff. Work will not be completed by the time this book appears, so no description is possible – but having seen the current Swansea displays and having visited the Cardiff museum in the past, one can at least be certain that what emerges will be well worth seeing. In the meantime, there are three vessels on view in the dock. The steam tug *Canning* was built in Selby in 1954, a powerful vessel with a triple expansion engine. She originally worked in Liverpool and then in Swansea from 1966 until taken out of service. Light Vessel No.91 was built in 1937 and was first used on the Humber, then later moved to mark the Helwick sandbank off Mumbles Head. She has been preserved just as she was in her working days. The vessel has no engine, being towed to her permanent station, but does have a staysail. The last vessel is one of the best-loved class of sailing boats, a Bristol pilot cutter. *Olga* was built in 1907, a typically fine-lined, gaff-rigged vessel. Pilot cutters needed to combine speed with stability. When a ship was spotted entering the Bristol Channel, the boats would race to meet her and the first one there got the job. The crew consisted of a man and an apprentice, who were responsible for getting the two pilots on board the ship.

The original museum building, now to be extended, was a transit shed, and the old rail link can still be seen. It stands beside the South Dock, completed in 1859, when Swansea had an immense trade exporting coal and importing copper ore from Cornwall for the local smelters. Among the surviving structures is the former hydraulic pump house, now a pub, and an original wrought iron swing bridge. Behind the dock are the arches of the Oystermouth Railway, built before the age of steam locomotives.

LLANTWIT MAJOR

Summerhouse Point Seawatch Centre

Free; Three days a week; Tel: 01446 795203

The rather ambiguous note on opening times reflects the fact that opening times are indeed ambiguous. There is a variable pattern of opening, so that one week it might be Monday to Wednesday, the next week three quite different days, so it is essential to phone for the updated information. The centre is based on the former coastguard lookout, and the interior is styled like a ship's bridge. As well as providing an excellent vantage point for watching shipping in the Bristol Channel, it also features weather forecasting, a subject of the greatest importance to all seafarers. All the standard instruments are here for measuring wind speed and direction, atmospheric pressure and temperature. If that is not enough to create your own weather forecast, there is a text machine giving the expert opinion of what the future holds.

CHEPSTOW

Chepstow Museum

£; Monday to Saturday and Sunday afternoon; Tel: 01291 625981; Website: www.chepstow.co.uk

The very prosperous looking house in Bridge Street was built in 1796 for a local apothecary and makes an elegant setting for the town museum. It is perhaps surprising to find that Chepstow was once a busy port and an important shipbuilding centre. They began building ships for the Navy here in the late seventeenth century, and the first, a 30-gun man o' war, was aptly named *Forester*. It was indeed the combination of the navigable river and the nearby Forest of Dean that created the industry. In later years the yards produced merchant shipping, including trows, the sailing barges of the Wye and Severn. The timber from the forest was also exported to other yards, keeping the Chepstow quays busy. The story of shipbuilding and the port are told in the museum. The other watery connection, if not exactly maritime, is salmon fishing.

The Seawatch Centre at Summerhouse Point, a former coastguard lookout where visitors can learn about the weather or simply watch the ships go by in the Bristol Channel.

MONMOUTH
Nelson Museum and Local History Centre

£; Monday to Saturday; New Market Hall, Priory Street; Tel: 01600 713519

It is perhaps rather bizarre that the last entry should be for an inland town that would seem to have no connection with Nelson. However, Lady Llangattock kept Nelson memorabilia and presented her collection to the museum – and a very fine collection it is too. Here one can see letters, commemorative ware and personal possessions, including his fighting sword. Surprisingly, this is not quite all there is to see. On top of the Kymin, a hill on the far side of the Wye, is

The Kymin Round House, where Nelson and Lady Hamilton breakfasted, stands by The Naval Temple.

The Naval temple. There is a little castellated cottage, the Round House, a ceremonial arch dedicated to sundry 'noble admirals' and a pair of cannon. It all began as parkland in 1794, and the Monmouth Dining Club met in the cottage. And here the Neslon connection comes in. In 1802 the occupant of the Round House was looking through a telescope at a vessel sailing up the Wye and recognized the passengers as Nelson and Lady Hamilton. The cannon were fired and the Mayor was alerted to greet the famous visitor. Nelson came to breakfast in the house and declared the view from the Kymin as one of the finest he had ever seen. Perhaps it is not a bad place to finish after all: sharing a view that was once enjoyed by Britain's most famous Admiral.

See Also
Barmouth RNLI Museum

Free; Easter to October daily; The Promenade Tel: 01341 280940

The museum has models and photographs of Barmouth lifeboats, and at the time of writing was about to be moved to the new RNLI boathouse. An interesting local feature is the viaduct across the estuary, which when it was built in the 1860s had a rolling central section to allow ships through. It was not very efficient, as it took two men over half an hour to open and close it. It remains one of the rare examples of a timber viaduct in Britain.

Aberdyfi, Snowdonia National Park Visitor Centre

Free; Easter to November; Tel: 01654 767321

Not an area one thinks of in terms of maritime history, but there was a busy trade in slate from the mines and quarries of the mountains, and schooners were built here in the nineteenth century.

Mumbles Head

Free; Open Access

There is an interesting little group here. The pier with its traditional concert hall stretches out into the bay, and the lifeboat station has been built at the far end, with a ramp leading down into the water. The lighthouse stands on the Head itself, with the former coastguard lookout alongside.

NELSON

It is not difficult to see why Horatio Nelson has become one of the great romantic heroes of British history. He not only won great battles, but did so with panache, defying convention and, on occasion, his superior officers. Then to cap it all he enjoyed a scandalous love life. The combination is irresistible.

He was born at Burnham Thorpe in Norfolk in 1758. His father was the rector, and the local church still has a range of Nelson memorabilia: the lectern is made out of wood from his last flagship, *Victory*. He contrived to attend three schools before joining the Navy in 1770, serving in the *Raisonnable* commanded by his uncle. He was encouraged to learn practical sailing skills in small boats and proved such a good pupil that at the age of fourteen he was appointed captain's coxswain on an Arctic expedition. Family connections helped, but it was natural ability and inspiring leadership qualities that brought him promotion at a startling rate: lieutenant in 1777, commander in 1778 and captain the following year while

A portrait of Nelson painted in 1797, when he was Rear-Admiral of the Blue and had lost his arm at the Battle of Santa Cruz in the same year.

still only twenty-one years old. Whatever the reason for his rapid rise, it was certainly not down to kow-towing to superiors. Early in his career he was sent to the West Indies. Here the commander-in-chief had granted colonial registration to American ships, which Nelson considered he had no right to do. On his own initiative he seized five American ships for trading illegally and was promptly arrested for disobeying orders. In the event he was justified, but even so he was laid off and returned to Burnham with his wife. There he would probably have languished if war with France had not broken out in

1793. He was called back to active service and given command of the 64-gun *Agamemnon*, built at Buckler's Hard (p.46).

His first major action was the siege of Calvi on Corsica. It was here, standing on the ramparts of the fort, that a shower of dust and stone from a cannon ball hit flew up in his face, resulting in the loss of his right eye. He was soon back in action, and by 1797 as commander of the *Captain* he was involved in the Battle of Cape St Vincent. Admiral Jarvis with a fleet of fifteen encountered a Spanish fleet of twenty-seven. Jarvis smashed through the Spanish line, dividing the enemy. The manoeuvre was still incomplete when Nelson recognized that there was a real danger of the gap being closed. He turned his own ship to take on seven of the Spanish, and held them off until reinforcements arrived. It was this action that assured victory. It was typical of Nelson: daring, successful and taken entirely on his own initiative. In a later attack on Santa Cruz he was hit by a bullet in the elbow and his right arm was amputated.

In 1797 Nelson was appointed Rear-Admiral of the Blue, and the following year he achieved the first of his famous victories. He discovered thirteen French ships at anchor in the Bay of Aboukir in Egypt. The French had assumed that nothing could pass between them and the rocky coast, so all the guns were trained out to sea. Nelson had other ideas, and sent five of his ships inland of the French, so that the anchored fleet was caught helplessly between the British lines. Only two French ships escaped what became known as the Battle of the Nile. Nelson was again injured and sent back to Britain to recover. By now he had begun his famous affair with Lady Emma Hamilton, and as a result his stay with his wife was brief and acrimonious. They separated and never met again.

In 1801 Nelson was appointed Vice-Admiral of the Red and set off for Scandinavia under the command of Sir Hyde Parker. Nelson led the fleet against the combined firepower of the Danish fleet and gun batteries of Copenhagen. After three hours of fighting, Parker flew the signal to withdraw; Nelson's response became famous: 'Leave off action? Now, damn me if I do! You know, Foley, I have only one eye – I have a right to be blind sometimes', at which point he held his telescope to his blind eye. The Battle of Copenhagen was to be Nelson's second great victory.

In 1805 Nelson went to Portsmouth, where crowds turned out to cheer him as he made his way to his new command, *Victory*. The British fleet sailed out to encounter the combined French and Spanish fleets off Cape Trafalgar. Attacking in two lines, the *Royal Sovereign* was the first to break through, followed shortly after by *Victory* leading the second line, devastating Admiral Villeneuve's *Bucentaure* with a close-range broadside. An hour later Nelson was dead, shot by a marksman. As the news of his death went round the fleet, one seaman reported how the ordinary sailors who had served under him sat down and wept. Trafalgar was the greatest of all Nelson's victories, for it established Britain's complete domination of the seas and ended Napoleon's dreams of invasion. Monuments to Nelson were erected all over Britain, most famously in London's Trafalgar Square. His most fitting memorial, however, must be his last ship, *Victory*, fully restored and resplendent in dry dock at Portsmouth (p.50).

A French view of the Battle of Trafalgar by Louis Philippe Crepin. It gives a very good impression of the devastation that could be caused by broadsides at close quarters. It was the last and greatest of Nelson's victories.

LIFE AT SEA

Conditions at sea varied enormously over the centuries of seafaring, so much so that it would be quite impossible to give a single account of what life at sea was like. Therefore, in order to give a flavour, here is a brief summary of life as experienced by the ordinary seamen of the eighteenth-century Navy.

Not all who joined the Navy did so voluntarily; as many as half the crew found themselves there as the result of the press gangs. The arguments in favour of impressment were set out in a pamphlet by Charles Butler. Service in the Navy was, he said, 'a disagreeable duty' and 'must fall to the lot of that part of mankind which fills the lower ranks of life'. The impressed men found life aboard to be a misery, often forcibly separated from their families and knowing that any attempt to desert would be harshly punished. In theory, only experienced seamen were impressed; in practice, the press gangs took whoever they could find. Once on board, much of daily life was given over to dreary routine, the day divided up into four-hour watches. There was the endless cleaning of the decks, washed with seawater, scattered with sand and scrubbed with 'holystones'. But there were also moments of high drama, not necessarily associated with actually going into battle. Few of us can imagine what it would be like to be caught in an Atlantic gale. Sailors would have to turn out, possibly in the dark, climb the soaking ratlines as the ship swayed and bucked beneath them and make their way out along a yardarm with just a rope slung underneath as a foothold. There they would wrestle with stiff canvas and hemp rope made as inflexible as a steel hawser by the cold. Safety precautions were non-existent – and remained so throughout the working life of sailing ships. In a storm the possibility of being blown off a yard or washed overboard by the sea that swilled across the decks was always there. In such circumstances a man who went overboard was dead: there was no question of attempting a rescue. This is one reason why so few sailors bothered to learn how to swim.

Discipline was notoriously harsh and the standard punishment was flogging with the cat-o'-nine-tails, a lash with a wooden handle and long, knotted cords. In naval law the maximum sentence that could be passed without a court martial was twelve lashes, but the law meant little in practice. A sailor who got drunk would probably curse an officer, try to hit someone and would

One of the more miserable aspects of life at sea in the Royal Navy was flogging, often for comparatively minor offences, in front of the entire ship's company. This is the scene as depicted by George Cruikshank in a lithograph of 1825.

certainly be unfit for duty – each offence earning its separate punishment. The result was that the unhappy drunk could receive forty-eight lashes carried out in front of the entire ship's company. Attempted desertion could be punished by as many as 500 lashes. It is little wonder that on the worst ships the men's morale was low. One officer reported of a particularly brutal captain that 'he got the men so scared of him they were completely bewildered in working the ship, pulling the wrong ropes and upset things generally'.

Nothing caused more grievance on board ship than the quality of the food. It was plentiful enough. The recorded allowance for a naval vessel in 1720 was 1lb of biscuit a day, 2lbs of salt beef twice weekly, 1lb of salt pork twice weekly, 8oz pease four days a week, 2oz dried fish three days a week, 2oz of butter three days a week, 4oz of cheese three days a week and a gallon of beer a day. This was more than adequate to meet the energy requirements of the men, and the beer

The quarterdeck of the sixth rate *Deal Castle* in 1775. Officers stroll under the shade of an awning, sharing the space with a goat and hens kept to supply fresh food.

ration seems more than generous. There were two problems. The first was that the food was often disgusting. A writer describing the reality of meals in the Navy in the 1760s wrote that the men carved the cheese into buttons because it was harder than metal, the flour was full of weevils and the bread so packed with maggots that the men had to close their eyes before they could bear to eat it. The preserved meat was board-like and required long soaking and cooking, which it did not always get. The cooks were not exactly noted for their culinary skills. A law of 1704 decreed that they should be chosen from the

ranks of 'cripples and maimed persons' receiving naval pensions. One-legged Long John Silver of fiction would have surprised no one on a man of war. An idea of the nature of the food can also be gauged from the fact that when meat was boiled it produced fatty scum called 'slush', which was used to grease the running rigging.

There was a saying at the time that 'God sends the meat but the Devil sends the cooks.'

Looking at the daily allowance, one is struck by a notable absence. There is no mention of fruit and vegetables. This resulted in a serious vitamin deficiency, which gave rise to the fatal disease scurvy. It has been estimated that in this period more seamen died of scurvy than were lost in battles and accidents. During Admiral Anson's circumnavigation of the 1740s, he lost over 1000 men from his fleet to scurvy. A ship's surgeon, James Lind, was so appalled that he began a systematic study of the disease and after trying many treatments found the remedy – fresh fruit. He published his results in 1753; Captain Cook was one of the few who took any notice (p.99). The Admiralty only acted on his findings forty-two years later.

Poorly paid, with accommodation limited to a hammock slung between the guns, fed rancid food and subject to harsh discipline, it is perhaps no surprise that the eighteenth century ended with the mutinies of *Spithead* and the *Nore*. As an old naval proverb had it: 'those who would go to sea for pleasure would go to hell for pastime'.

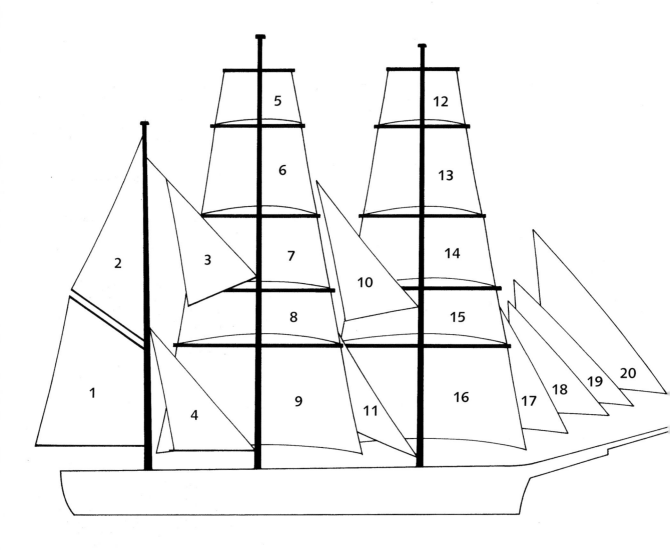

The sails of a fully rigged ship.

1. Jigger or spanker
2. Jigger gaff topsail
3. Mizzen topmast staysail
4. Mizzen staysail
5. Main royal sail
6. Main top gallant sail
7. Main upper topsail

8. Main lower topsail
9. Main sail
10. Main top gallant staysail
11. Main topmast staysail
12. Fore royal sail
13. Fore top gallant sail
14. Fore upper topsail

15. Fore lower topsail
16. Foresail
17. Fore topmast staysail
18. Inner jib
19. Outer jib
20. Flying jib

GLOSSARY

Adze: A tool used for shaping ships' timbers. It is similar to an axe, except that the cutting edge is at right angles to the shaft.

Barge: A flat-bottomed vessel used for carrying freight on inland waterways and estuaries.

Beam: The width of a vessel amidships; also the name for part of the framework supporting the decks.

Binnacle: The housing in which a ship's compass is suspended.

Block: A pulley or pulleys, mounted in a case, used to guide a rope and to help with the raising and lowering of heavy weights, such as yards and sails.

Bowsprit: A sprit or spar that runs forward from the bow of a vessel to support sails such as jibs.

Carvel: A carvel-built vessel is one in which the outer planks of the hull lie flush and are attached to a previously constructed frame.

Caulk: To make a ship watertight by forcing material such as oakum – the fibre from old ropes – between the planks and then covering the seams with pitch.

Clinker- or clench-built: This describes a vessel in which the hull is constructed from overlapping planks.

Coaming: The raised edge round a hatch.

Drift netting: A form of fishing in which the drifter sets out nets suspended vertically in the water, then drifts with the current. Bottom feeding fish, such as herring, are caught as they rise towards the surface.

Fathom: The traditional measurement for sea depth, equal to 6ft.

Fore and aft rig: A rig in which sails are set along the fore and aft axis of a vessel, as, for example, in a schooner.

Forecastle or fo'c'sle: Originally a fighting platform erected in the bows to convert a merchant ship into a man o' war. As this was above the crew quarters, it came into general use for crew quarters.

The drifter and its drift net.

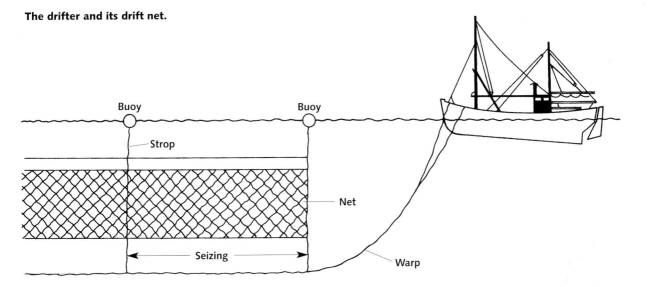

Foremast: The mast of a vessel nearest to the bows.

Gaff: The spar that holds the top edge of a four-sided fore and aft sail.

Gunwale: The upper part of a ship's side, standing above the level of the deck.

Jib: A triangular sail, usually running from the main mast to the bowsprit.

Keel: The lowest member of a ship's frame around which the rest of the vessel is constructed; a shallow-draught coastal vessel.

Knee: A bent timber or angled iron piece securing beams to the ribs of a ship.

Knot: The unit of measurement of a ship's speed, defined as one nautical mile per hour. A nautical mile is roughly equivalent to 1.25 land miles, and is based on one minute of latitude, so a ship making 20 knots would be travelling at 23mph.

Lee Boards: Sometimes known as barge boards, these are roughly triangular-shaped boards which are lowered over the side of a shallow-draught sailing vessel to prevent it slipping sideways through the water. They are used, for example, on Thames barges.

Leeward: The side of the ship sheltered from the wind.

Lug sail: A four-sided sail that is hung asymmetrically so that the greater part of the sail is aft of the mast. In a dipping lug the yard is lowered, carried round the mast and raised again when tacking.

Mainmast: The principal mast of a ship.

Mizzen: The mast nearest to the stern.

Port: The left-hand side of a vessel when looking to the bows – so called because it was originally the side of the ship next to the quay when in port.

Rating of Ships: In the days of sail, naval ships were rated according to the number of their guns. A first rate ship had over 100 guns, and the lowest ranking, a sixth rate, had up to 32 guns.

Reef: To shorten a sail by rolling up the bottom. In older systems this was achieved by rolling up and then securing it by means of a series of short lines attached to the sail – using, of course, a reef knot.

Rigging: The lines that hold masts, spars, etc. in place. Standing rigging is permanently fixed; running rigging controls the movement of spars and sails through blocks.

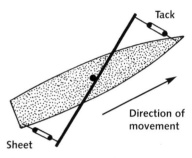

The running rigging of a square rigged vessel.

The cross section shows the construction of a typical wooden sailing ship.

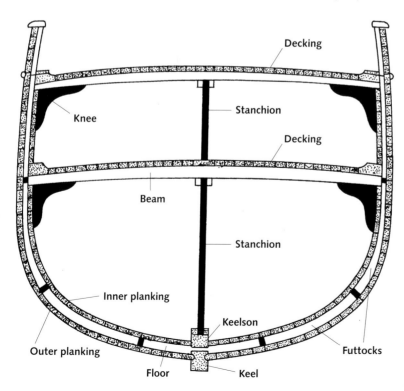

Scarfe: A joint used to join pieces of timber in a straight line. It is commonly used in shipbuilding where long sections are needed, for example in the keel.

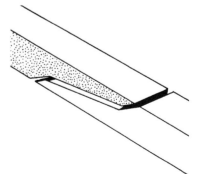

A scarfe joint for joining timbers, e.g. in a ship's keel.

Sheet: A line running from the bottom aft corner of a sail, which can be used to adjust the position of the sail to make best use of the wind.

Spritsail: A sail in which the peak, the top corner furthest from the mast, is extended by a spar, the sprit, running diagonally from the mast.

Square rig: A rig in which four-sided sails are hung symmetrically from a yard at right angles to the fore and aft line.

Starboard: The right-hand side of a vessel when looking to the bows – originally 'steerboard', as in older ships the 'steering oar' was set on this side.

Stay: Standing rigging supporting a mast and running in a fore and aft direction, to which staysails are often attached.

Strake: A continuous line of planking running fore and aft along a ship's hull.

Tack: Unless a vessel has a wind from astern, it needs to take a zigzag course to make headway. This is tacking. If the wind is coming from the starboard side, it is on a starboard tack, from the port side, on a port tack. Also the lower forward corner of a square sail when sailing towards the wind.

Trawler: A fishing boat that drags an open-mouthed net along the seabed.

Tumblehome: The curve of a hull which makes the upper deck of a vessel narrower than the deck at the water line; this can be seen, for example, in warships such as *Victory*.

Windward: The side of a ship facing towards the wind.

Yard or Yardarm: A spar suspended from the mast to carry a sail.

Site Index

Ship and Boat Index

PICTURE CREDITS